DON'T COUNT ON IT!

WHY YOUR PENSION MAY BE IN JEOPARDY—AND HOW TO PROTECT YOURSELF

THOMAS G. DONLAN

SIMON & SCHUSTER

New York London Toronto Sydney Tokyo Singapore

SIMON & SCHUSTER
Rockefeller Center
1230 Avenue of the Americas
New York, New York 10020

Designed by Irving Perkins Associates
Manufactured in the United States of America

1   3   5   7   9   10   8   6   4   2

Library of Congress Cataloging-in-Publication Data

Donlan, Thomas G.
Don't count on it!: why your pension may be in jeopardy and how to
protect yourself/Thomas G. Donlan.
p.   cm.
Includes bibliographical references (p.   ) and index.
1. Old age pensions—United States—Finance.   2. Pension trusts—
United States—Finance.   3. Retirement income—United States—
Forecasting.   4. Retirement income—United States—Planning.
5. Retirees—United States—Finance, Personal.   I. Title.
HD7105.35.U6D66   1994
331.25'2'0973—dc20   94-22136
                                                                          CIP

ISBN: 0-671-87466-7

to Nick and Alice

in the hope that their generation will not
have to pay for my generation's mistakes

Contents

Part Four
ESCAPING THE PENSION SYSTEM

LEGAL LOOTING

WILLIAM J. DE LANCEY, the chairman of Republic Steel, walked out of a board meeting on September 15, 1981, to avoid the appearance of a conflict of interest. In a preparatory memo to the members of the board's Management Development and Compensation Committee he wrote: "Since I have a personal interest in the first topic and a technical or nominal interest in the second, you may want to consider these matters in my absence."

The second matter was indeed a minor question about which company executives would have company cars. The chairman of the board certainly would have one, and De Lancey would be retiring soon anyway. But the first topic was worth $275 million to the pension fund covering past and current nonunion employees of Republic Steel, from De Lancey down to the secretaries and clerks.

After De Lancey left the room, four outside directors ratified a change in the pension plan. (The power to implement the change actually lay with three Republic executives, but, as De Lancey told the four directors, "they would be guided by your views.")

The change was technical: reducing the rate of interest used to calculate a lump-sum retirement disbursement in lieu of a pension. The change had been approved by the company's actuarial consultant, and seemed routine. But changing this number opened a window of opportunity for De Lancey, other senior officers of Republic Steel, and about 3,800 lower-ranking salaried workers. Over the next three years, they all retired and took lump-sum payments in lieu of a pension. When they were through, nothing was left in the pension fund; a $275 million fund was legally looted and drained. Among those benefiting were Chairman De Lancey, President E. Bradley Jones, and Chief Financial Officer John J. Loftus—each to the tune of more than $1 million.[1]

Underfunded to begin with (the $275 million only covered 44 percent of the $625 million in benefits already earned), the pension fund should not have been paying lump-sum retirement benefits at all. Anyone who took a lump sum received the full value of his pension benefit right away, while 3,200 retirees were taking theirs one month at a time, until the money ran out. Only if the pension plan were fully funded to cover all projected benefits would the lump-sum payments represent a fair share of the total assets.

The interest change made matters worse. The rate for computing lump-sum settlements was slashed from 11.25 percent to 8 percent. The 8 percent rate reflected the pension fund's historic average investment performance, but it was put into effect as long-term bond rates were cresting above 14 percent. The huge difference between the two made cashing out almost irresistibly attractive. Every dollar of monthly pension benefit would buy $81.68 of lump-sum payment before the switch and $98.35 afterwards—a 20 percent sweetening of the pot. A person retiring in mid-1982, such as De Lancey, could take his lump sum, invest it in long-term government bonds, and receive interest payments for thirty years nearly equal to what his pension would have been, while preserving the principal for his estate. Or, if he chose to take a little more risk, he could have bought an annuity from an insurance company that would have paid him a monthly income for life, just like a pension, that would have been double the Republic Steel pension benefit.

Eligible Republic workers headed for the exits. The annual retirement rate at Republic more than doubled in the year after the change, and nearly everyone who retired took the lump-sum benefit. After that, retirements increased even more as Republic suffered through a deep recession and then was taken over by

LTV Corp. of Dallas. In the merger discussions, Republic executives won a clause that guaranteed continuation of the lump-sum payments, figured at 8 percent, for at least a year into the merged operation. The negotiators thus were able to join the ranks of the fortunate retirees with lump-sum payments.

Anybody who got out was lucky. The salaried workers' pension fund was out of money by April 1, 1985, though LTV kept paying benefits on a pay-as-you-go basis for another year and a quarter. Then, on July 17, 1986, LTV filed for reorganization under Chapter 11 of the federal bankruptcy code. LTV terminated the Republic salaried workers' plan and three other underfunded company pension plans, throwing more than $2 billion in liabilities onto the federal Pension Benefit Guaranty Corp.

A battle over the husk of LTV ensued, in which the PBGC tried to establish that LTV's first obligation was to pay pensions, while LTV's creditors tried to push the PBGC aside and LTV itself tried to shed debt of all kinds and to reorganize.

There were pension issues galore in the reorganization. LTV tried to fund new pension plans while leaving the old ones supported by federal insurance. It tried to use pension assets to pay health benefits for retirees. The company emerged from Chapter 11 in 1993, having left the Republic salaried workers' pension plan in the care of the federal Pension Benefit Guaranty Corp., which forced the new LTV to keep operating the other three underfunded plans.

Nobody—not LTV and not the federal government—ever pursued De Lancey or other Republic executives or other salaried workers or the board of directors. They took their money and they didn't even have to run. But thousands of other Republic salaried workers, a little bit younger, a little bit less savvy, or a little bit less fortunate, found their retirement plans on the rocks.

There are thousands of ways to loot a pension plant legally, and to leave little or nothing but federal pension insurance to back up the empty promises made by employers. What happened at Republic could happen to anyone in America who counts on receiving a defined benefit pension plan. And federal pension insurance itself is not secure.

THE REAL STORY

We Americans think we are so rich. We can retire at sixty-two
and spend twenty or thirty years in luxurious bliss in Palm
Beach. Then we will die painlessly in our sleep and leave a
million dollars to our loving children.

This American Dream of a luxurious retirement has always
been a fantasy, enjoyed only by a lucky few. Sadly, it has become
more widely believed as it has actually grown more unrealistic.
The financial and political faults in our retirement system have
shattered this dream for many older people today, and guarantee
a broken dream for younger people who will retire in the twenty-
first century. In particular, members of the baby-boom generation, born between 1945 and 1970, are like ships without radar
running confidently through a field of icebergs.

Financial, political, and economic icebergs have sunk many
ships. If we look, we see the wreckage in the union halls and
social clubs of decrepit midwestern cities. Over the past twenty
years, retirement disasters have blighted the steel industry and
the rest of the Rust Belt. They are punishing aging airline and
aerospace workers now.

But the real disaster of the American pension system is yet to
come. We have made empty promises to ourselves, and we will
be unpleasantly surprised when we try to collect. Today's hand-
ful of cases are relatively minor compared to the sad plight of the
future, when the 80 million Americans of the baby-boom generation reach retirement age. Most of the unknowing victims are
in their thirties and forties, and they don't see the danger. By the
time their retirement dreams are drowned, it will be too late.

This book is meant to warn them now that:

- The finances of the pension system are shaky—one pension
  plan out of five does not have the money to pay promised
  benefits, and many employers are making new promises
  faster than they are contributing money to pay for them. We
  have an unstable private pension system, which too often
  defines benefits without putting aside enough money to pay
  for them and leaves workers' assets vulnerable to desperate
  corporate managers and greedy raiders.
- An elaborate government structure to regulate pension plans

and protect pension benefits is a hollow shell without the financial strength to save the system when the crisis comes. Worse, the federal government's insatiable demand for tax revenue is reducing the tax incentive to create and contribute to pension plans. And the ill-designed, overburdened federal pension insurance scheme promises far more safety than it can deliver and actually encourages raids on the pension plans it's supposed to protect.

- The nation faces a demographic crisis when the retiring baby-boom generation must depend for the sustenance of its pensions on the economic productivity of much less numerous younger generations. The most numerous generation in American history will also be the longest-lived. The most demanding generation in American history will be hardest to satisfy in the twilight of their lives.

- The basic foundation of every American's retirement plans, Social Security, is vulnerable to the same financial and demographic pressure. We have built it up as the holiest of sacred cows and it will tear our society apart one day when its promises fail.

- There is nothing and nobody that will guarantee people a comfortable retirement except their own determined action now to save and invest wisely and aggressively.

FOLLOWING THE S&Ls

More than a decade ago, the savings-and-loan insurance system was under stress and threatened a financial disaster for the nation that brought falling real estate prices and years of economic blight to communities in Texas, California, Colorado, New England, Florida, and New York. The only monies that could not be confiscated as a result of the S&L collapse were the savings of ordinary citizens, and that was averted by wholesale federal borrowing whose consequences may not yet be completely visible.

The pension insurance system is now under stress. Unless we reform the pension system now, it will be a financial disaster for the nation in the twenty-first century. And the coming collapse of the pension system is much more likely to take away the savings of ordinary citizens.

Savings and loans collapsed because they borrowed short and loaned long. They took in deposits that could be withdrawn easily and paid a floating rate of interest for those deposits, while they made mortgage loans with a term of thirty years at fixed rates. This worked as long as the U.S. economy dominated the world and the United States kept interest rates frozen.

It could not last forever. Capital fled to higher returns overseas, and had to be lured back with higher interest rates at home. When interest rates rose, S&Ls had to pay more interest on deposits but could not earn more on their old loans. (Banks were in a somewhat better position because their commercial loans were usually shorter-term.) To earn more money, S&Ls had to make new loans at high rates. Unfortunately, there was not enough new good real estate—housing developments, apartments, and office buildings—to lend to, so the savings and loans made loans on bad projects instead. The bad projects stopped paying and the savings and loans collapsed. When they collapsed, they of course stopped lending and even sound borrowers found it hard to get loans for good business ideas. Without a steady supply of capital, real estate markets dried up, prices fell, and loans exceeded the value of their security.

A defined benefit pension fund has much the same structural defect as an S&L. A company agrees to pay a certain benefit for the life of its workers, beginning at retirement. It takes capital from the firm and deposits it in a pension fund, and the fund assumes the obligation to pay the pension. Actuarial calculations for pension plans require assumptions about investment returns, about the life expectancy and retirement plans of workers, and a host of other assumptions that no outsider ever regulates, tests, inspects, or criticizes. The earnings of the pension fund go up and down with the markets, but the obligation to pay pensions remains fixed or rises. The problem gets worse whenever asset values fall, as in a decline of the stock market or real estate, and whenever the earnings of the assets fall, as in a recession.

The difference between thrifts and pension funds is that pension funds take risks on the other side of the balance sheet. They put sound assets in the service of questionable liabilities while risky thrifts backed certain liabilities with questionable assets. Pension funds run risks when they accept new unfunded obligations such as shutdown benefits, early retirements, and benefit increases. Eventually, the bad liabilities must be paid or the pension fund—and probably its sponsoring company—will collapse.

Federal pension insurance stands behind the system, but only to pick up the pieces from a system that is exploding, a system that has to explode. Many people who believe they are going to retire in comfort will instead be forced to keep on working, if they can. Some will be forced to find new jobs taking airline reservations or fast-food orders. Others will be dependent on their children, and others will live out their lives on the federal dole, barely surviving, on the margin of society.

PENSION ACCOUNTING

The glossary of pension terminology at the end of this book may be helpful to those unfamiliar with such terms. Two that you should understand at the outset are a *defined benefit pension plan* and a *defined contribution plan*, and the difference between them. A company with a defined benefit plan promises to pay workers a specific monthly amount on retirement. It puts a certain sum for each worker into a trust fund each year to save up for the day when the worker becomes a retiree and receives a pension. The precise amount of the deposit is determined by estimates of the earnings of the investments of the plan, but the pension is supposed to be paid regardless of the plan's earnings. A company with a defined contribution plan doesn't promise any specific benefit. Instead it specifies how much it will deposit each year to an account for each worker, and lets the actual pension benefit be determined on retirement by the amount of money saved and the amount of investment earnings on that savings.

Most of the big problems of pension finance concern defined benefit plans. Defined contribution plans also pose problems of their own, but not the most dangerous problem of overfunding and underfunding. If you understand that a defined benefit pension plan funds a worker's future benefit by putting aside smaller sums of money during each year of employment, then you will see that these invested contributions, plus the earnings on the investments, are supposed to be enough to pay the promised monthly pension when retirement comes. Mathematical engineers called actuaries estimate future pension liabilities for the members of each pension fund and also project future earnings of the assets deposited for them. When liabilities—the projected future pension payments—are larger than assets—the projected future value of the fund—a plan is underfunded. When liabilities are less than assets, a plan is overfunded.

Full funding of a pension plan means that the money currently being deposited in a pension fund, invested at a realistic rate of return, will grow sufficiently to pay the benefits to current employees as they retire. Underfunding means that the benefits promised have grown faster than the assets were deposited. Many people think this is impossible, illegal, and immoral. It is only the last.

More than fifty major American companies have pension funds that are out of balance by more than $100 million. The total underfunding of pension systems in the United States exceeds $51 billion, and can easily grow. General Motors leads the list with underfunding approaching $25 billion, and that debt was created legally in only a few years of bad business and unfair pension policies.

All too often industrial managers have tried to buy labor peace with a generous-looking package of salary and benefits, light on the cash and heavy on the benefits. All too often the unions have collaborated in order to preserve jobs, even at the expense of pension security. What is worse, these companies are weighing down the labor market so other companies without systemic industrial weakness and without unions have been forced by competition to offer similarly self-destructive benefits. One bad apple rots the barrel—it's true in business and finance as much or more than it's true in farming.

We cannot tell when the American pension system will provide us with a barrel full of rotten apples. We can only see that rotten apples exist, that they are in the barrel with all the other apples, and that many of us have staked our future happiness and comfort on receiving good apples at the end of the journey.

A pension fund ought to be a sacred compact between a company and its workers, but neither employers nor workers give much thought to their rights and obligations until it is too late.

Time and again, money that was thought to be secure was gone before anybody noticed that it could be taken.

PLAN OF THE BOOK

Accounting is the professional discipline that provides financial information to the owners of a corporation, so that they can make decisions to manage the company—or to buy or sell its shares—with full knowledge of the essential facts about the corporation's worth.

We Americans, however, are working without full understanding of pension finance. This book is an attempt to provide the accounting that most of us never receive.

An accounting begins with an inventory, so Part One of the book sums up the evolution of the American pension system and reports on the status of pension plans—private and governmental—today. It relates the funding problems and abuses of the recent past and reports on similar problems that are arising today.

An accounting also tests the security of the system; therefore Part Two concentrates on the regulation of American pensions. Congress adopted the Employee Retirement Income Security Act in 1974 to regulate pension funds and preserve pension assets for the "exclusive benefit" of the beneficiaries. Even though it's backed up by three federal agencies and an elaborate insurance scheme, federal protection is an empty promise.

An accounting requires an estimate of future stress on the system. Part Three reports on the overwhelming demographic pressure that will be generated during the retirement of the baby-boom generation. Pension sponsors cannot be expected to provide adequate responses to the funding crisis of the twenty-first century, so Part Three also offers some suggestions for reforms to enact now. Although radical and painful, they would be preferable to the misery and suffering that a collapse of the American pension system would cause.

An accounting requires specific recommendations for action by the responsible people. There's little hope for legislative reform without an impending crisis, so Part Four consists of financial advice for readers to use to protect themselves from the all-too-likely possibility that their pension benefits will be far less than they have been led to believe.

In the Afterword, there are suggestions for how any reader can investigate the current health of his pension.

PROTECT YOURSELF

The American pension system's problems do not mean that every single pension will be reduced to nothing. Some employers will default on their pension promises; the protections that the government has erected are too weak to prevent that from happening and too restricted to provide full protection to those who lose their benefits. Unless we act now, our country will face a financial and political crisis when it will be too late to repair the collapsing pension system.

We cannot accurately predict who the victims will be, although we ought to acknowledge that for many Americans, the private pension system does not exist: About a third of the adult population has no employer-sponsored pension plan.

Thus this book is written as an alarm bell to the entire postwar generation, warning that they are depending on an economic system that is not strong enough to bear their weight. It is a call to action to reinforce the American pension system and a survival kit that can reduce our reliance on that system.

PART ONE

THE
AMERICAN
PENSION
SYSTEM

1

CONSTRUCTION

IN AMERICA BEFORE the twentieth century, as in almost every society, people worked until they could not work anymore. A few wealthy people didn't have to work at all, but society as a whole did not produce enough to support many idle people.

The Industrial Revolution created the need for a pension system, and then created the wealth necessary to pay for it. Before the Industrial Revolution, when a worker was disabled by age or injury he became dependent on his family, his friends, or his church. He had no other refuge. The closest thing to a source of retirement income was the accumulated property of a small business—real estate, tools, or other means of production. A proprietor might pass on these physical assets to a successor in return for support in his old age. Usually these arrangements were an understood part of a family business.

The industrialization of America after the Civil War broke down the independent system of small farms and small businesses. Farmers who left the land to become industrial workers also became dependent on capitalists for the means of production, receiving cash wages instead of growing their subsistence, and using financial institutions to accumulate capital in the form of a home or an insurance policy.

It was common—though far from universal—for factories to

put disabled people on light-duty jobs, perhaps at reduced wages. Outstanding employees might even receive a cash pension. Such arrangements depended on the profitability of the factory and the willingness of the owner to take money out of his own pocket for the benefit of his employees.

Gradually, industrial society became too complex for ad hoc arrangements based on need and the whim of a single owner. When a personnel office hires the workers and a board of directors hires professional managers, nobody knows which workers ought to be pensioned off. Some companies decided that it was more efficient to retire all workers at a specified age with a specified support, rather than to retain some, dismiss some, and pension off others.

The American Express Company started the first formal retirement and pension plan in 1875, and the Baltimore and Ohio Railroad followed five years later. Other railroads—the most important and wealthiest industry of the time—soon imitated the B&O. They experimented with different structures, some requiring worker contributions and strict savings accounting, others simply stating a promise to pay. In 1900 the Pennsylvania Railroad started the new century with a new, simplified pension plan that required retirement at age seventy and paid a percentage of wages to anyone with thirty years of service. To make this system universal among its workers, the railroad also established a maximum hiring age of thirty-five years. In the next three decades, hundreds of major American companies—railroads, utilities, banks, and factories—adopted the Pennsylvania plan.

HIGH TIDE

By 1930, more than 4 million workers were employed in 462 U.S. firms with employer-provided pension plans, mostly in railroads, telephone, telegraph, and cable companies. There were also about a half-million workers covered by union pensions and about 1 million government workers covered by public pensions. Manufacturing had only about 20 percent of workers covered. The largest companies were more likely to have pension plans:

64 percent of covered workers were in companies with more than 25,000 workers and only two of the seventeen firms with assets of more than $750 million did not have pension plans. (They were General Motors and Standard Gas & Electric.)[1]

Virtually all the new retirement plans were *defined benefit plans*, meaning that the employer promised to pay a pension of a defined amount. In a defined benefit plan, each worker who qualifies receives a set benefit, guaranteed by the employer and backed by invested contributions to a pension account. The benefit for every worker may be defined as a dollar amount, or it may be adjusted for years worked, or pay scales.

More than 70 percent of all the firms in the Depression-era studies used a formula to compute benefits that averaged the salary of the last ten years of service and multiplied it by 1 percent and by the number of years of service. For example, forty years of service would produce a pension equal to 40 percent of the average salary in the last ten years of service.

(Today, some plans promise a flat dollar benefit, but most use a complex version of the percentage formula. The formula may use the highest year's pay or the last year's pay instead of the ten-year average; the generosity factor may vary in order to make early retirement somewhat more attractive than retirement at the "normal" age.)

Being employed in a company with a pension plan by no means guaranteed that a worker would receive a pension. Being fired or quitting before retirement age, or being laid off for more than a year during long service, would disqualify a worker from receiving a pension.

(Today, workers obtain vesting rights, which means that a worker leaving a job for any reason will still receive his vested benefit at retirement. The typical vesting period, mandated by law for private defined benefit plans, is five years.)

The payment of a pension depended on the survival of the employer who paid it. Only 29 percent of the companies surveyed in 1930 had even established trust funds to pay benefits, and they generally contained only a small portion of the assets that would be needed to back up promised pensions completely. Companies did not make deposits to these funds systematically, but only as needed and when they felt profits allowed. Another

13 percent of companies had set up reserves on their books, but had not segregated funds. The rest paid pension benefits out of operating expenses, if they could. (After 1926, they enjoyed the right to deduct pension expense from the federal corporate income tax.)

The total accrued liabilities of pension plans in the United States in 1928 were about six times their assets. In an era when the employer set the terms and conditions of employment, free to hire or fire and to raise or lower pay subject only to the supply and demand for labor, it was natural for pensions to be set up without much advance funding. Railroads in particular could not accumulate funds for pensions because of Interstate Commerce Commission rules intended to hold down rates by regulating expenses, and most companies preferred not to spend today's profits on tomorrow's expenses. Also, employers did not (and still don't) want their workers to think of pension fund assets as their property.

In the Great Depression, the fortunes of pension plans followed the fortunes of the employers who sponsored them. Some failed and many cut benefits, though most survived.

THE FIRST PENSION CRISIS

It didn't take long for the first pension system to generate the first pension crisis. Pension expense at the Pennsylvania Railroad grew from $300,000 in 1903 to $3.5 million in 1925.

"How long can American Railroads stand the financial strain of their present pension plans?" asked the trade journal *Railway Age* that year. "What assurance has anyone that current revenues in 1950 will be sufficient to stand the strain of pension liabilities accruing in 1925?"[2]

By the Great Depression, few in the railroad industry were worried about making their pension system last until 1950. They were more concerned about making it until next year or next month. Congress and the Roosevelt administration, already looking ahead to enactment of Social Security, decided to experiment first with the railroad industry. A national pension system might have constitutional problems, but the federal government clearly had the power to regulate and rule interstate commerce.

Thus the Railroad Retirement Act assumed all the liabilities of the largest employer in the United States, with more than a million workers. The new federal system levied a payroll tax on workers and companies to pay retirement benefits. But the railroad industry was already past its prime. Track mileage and employment both peaked in the 1920s. The inevitable result was that there would be more retirees but fewer workers and fewer profits to support them. The payroll tax had to be increased over and over again.

In 1993 there were more than 900,000 railroad retirees drawing benefits and about 300,000 railroad workers paying taxes of nearly 15 percent—twice the rate on Social Security. Railroad companies were paying more than 16 percent on payroll, even new short-line railroad companies that had few if any retirees. The federal government had to subsidize the system from general tax revenues to the tune of $2.8 billion a year.

PROSPERITY AND PENSIONS

Few new pension plans were created during the Depression, and only about 17 percent of the labor force in 1940 worked at places with pension plans. Then, after 1940, pension coverage rose dramatically, reaching 52 percent of the work force by 1970.

The wage and price freeze during World War II explains some of the early growth in pension coverage; pensions were a convenient form of deferred compensation when cash pay increases were made illegal. (The American system of employer-paid health insurance arose at the same time, for the same reason.) Pension expense also looked more attractive in the light of the nearly confiscatory corporate income tax rates of the period; the company got some benefit from promising pensions to workers, and no direct benefit from paying taxes. Also, national policy in the war years encouraged the unionization of large industries, and unions were more inclined to bargain for benefits than employers had been to award them.

In 1949 the U.S. Supreme Court put pensions on every bargaining table by holding that the terms of pensions would be subject to collective bargaining. Once unions became partners in setting pension policy, it was inevitable that trust funds would become more important in pension finance. Antagonists in labor negotiations needed a way to divide responsibility for the safety of pensions and to guard against misappropriation by either side.

In the 1950s and 1960s, corporations improved the funding ratios of their pension plans substantially, reaching an average of nearly 50 percent by 1970. But the double-dip recession that began that year placed new stress on the pension system at a time when Congress was ready to write a law to right any wrong. After too many companies with underfunded pension plans, such as Studebaker-Packard and Raybestos-Manhattan, closed plants and failed to pay all the benefits that workers and their unions thought were coming to them, Congress tried to carve pension promises into granite.

A FEDERAL LAW

The result was a new law called the Employee Retirement Income Security Act of 1974, known as ERISA (pronounced *ee-RISS-uh*). ERISA set funding standards and demanded that companies sponsoring underfunded pension plans make a start on depositing enough assets to cover their expected future payment liabilities. It defined the limits of accounting rules to govern pension plans so that workers would not be cheated of promised benefits. It set standards for coverage and set a maximum of ten years (now five years) of service for a worker to acquire a vested legal right to his promised pension benefits. ERISA established a legal structure to maintain the crucial point that the money in a plan is a trust that must be used exclusively to benefit plan participants. It also created a federal insurance agency, the Pension Benefit Guaranty Corp., to pay pensions to the beneficiaries of failed plans. The authors of ERISA did not expect many claims on this insurance. They thought their regulations were tight enough to cover all but a few unusual accidents.

All unfunded benefits were insured by the federal government from the start of ERISA, although Congress didn't levy sufficient

premiums or require more rapid funding to cover the large liabilities. But the people who had worked for companies that had
gone belly-up before passage of ERISA got nothing. More than
100,000 workers whose plight had motivated the Congress to
pass ERISA, whose pension expectations had been dashed on the
rock of bankruptcy, received no federal help. They complained
that Congress pledges relief to the victims of other disasters,
such as floods and earthquakes—it doesn't just build flood barriers to protect against future floods.[3]

But what had happened was different from flood control or
disaster relief: the government had flown over the pension system in a helicopter, landed briefly at the airport to promise help,
and flown back to Washington without accomplishing anything.
Those who had sponsored and supported ERISA were trying to
have their cake (secure pensions) and eat it, too (not harm any
plan sponsors). Therefore ERISA was shot through with loopholes and exclusions and waivers so that it could not weigh so
hard on any employer that its burden could be said to have
destroyed a company.

ERISA also did not take away the right of companies to terminate a plan at any point and pay only what benefits had been
earned up to that point. Lawmakers had not forced employers to
create pensions, so they reasoned that they could not force employers to keep a pension plan going. It was a far-enough reach
for Congress just to say that pension promises had to be funded
at all.

Private employers and the federal government spent the rest
of the 1970s learning to live with ERISA and its rules. Their
attention was diverted by two oil price increases, a major recession and stock market crash, and inflation that exceeded anything in living memory.

Against these immediate crises, the biggest concern in the
pension field was underfunding. Since so many plans had started
deep in the hole, it would take a long time to come up to par.
ERISA provided a gentle requirement that gave companies forty
years to make up for past underfunding, but even that was a
serious financial burden for some companies.

Curiously, though, ERISA's authors allowed and even encouraged companies to let their underfunding get worse by allowing
amortization of benefit improvements over thirty years. This

meant that when a company increased pension promises for all workers, creating a new unfunded liability, it would pay for that new promise over thirty years. This would not be a problem if all workers waited that long to receive the new benefits, but some workers would retire the same year, and nearly all would be retired and drawing the new higher benefits before the company finished contributing the necessary cash to pay them.

Every two or three years, when a new contract would roll around, unions would negotiate pay increases and pension improvements, but the company would only need to pay for the pension improvements over thirty years. It was inevitable that funding shortages would grow.

Even worse, companies were allowed to suspend required pension contributions if they ran into financial difficulties. In the next chapter, we'll see how ERISA went wrong.

2

OVER- AND UNDERFUNDING

PAN AMERICAN WORLD Airways is a classic example of a troubled company that liquidated everything, including pension assets, in a desperate bid to stay alive.

Once the world leader in aviation, Pan Am made money in only two years between 1980 and 1991. The airline had increased pension benefits in the late 1970s after a merger with National Airlines. The idea was to keep labor peace by bringing all workers from National to equality with Pan Am's more generous compensation package, then to reduce the workforce with early retirement offers. It failed miserably, as did the merged operation of the two airlines. Operating losses exceeded $3 billion, and the airline kept itself afloat with a series of asset sales and peculiar transactions. In 1980 it sold its headquarters building on Park Avenue in New York; in 1981 it sold the Inter-Continental Hotel chain.

In 1986 Pan Am sold its transpacific routes to United Air Lines. In 1989 it sold a subsidiary, Pan Am World Services, which did technical support, including management of the ground crew at the Kennedy Space Center in Florida. In 1990 it sold the Pan Am shuttle service in the Northeast Corridor, and finally the transatlantic routes that were its reason for being. All through the 1980s it sold and leased back its own airplanes, except for those that were completely mortgaged.

In 1980, 1981, 1982, 1983, and 1985 Pan Am suspended payments to its three pension funds, and the Internal Revenue Service approved this silent subtraction of more than $200 million worth of pension security. In 1987 Pan Am won special permission from the IRS and the Department of Labor to stage a transaction normally prohibited by ERISA: it sold to its pension plans a leasehold on its Worldport terminal building at JFK airport in New York. The deal was completed in 1989.

ERISA sensibly prohibits transfers of assets from employer to pension plan, on the grounds that the management officials overseeing the pension plan may too readily accept the company's valuation of property, and allow the pension plan to come off badly in a deal.

And there were questions about the value of the Worldport building. The Connecticut National Bank, which had been hired to give the pension plans impartial advice about the value of the building, backed off and advised the Labor Department that it could not estimate the potential cost of eliminating an asbestos hazard in the building. Result: the airline found another adviser. The new adviser was a subsidiary of the Wall Street firm of Bear, Stearns, which supplied a former Labor Department solicitor general to represent Pan Am at the Labor Department.

The Labor Department and the IRS eventually approved a deal that allowed Pan Am to give its pension plans the leasehold on the building instead of $104 million in back contributions. But the most amazing feature was that the leasehold was appraised at $170 million, so the desperately underfunded (by more than $600 million) pension plans ended up giving Pan Am $66 million in cash.

It would be hard to imagine a more improper deal that does not include use of a mask and a gun: Pan Am was a wretched risk for the required monthly rent payments of $2.8 million; the leasehold was a wasting asset that would expire in less than ten years; the lease became the pension plans' largest asset, some 29 percent of total assets.

But the airline had the workers over a barrel, because they were, by this time, forced to choose between jobs and the diminished security of their pension plan. Pan Am did not have the cash to make a real contribution to the pension plans that year. One union spokesman said it was a case of "damned if you do and damned if you don't," and within two years he was proved right. Pan Am was liquidated in bankruptcy and the pension plans were thrust onto the Pension Benefit Guaranty Corp.

Many workers lost their uninsured benefits and their jobs. The Pan Am pension plan had subsidized early retirement, so that many employees could collect a full pension at age sixty-two and 79 percent of full benefits at age fifty-five. They found that PBGC would cover an early retirement at only 45 percent of full benefits for a fifty-five-year-old. And the PBGC did not cover Pan Am's supplemental payment that replaced Social Security for early retirees. Some pensioners saw their monthly income cut in half.

The unfunded pension liabilities had made it impossible for any competitor to buy the whole airline and preserve most Pan Am jobs. Any company that bought Pan Am would have started out more than $600 million in the red. Pan Am was forced to sell routes and airplanes, and most employees did not go with those assets. More than 20,000 workers lost their jobs when Pan Am finally shut down in 1991.

MARKETS FLUCTUATE

The 1980s brought change to an unstable defined benefit pension system. Several trends combined in the early 1980s to create pension surpluses at many formerly underfunded plans. Underfunding, the predominant pension crisis of the 1970s, almost disappeared. Federal Reserve chairman Paul Volcker switched the Fed to a strict monetary policy that brought down inflation. A historic bull market in stocks began in August 1982. A recession in 1981–82 began the Rust Belt Depression by forcing the permanent layoff of many workers who had little seniority and hence weren't vested in their pension plans. Pension funds held as much as nine years' worth of contributions for these now-disappeared workers, but would never have to pay them a dime.

Probably the most significant force on pension economics was the Volcker combination of low inflation and high interest rates. Wage settlements, which had been running above 10 percent to keep pace with inflation, suddenly dropped to 5 percent or less. The forecasts of future wage growth embedded in pension actuarial assumptions were changed, and this held down projections of future benefits. But interest rates were still high, keeping up the future value of every dollar contributed.

Although more than half of U.S. defined benefit pension plans were underfunded in the mid-1970s, by 1983 only about 30 percent were still underwater. Take Lockheed, the aerospace company. In 1977 its pension plan was underfunded by $276 million. By 1983 it had recovered and the fund was in surplus by $702 million, even though the company had gone through a period of heavy losses and only survived with the help of a government loan.

SURPLUS ASSETS

The existence of overfunding quickly turned from a happy accident to a controversy. The authors of ERISA had been at pains to keep the U.S. private pension system voluntary, and so did nothing to restrict the right of an employer to terminate a pension plan at any time for any reason. High interest rates and competition among insurance companies also made annuities relatively cheap. Annuities are insurance contracts under which an insurer provides a stream of payments for a lifetime, the equivalent of a pension, in exchange for an up-front cash payment. When a corporate pension plan is terminated, the sponsor purchases a set of annuities to cover the plan's obligations to each beneficiary.

Although plans can be terminated at will, ERISA requires pension plans to be funded as if they would go on forever—always taking in new members and always pensioning off those workers who reach retirement age. Actuaries spend a great deal of time estimating how many workers will actually retire and what benefits they will be entitled to receive. The company then puts aside money to fund that future obligation. But if a plan terminates, the company obligation freezes. Employers must fund only what has been earned up to that point. A company's obligation to a terminated pension plan is usually much less than its obligation to a continuing plan. Terminating a plan can thus create overfunding.

ERISA made it clear that money in a pension fund was to be used for the exclusive benefit of participants. But it was not clear who really owned a pension fund surplus left over after a pension plan was terminated. The employers who had made contributions believed the surplus in a plan belonged to them after all benefits had been provided for by the purchase of an insurance annuity. Workers, if asked, probably assumed that the whole pension fund belonged to them. But they were rarely asked.

The newly overfunded pension plans of the 1980s suddenly began to look like a new source of corporate cash. Managements awoke to the idea that they could terminate a pension plan in order to grab the surplus. They would cash in the high market values of the plan assets, purchase annuities to cover the plan's liabilities, put the difference in the corporate treasury, and call it an asset *reversion*.

The U.S. Labor Department, in collaboration with the Internal Revenue Service and the Pension Benefit Guaranty Corp., allowed employers to terminate a plan, capture a surplus, and create a new plan to continue the promise of pension benefits.

Originally, the Labor Department just wanted to turn its back and allow employers to seize surplus assets at will, but the Internal Revenue Service was afraid employers would play tax games and the PBGC was afraid of weakening plans so much that its insurance fund would be overburdened. The three agencies compromised and allowed companies to use two kinds of reversions. The first was a "spin-off termination," in which retirees would be paid off with insurance annuities and the surplus attributable to them would revert to the employer, while the plan carried on as before for current workers. The second was a "termination-reestablishment," in which companies could end a plan, capture the surplus attributable to all employees, and then start a similar plan all over again.

Now you see it, now you don't: government regulators who should have been responsible for protecting pension assets held these versions of the old shell game to be an inescapable consequence of the voluntary private pension system.

PENSION PARTY

When the rules were published it was as if the government had issued an engraved invitation to capture pension surpluses. Companies responded accordingly:

Exxon Corp. set a record by extracting $1.6 billion from a $1.8 billion pension plan. The American Red Cross grabbed $400 million from a $740 million plan. In perhaps the most outrageous reversion, Continental Airlines grabbed $19.6 million by liquidating a pension fund in 1982, a few months before going into bankruptcy and laying off many of the workers who had been part of the plan.

Occidental Petroleum Corp., up to its ears in debt from its $4 billion acquisition of Cities Service, decided in 1983 to force employees to help finance the deal. It canceled four Cities Service pension plans and captured $541 million in surplus.

Another $150 billion in surplus was waiting for more corporations to catch on to the gold in their bank accounts. In 1984 an analyst for Oppenheimer & Co., Norman Weinger, made waves by listing dozens of companies that had overfunded pension funds that were ripe for the picking.

Weinger's job wasn't as easy as picking information off the footnotes in an annual report; he had to find out the interest rates on which hundreds of fund reports were based. A low earnings assumption means a pension fund is conservatively funded, which from Weinger's point of view meant that the company was undervalued. "If you're paying $575 million for a company and the overfunding in the pension plan is $350 million, you're really paying very little for the firm," he advised investors.

Some overfunded companies, such as U.S. Steel, did not seem to have the kind of prospects that would bring a corporate raider sniffing around. But U.S. Steel had a pension fund surplus equal to 54 percent of its total capitalization in the stock market. Carl Icahn arrived within a few years to take over U.S. Steel, proving it was possible to make good money in the market just by purchasing the stocks on Weinger's list.

In 1985 Union Carbide was sitting on a $1 billion pension fund surplus and had drawn unfriendly suitors like honey draws flies. (GAF, which had taken $18 million out of its pension plan the year before, was one potential acquisitor.) Carbide wanted to stop being so attractive, so it terminated its pension plan. For a twenty-year employee earning $60,000 who retired that year, the substitute annuity would pay about the same as the old pension plan—$1,200 a month. But Carbide was noted for giving periodic cost-of-living adjustments, and nothing like that would come from the insurance company to fight inflation. Still, Carbide managers were comparatively generous; they planned to take only $500 million of the surplus and they offered to use the other $500 million to create a kind of poison pill they called a pension parachute. In the event of a hostile takeover, the parachute would open and pay pension beneficiaries the other $500 million of the surplus.

Best-Laid Plans

Sometimes pension tricks could backfire: when AMF filed paperwork to lay its hands on a substantial pension surplus, managers found that they had tipped off raider Irwin Jacobs to the underlying value of the company. Shareholders accepted Jacobs's hostile offer for $550 million, and he soon reduced his expenditure with a $97 million raid on the AMF pension fund.

By 1988 Occidental Petroleum had terminated thirteen pension plans in companies it had taken over and grabbed about $624 million—or nearly a quarter of the company's entire net income from 1983 to 1988. Only Dresser Industries of Dallas had terminated so many plans, and Dresser only seized $177.2 million. In dollar terms, Exxon was the champion terminator, taking $1.64 billion through 1986. FMC Corp. of Chicago took $803 million, although $470 million was in the form of company stock and some of the proceeds had to be paid to the Defense Department. The St. Regis Corporation collected $88 million in pension assets after taking over Champion International.

United Air Lines found more than $1 billion in its pension fund at a time when the stock market valued the whole company at only $1.5 billion, but its strong unions fought so bitterly that the parent company, Allegis, was only able to take $187 million.

AM International made as dirty a play as could be imagined. The company terminated two plans, grabbing the surplus in one that was overfunded and dumping an underfunded plan on the Pension Benefit Guaranty Corp. (Remember this stunt when companies lump the reports of many pension plans into one bright and optimistic average: every pension fund is independent, and the assets of one will not be used to cover the deficits of another.)

DISHONOR ROLL

In 1980 nine pension plans terminated with surpluses of more than $1 million, and the total surplus handed over to employers was $18.5 million. In 1985 employers laid their hands on $6.1 billion by terminating 582 overfunded plans.

Workers protested in vain. In case after case, federal judges found against the workers by accepting managers' contention that a defined benefit plan means that only the benefit is defined. As one judge said, "Employees will continue to be protected to the extent of their specific benefits, but will not receive any windfalls due to the employer's mistake in predicting the amount necessary to keep the Plan on a sound financial basis."[1]

The employees of the *Washington Star* newspaper discovered to their amazement that even a specific prohibition in the pension plan barring any payment of any surplus to the employer was useless: the employer had the right to amend the plan and the judge held that the language was just contractual "boilerplate."[2] It was boilerplate that cost the workers $4 million when Time Inc. closed the newspaper and eliminated their jobs.

What the judges did not take into account was that pension surpluses do not usually arise by the will or the miscalculation of an employer. Pension surpluses arise by accidents of the securities markets and accidents of the economy. The same forces can make them vanish again. When a plan is terminated and replaced by an insurance contract, the securities markets and the economy keep on changing. The difference is that the insurance company that wrote the annuity contract picks up the market and economic risks that the employer lays down.

THE ANNUITY GAME

The idea that an insurance annuity contract was a fair substitute for a pension was another misunderstanding. Not all insurance companies that wrote annuities were sound. Consider Revlon, where a defined benefit plan was converted to Executive Life annuities after Revlon was taken over in a leveraged buyout financed by Michael Milken at Drexel Burnham Lambert. The $50 million surplus in the plan helped finance the leveraged buyout. Then Executive Life bought $400 million of the Revlon junk bonds. This circle game left both Revlon and Executive Life deeper in debt and less able to pay benefits. Members of the Milken junk bond ring employed similar tactics at many companies, and Executive Life was often involved at both ends, as the seller of annuities and the purchaser of junk bonds.

The 1991 collapse of Executive Life was the most spectacular failure of an insurance company in recent years, resulting in 30 percent reductions in its annuity payments, including those annuities that had been purchased to fund pension benefits from terminated plans. (It took several years and fortunate increases in both the stock and bond markets for the beneficiaries of Executive Life annuities to gain back what they had lost.)

The most important change for workers when a company converts a pension plan to an annuity is almost invisible: The pension plan was insured by the federal Pension Benefit Guaranty Corp., while insurance companies and their annuities are not. The federal insurance, while not completely reliable, is still far better than the promises of state insurance guaranty funds. Some of the state funds are so weak as to be useless; others are in better shape, but all would require months or even years of legal wrangling to bring any benefit to the policyholders when a company collapsed. If a large company collapsed, overwhelming the cash reserves in a guaranty fund, the state insurance regulators would have to liquidate the company and assess surviving companies to make up any deficit. The process could take years.

HARDER TERMS

Once reversions became popular and experience showed that there would be few penalties, the terms became tougher. Many companies terminated their plans outright. They followed up their old plans with less generous plans or with nothing at all and dared their workers to protest or quit. A 1986 Labor Department study found that workers lost up to 45 percent of the benefits they might have been entitled to if the old plan had been carried on.

A survey of pension data showed depressing results for 694 pension plans with more than $1 million in surplus funds that were terminated in 1986, 1987, and 1988. Only 39 percent gave workers the same coverage; 100 percent of plans were replaced with plans that were not as generous or secure; and there was no new plan at all in 25 percent of the cases.[3] A survey conducted by the American Academy of Actuaries in 1992 found worse results: 39 percent of the plans were not replaced, 30 percent were replaced with less generous plans, 23 percent were replaced with roughly similar plans, and 7 percent with more generous ones.[4]

The employers' argument was simple: if employers bear all the risk of paying for a defined benefit, then they should reap the reward if their invested contributions do better than expected. They also argued that changing the rules would discourage the creation of new defined benefit plans.

Kathleen P. Utgoff, executive director of the PBGC from 1985 through 1988, took the employers' position and warned that reform would mean the decline of the defined benefit plan.

"Imagine if we said that if you ever started a pension plan, that's your pension plan in perpetuity. No matter what happens, that pension plan has to continue to infinity," Utgoff said. "Employers would never start pension plans if they didn't have flexibility."[5]

Unfortunately, "flexibility" still means the freedom to sacrifice a pension plan to other corporate interests. Pensions are nobody's highest priority. They will be sacrificed to other concerns whenever necessary to preserve a company or preserve jobs.

Utgoff's predecessor, David Walker, who also served the Reagan administration as pension and welfare benefits administrator at the Department of Labor, was even more adamant: "If the employer bears the risk, he should be able to reap the benefits."[6] Another official who held the Labor Department job, Alan Lebowitz, acknowledged that reversion "certainly does hurt some workers in some companies," but added, "All I can observe is that the law is clear and unambiguous on the right to terminate a plan. . . . Questions of morality are for someone else, a higher authority as they say."[7] It was not his job to wonder how many people suffered financially, nor did it ever occur to him or anyone else who held his job that the Labor Department could write rules governing the termination of plans.

To Utgoff, the best government rules help both sides "voluntarily enter into the kinds of arrangements that are best for both the employer and employee." The observation is so true that it defies implementation. The only rules that can improve on a truly voluntary system are those rules of contract that require people and corporations to live up to the promises they make. Even if nobody forces an employer to create a pension system, the beneficiaries ought to be able to force employers to provide airtight funding for pension promises they do make.

Neither the PBGC nor the IRS nor the Department of Labor ever challenged a pension fund reversion. A few private individuals got some satisfaction in court. A retired executive, William I. Walsh, sued the Great Atlantic & Pacific Tea Co. when it tried to grab $250 million of a surplus largely created through massive layoffs. An out-of-court settlement wrung $50 million for the pension beneficiaries.

Two suits were filed against Harper & Row, the publishers, which grabbed $10 million by canceling its pension plan so that management could buy a controlling block of the firm's stock from Cowles Media Co. The point of controversy was that management paid Cowles twenty dollars a share for stock that was trading for less than thirteen dollars. Harper & Row management also maneuvered an employee profit-sharing fund into buying some of the shares. Former chairman Raymond C. Harper, who was both a pensioner and stockholder, sued to block the deal, as did a union representing clerical and editorial employees.

Interest rates and annuities were also controversial in the Harper & Row case. The publisher offered employees a choice between a Prudential Insurance Co. annuity and a lump-sum payment allegedly representing the present value of future benefits under the discontinued plan. But the lump sum was based on a 15 percent discount rate, which so reduced the lump sum that workers were effectively forced into the annuity. Former chairman Harper and the union settled out of court for cash payments; they could not block the deal.

The only action that the government took in the 1980s to defend any financial interest was the defense of its own tax revenues. The Treasury Department and congressional tax writers decided to demand that corporate asset-grabbers return some of the tax subsidies that helped create pension surpluses. So Congress levied a 10 percent exit tax on pension asset reversions in 1986 and raised it to 15 percent in 1987 and 50 percent in 1990.

CHAPTER

3

THE LOOTING CONTINUES

THE EXCISE TAX on pension asset reversions hasn't stopped the decade-long raid on pension funds. Terminations continue. More than 30,000 employers terminated defined benefit plans between January 1990 and June 1992.[1] And companies have found other ways to raid the assets of their pension funds. ERISA's loopholes often let them stop paying pension contributions for years, and that can be worth as much as a straightforward reversion. One of the most aggressive of the silent raiders is General Motors.

Around Christmas of 1992, General Motors concocted a pension humbug worthy of Ebenezer Scrooge's treatment of Bob Cratchit. In creating new incentives for early retirement, General Motors disguised a lump of coal as a plum pudding.

The name of this alleged Christmas gift was the Special Accelerated Attrition Agreement. The bureaucratic weight of the name alone should have been a warning, as should the use of the military term "attrition." A war of attrition is the methodical destruction of the enemy and his defenses, regardless of one's own casualties.

The key retirement incentive went to union auto workers aged fifty to sixty-one who had at least ten years of service. If they retired, they could start collecting full pension and health-care benefits, with no cap on outside earnings to limit their pension payments. They would also continue their life insurance coverage.

There was no difference between this plan and raiding the pension fund to pay line workers, except that clever lawyers worked it out so this plan was legal. The $34 billion General Motors pension fund for union workers was already $11 billion short of the assets necessary to pay all earned future benefits; the new plan simply increased the pension deficit and made it more likely that the fund will eventually collapse.

GM's Christmas humbug was an act worthy of a bankrupt corporation attempting to postpone the day of reckoning. And indeed, GM's unfunded pension liability of $11 billion, and its unfunded retiree health-care liability of at least $16 billion, together exceeded shareholder equity. In other words, on a long-term basis General Motors is worth less than nothing. The only value it has is the chance that it can earn its way out of the hole, reversing the trend, for liabilities grow faster than company assets. The pension liability at the end of 1993 swelled to $25 billion.

The United Auto Workers union, which supposedly represents the interests of all GM workers, approved the humbug plan, even though it multiplied the risk that workers eventually will lose some or all of their pensions and retirement health benefits. In fact, the union helped the company create the mess that the humbug plan was designed to cover up. The union contract provided job-security benefits that pay laid-off workers virtually full salary. With about 13 percent of GM's labor force on furlough, the support fund ran through $3.3 billion in less than three years. Both company and union found it imperative to find some other way to support these nonworking workers.

Normal retirement policies at GM are generous. The pension in 1992 was $30.70 for each year of service. That's $1,074.50 a month, plus Social Security of about $1,100 a month, for a worker who retires after thirty-five years on the job. The regular early-retirement program allowed those with thirty years of service to quit and receive $1,800 a month from the pension fund until they hit age sixty-two, when Social Security kicked in.

But the special early-attrition program of 1992 started to pay workers as much as twenty years before they could have collected benefits under the regular programs. Retirees could receive $30.70 per month for each year of service and a supplemental $21.40 per month per service year, even if they worked at other jobs. The supplement would last until the worker started to collect Social Security.

Even before the early-retirement plan of Christmas 1992, the acknowledged underfunding of the GM pension fund system increased by about 35 percent in 1991 and 1992. The company had to admit that it had been too aggressively optimistic in projecting its interest rate assumptions. Simply put, the company projected high returns from pension assets and short lifespans for pensioners.

A simple mistake that could happen to anyone? Hardly. GM had ratcheted up those earning assumptions and cut life-expectancy estimates to hold down the expense of pension contributions. GM was able to avoid making any cash contribution from 1987 to 1991. In 1990 GM raised its rate-of-return assumption to 11 percent in order to cut its cash contribution, and as it turned out, the pension fund lost 2 percent that year. The next year, though, a rising stock market helped boost earnings to 23.1 percent for the year, so the company stuck to its 11 percent long-term assumption. The next year, 1992, saw fund earnings of 6.4 percent. The three-year average was 8.7 percent a year.[2] GM, however, stuck to the justification that the fund averaged 14.4 percent a year from 1983 to 1992. The company did cut its rate-of-return assumption for 1993 to 10 percent, and it did give the fund a special contribution of its own stock, valued at $500 million for the time being. But the pension fund still fell further and further short.

During 1993, GM acknowledged that its underfunding grew from $11 billion to $14.2 billion. The company said the shortfall in earnings was responsible for $7 billion of the admitted deficit. Negotiated benefit increases that had not yet been funded were responsible for $2.7 billion. Early-retirement programs, including the Christmas humbug of the previous year, were responsible for $2 billion of underfunding. And $2.5 billion had occurred because GM had contributed more than its minimum funding in years gone by, and spent the late 1980s using up that cushion.

MAKING MATTERS WORSE

General Motors said its year-end reckoning of the pension underfunding might rise to as much as $19 billion. But even before the year could end, GM faced another pension crisis.

In a world that has too many automobile companies, competition can take many forms. Ford Motor Co. used its solid pension funding as a stick to beat General Motors.

The United Auto Workers selected Ford as the 1993 "target" for contract bargaining, meaning the union thought it could get the best deal from the company in the best financial and managerial shape and then use that as the pattern for the other two unionized American car companies.

Ford fought hard, but not too hard. The union came away with a contract that continued income protection for laid-off workers, increased pensions, and a lower wage for new employees. By comparison with GM, Ford had fewer laid-off workers, better prospects of needing to hire new workers, and a better-funded pension plan, so each of the major provisions would help Ford more or hurt Ford less than they would GM.

"The new contract played into Ford's strengths: 100 percent capacity utilization, full employment, and the likelihood Ford is not going to go through any huge painful job cuts," said auto analyst Maryanne Keller.[3]

But GM was a different case. During the previous three-year contract, GM had depleted a $3 billion income protection fund because of its layoffs. Continuing the costly program for another three years seemed almost certain to force more huge losses. GM's answer to the layoff squeeze in 1992 had been to put as many laid-off workers as possible on early retirement, where their pensions could pick up the cost of supporting them.

When the union came to General Motors, its negotiators were determined to continue to protect workers from layoffs. They demanded restoration of the income protection program and a match for the increase in pension benefits at Ford. GM was unwilling to take a strike, which would have been an immediate disaster. So the company caved in quickly, bringing its unfunded pension liability to $24 billion.

Pause for a moment and consider how fast the General Motors

pension disaster happened: At the end of 1987, GM's union plan was overfunded by nearly $2 billion. It took seven lean years to take the largest industrial company in the United States from a tower of financial security to a deep pit of danger. Incidentally, the company management somehow managed not to do the same thing to their own pension plan, which was still $2 billion in surplus at the end of 1993.

DAY OF MISRECKONING

At the end of 1993, General Motors acknowledged the need to do something about the sorely underfunded pension plan for union workers, and then proposed to fix it by making it worse. GM proposed a $5.5 billion extra contribution to the fund—which sounded good until it turned out that this contribution would come in the form of GM's own stock. And it wouldn't be just any stock, it would be the screwball Class E stock that was created to accomplish the takeover of Electronic Data Systems. Class E stock is a hybrid, with its value tied not simply to GM's value but to the earnings performance of the EDS subsidiary. Class E stock is GM stock, with a promise of a dividend equal to 30 percent of what EDS earns each year—as calculated by GM.

Asked about the contribution, GM treasurer Heidi Kunz basically said take it or leave it:

"That a cash contribution is better than a stock contribution . . . is not the relevant issue in GM's case. A stock contribution that is incremental to cash contributions adds real economic value to the pension plan. How could this extra contribution of stock be harmful to pensioners or to the pension insurance agency?"[4]

Kunz asked the wrong rhetorical question. The right question is, How much was the stock really worth? If GM tried to sell 185 million Class E shares to the public, it would dilute all existing shareholdings and decimate the price of the stock. By contributing the stock as a block, GM avoids valuing its paper in the marketplace, avoids showing that it expects its pension beneficiaries to accept play money in satisfaction of real debts. It leaves to the pension fund the tedious job of turning play money into real money by selling the Class E stock into the market in dribs and drabs.

The stock market's judgment of the deal was swift. The new overhang of stock to be disposed of was a clear negative for Class E shares, and their price fell more than 10 percent in the first week after the announcement.

Only the U.S. Department of Labor stood between General Motors and the paper flood. Pension rules bar any plan from holding more than 10 percent of the sponsor's stock, and the GM contribution would push the union workers' plan into a position where about a quarter of all its investments would be Class E shares. The plan would also own 38 percent of all Class E shares, in violation of a rule that prohibits a plan from owning more than 25 percent of any issue.

Although they have approved waivers for many stock contributions before, federal officials immediately announced that they would not make a decision right away, and they hinted that it could take until 1995 to decide. It could be that GM overdid it, that 185 million straws finally broke the tolerant camel's back.

INGLORIOUS COMPANY

General Motors is not the only large American industrial company to run up a serious deficit in its pensions.

Since 1990, the federal Pension Benefit Guaranty Corp. has published an annual list of the fifty companies with the most underfunded pension plans. The PBGC takes annual report data and adjusts the numbers to provide equal and realistic discount rates, so the deficits counted by the PBGC are often larger and more realistic than those the companies report. The idea is to embarrass companies into making larger contributions to get off the list and to highlight the need for reform of the pension system. Shining the spotlight on these firms has been the most constructive thing the federal government has managed to do for the pension system in many years. But total underfunding increases every year. In 1992 the total for the fifty companies on the list was $38 billion, of which the federal insurance agency guarantees $31.7 billion. The total was $29.1 billion in 1991. See the Appendix for the whole list.

Every year some of the companies on the list scream and complain that their numbers were unfairly manipulated. Others say that underfunding is a perfectly normal result of good pension practices. Others simply state that their pension contributions were in accordance with minimum funding standards, or that they were the maximum permitted for tax deductible status with the IRS. Two sample responses:

"It singles us out as bad guys when we are complying with the rules and regulations," said Chrysler treasurer Thomas P. Tapo. "We have had funding the pension plan as a top priority of the company." [5] Indeed, Chrysler's underfunding fell from $3.6 billion in 1991 to $876 million in 1992.

"We don't think there is very much meaning in the report of our pension underfunding," said Alan Halpert, manager of public affairs of Bridgestone-Firestone, the Japanese-owned tire company. "We are certainly operating in full compliance of the law, and even the government acknowledges there is not a significant risk to anybody on pension. This announcement just creates anxiety. In all our years, we have never had a pension problem, and there is nothing to worry about now."[6]

There were twelve companies on the 1991 list that were not on in 1992, and ten of them were good-news stories because they improved their funding position. One, Sharon Steel, terminated its underfunded plans and threw the liability on the PBGC, and another, Cyclops Industries, was bought by Armco, which was on the list both years.

It's sometimes said that Americans should not worry too much about underfunded pensions because almost all the companies on the list are concentrated in a few industries, primarily metals, heavy machinery, and airlines. See the list in the Appendix to judge for yourself; it should be clear that underfunding is widely distributed through American industry.

To understand how a company gets into this kind of predicament, we can look at one of the biggest, best-known, and most respected American industrial corporations, IBM. The company that brought American business and finance into the computer age with mainframe computers and that popularized the personal computer in business and at home, IBM failed to move as fast as it had to in order to keep up with its rapidly evolving industry.

IBM held itself back with a rigid and bureaucratic corporate culture in which it was far easier to "non-concur" than it was to get a project moving to market. The company maintained a no-layoff policy for about half a century, and accumulated deadwood on its worldwide staff faster than it could create new jobs.

IBM restructured several times in the late 1980s and early 1990s, offering more and more enticements for people to leave the company. The 1991 restructuring, for example, eliminated the financial penalty for early retirement and added extra benefits besides. IBM paid out $122 million in special retirement incentives in 1991, $355 million in 1992, and $263 million in 1993.

New management eventually realized that the people most likely to leave the company were those best able to find other employment, leaving IBM with those who were too frightened or too conservative to strike out on their own. In 1992, IBM started forcible retirements and layoffs.

From 1988 to 1993, the number of retirees nearly doubled, from 40,567 to 77,664. The cost of the retirement plan—including non-U.S. plans—more than tripled, from $460 million in 1988 to $1.5 billion in 1993.

Also in 1993, IBM changed the discount rate assumption in its U.S. plan from 8.5 percent to 7.25 percent, bringing the rate more in line with reality. The company should be praised for not indulging in phony accounting; its new numbers cost it more than half a billion dollars in cash contributed to the pension fund. But the new, truer numbers still were disheartening. For the first time, IBM found itself with an underfunded pension plan. The projected benefit obligation disclosed in the 1993 annual report stood at $29.0 billion, with assets of $28.1 billion.

The computer industry continues to change rapidly, and IBM is trying to change just as fast. The security of its pension fund, which represents retirement security for hundreds of thousands of workers, depends on IBM's ability to hold on to its markets and its customers. The trend is in the wrong direction though, and every American ought to learn from IBM, and of course, from General Motors, where the trend has gone on much longer.

How can you know that your company will be around to support you in its old age? Can you trust it to use honest accounting? Underfunding is a natural consequence of the mismatch between benefit promises and benefit funding in a defined benefit pension plan. How this happens and how it might be alleviated will be addressed later in the book. However, another part of the American pension system, the pension funds operated by governments, will be discussed in Chapter 4.

THE GOVERNMENT EXAMPLE

MOST GOVERNMENT EMPLOYEES' pension systems are defined benefit systems. Interestingly, they are left to their own devices, not subject to the federal regulatory system. This freedom, this trust, has produced some of the worst pension systems in the United States.

The District of Columbia offers a leading example, with $7 billion in pension liabilities and $2 billion in assets. Promises are cheap—so the D.C. government keeps making them to its teachers, firefighters, police, and court workers. Local officials demand that Congress fund their promises, but Congress usually turns a cold shoulder to all pleadings from the people who run their capital city.

Cost-of-living increases are rare in the private sector, but government pensions typically feature guaranteed increases protecting retirees from any erosion of the purchasing power of their monthly checks. Cost-of-living benefits can eat a pension plan alive, yet 75 percent of state and local pension plans have COLAs, while only 28 percent of private defined benefit plans do.[1] It's a cheap promise at the beginning, but the expense grows and grows, and often leaves a city paying more to retirees than to working employees. The District of Columbia is extreme, awarding cost-of-living increases twice a year so that recipients get a pension that grows faster than inflation. In 1993 Washington, D.C., paid more money to retired police and firefighters than it did to those on active duty. The city of Chicago, for another example, spends three-quarters of its property tax revenues on retirement pay.

All too many public employment contracts treat sick time and vacation time as money in the bank, rather than imitating private industry and requiring workers to use it or lose it. Public-sector workers of long standing who are never sick and never take a vacation can build up some incredible sums. A Suffolk County, New York, school superintendent retired in 1992 with a golden parachute amounting to nearly $1 million.

"These are benefits that were granted during better economic times in an effort to lure qualified people from the lucrative private sector into public employment," said Thomas Gulotta, county executive of neighboring Nassau County, where union and management police were allowed to claim on retirement up to fifty-four vacation days, 235 sick days, and a bonus of five days' pay for each year of service.[2]

THE FEDERAL TROUGH

The federal government has more than a trillion dollars of pension liabilities, and an accounting system that covers up the future burden to American taxpayers. Though the federal budget accurately reflects the huge cost of pensions, which matches the payroll for current workers, the pensions are funded with government bonds—an IOU covering an IOU. Federal retirement trust funds are filled with Treasury debt, not with real assets of the productive economy.

Judy Park, legislative director of the National Association of Retired Federal Employees, works to protect the trust fund for civil service retirement benefits. When the subject of holding nothing but the government's IOU is raised, Park laughs nervously. "I'd just as soon nobody would talk about it," she says. But she bravely adds that she thinks it entirely appropriate. "Our feeling has always been that if you work for the government, you should invest in the government."

This actually makes no more sense than investing your retirement savings in the stock and bonds of your employer. You accept the risk that your employer may have financial trouble that may cost you your job. You should diversify your retirement investments away from the employer, whether your employer is General Motors or the President of the United States.

The civil service trust fund shows a surplus by the cash accounting system of the federal government. But in truth, only those workers hired after 1984 have benefits fully funded by even Treasury debt. The vast majority are only partly covered by the $214 billion of assets in the kitty as of 1990. The discounted present value of payments to be made over the next seventy-five years exceeds those assets by $486 billion. Since 1985, the military retirement trust fund has received contributions for benefits currently earned, but there's a $498 billion actuarial deficit for benefits earned before 1985.

Federal financial managers make up the difference by paying as they go, using today's payments for workers to pay today's retirees. They apparently hope that their successors will also be able to pay as they go.

There are only two serious ways to make real savings out of a government trust fund balance. These are to invest the balance in the private sector or to have the whole government run a consolidated surplus, so that the trust funds repurchase previously issued bonds from the public, driving down the amount of government debt in private hands.

POCKET PICKERS

Just as in private industry, hard-pressed local government officials often turn to the pension fund as a ready source of emergency cash.

Dennis Spice, who presides over a $3.5 billion deficit as executive director of the State Universities Retirement System of Illinois, blames politicians who answer to no higher authority. "Who makes legislators and governors ante up? That's the

question. Should they not be held to fiduciary standards? We
do not have a Pension Benefit Guaranty Corporation. We do
not have federal laws that our members could go to and file
some sort of petition for relief. . . . The health insurance crisis
of the next century is going to be the funding of public pensions. No one wants to realize how bad it is."[3] In fact, there is
no federal requirement for government pensions at any level to
be funded at all. Some states have required funding for municipalities, but they can do as they please to their own funds,
even to the point of going for a pay-as-you-go system if they
choose.

In a 1993 report, the General Accounting Office analyzed a
survey of pension plans from forty-seven states and Puerto Rico.
Of the 189 plans that provided complete funding data, most
were underfunded. One can only imagine the financial position
of those that didn't bother to provide complete figures. GAO
said the reporting group, eighty-nine statewide plans with assets
of $306.7 billion and one hundred local plans with assets of
$156.4 billion, had an average funded ratio of 83 percent of re-
ported liabilities.

Only sixty-one plans were fully funded. The underfunded
plans were short with a 76 percent average funding ratio,
and fifty-four of the underfunded plans were below even that
level.

As a group, government employees average a little older than
the national workforce. Most are over forty and many of them
expect to retire before age sixty. Of course, the ratio of active
workers to retirees is falling rapidly, so the cash flow of many
pension plans is likely to get worse, and soon. The GAO said
teachers' retirement plans in the District of Columbia, Maine,
Oklahoma, and West Virginia, and state employees' retirement
plans in Maine and Massachusetts don't even have enough assets to support current retirees, let alone the coming wave of
new pensioners.

"Inadequate contributions over the long term could seriously
erode the tenuous financial status of some plans, especially
those underfunded by large amounts," the GAO added. For the
politically circumspect accountants of the GAO, those were
strong words.

It's not hard to find other governments with pension problems unremarked by the GAO. Florida's pension system has always been underfunded. The good news is that the state contributes an extra $840 million a year to make up for past failure; the bad news is that underfunding keeps growing because the state would need to pay another $500 million a year to keep current. The unfunded liability hit $15.9 billion in 1991. The next year, though, the legislature added another $5 million by granting new unfunded pension benefits to five hundred of the state's highest-paid managers.[4]

COLD RECEPTION

Managers and public-employee unions greeted the GAO report with criticism.

"We are deeply concerned that this report paints a distorted picture of the financial health of public-employee retirement systems and that its publication has resulted in undue worry for many state and local pensioners," said Michael Mory, chairman of the Public Pension Coordinating Council. He complained that GAO didn't mention that the average funding ratio of public-employee retirement systems had increased from 51 percent in 1975 to about 85 percent in 1990. "While our members are working to see these circumstances improve, we do not believe that the situation is as pessimistic as the GAO report suggests," he said.[5]

The National Council on Teacher Retirement complained that the report gave "the misleading impression that state and local pension plans are about to collapse. Nothing could be further from the truth."[6] The council also seemed more annoyed by the upset that the report caused among retired teachers than by any financial problems that exist: "GAO's biased view also had the unfortunate consequence of panicking thousands of public-sector retirees," the council said, asserting that GAO was off the mark in its strict assumption that anything less than 100 percent funding represents a financial risk. "State and local governments . . . don't go out of business, so the need for full funding in every instance is subject to debate."

LONG-TERM PROBLEM

As with virtually all pension problems, it's hard to mobilize for a crisis that seems a long way off. The Illinois teachers' fund will cover its payments until around 2020, assuming its funding doesn't get much worse. The only justice in that is that some of the people who are not now fixing the problem will be among the victims of the twenty-first-century crisis. But they will not be in the jobs where they are now shirking responsibility, and they won't be available to shoulder blame.

Even in the District of Columbia, which is widely recognized to be on the verge of bankruptcy because of its pension obligations, there is more of a sense of public relations problem than of urgency.

In January 1994, Mayor Sharon Pratt Kelly proposed a plan to reduce the $5 billion unfunded liability by cutting benefits slightly, raising employee contributions from 7 percent of pay to 8 percent, and asking Congress to increase the federal contribution by 5 percent a year. But her administration spent more time explaining how the federal government had caused the problem than on how the numbers would add up to a safe, secure pension system. In fact, the let-Congress-do-it proposal simply postponed the problem to another day; its most significant financial feature was to extend federal contributions for thirty-one years beyond the intended termination date in 2004.

LOCAL PROBLEMS

Illinois, Louisiana, Rhode Island, West Virginia, Oklahoma, Connecticut, Massachusetts, and Maine have severely underfunded pension plans. Kansas and Alaska suffered well-publicized losses on unwise investments. Incidentally, averages are not relevant in pension finance. The annual Wilshire Associates survey of large public plans finds funding all over the map: New York State employees have a $10.3 billion surplus and the state employees fund in Massachusetts is $3.1 billion in the hole. On average, they both look healthy, but one is sick and one is not.

The West Virginia Teachers Retirement System has the dubious distinction of coming in dead last in the Wilshire survey, being only 14 percent funded. State funds for judges and state police aren't much better off, with funding ratios of less than 40 percent. The state plans to make up the underfunding over forty years.

State governments, which haven't gone bankrupt since shortly after the Revolutionary War, are nothing compared to municipalities, school districts, and other small government agencies, which can and do go bankrupt regularly. Many of them also have pension obligations, and nobody has ever kept tabs on them all.

Teachers' pension funds are often found among the most troubled. This is partly because there are so many different school districts and partly because teachers tend to stay in one job for a whole career and build up the maximum pension promises, too expensive to fund adequately.

Many public employees ought to worry because they have nothing except their pension. Congress did not draft most of these workers into the Social Security system until recently, so that few pensioners and only about a third of current workers are eligible for full Social Security benefits.

But nobody worries about public pensions because the governments responsible for them can always fall back on taxation. No public pension fund has ever gone under and all the experts say that none ever will, even while governors and mayors balance their budgets on the backs of pensioners by reducing contributions and selling state assets to captive pension plans.

In California Republican governor Pete Wilson and a Democratic legislature collaborated in 1991 to raid $1.9 billion in pension surplus that the California Public Employees Retirement System had set aside for cost-of-living increases. The California State Teachers Retirement System allowed the state to defer a $477 million pension fund payment. The legislature promised to change actuarial assumptions and make up the lost money in future payments.

In 1990 New York did not make a $843 million state education aid payment that local school districts were depending on to make their teachers' pension fund payments. Not all the districts made up the shortfall out of their own revenues.

MISREPRESENTATION

Public officials are constitutionally and practically responsible to their constituents, but problems arise when their constituents are also their employees. More problems may occur when those employees are represented by unions. All too often, public pension interests become lost in the shuffle.

In 1990 municipal employee unions acquiesced in New York City's funding raises for workers by decreasing their pension contributions. The method was to increase the interest rate estimate of how much the city pension portfolio would earn each year. Increasing the earnings assumption decreased the required pension contribution, freeing up current cash to pay raises.

We might imagine that changing the interest rate assumption was warranted by the funding status of the pension fund, but this was New York City, a city that almost bankrupted itself by spending its capital fund for operations and by borrowing against anticipated revenues that did not materialize.

The city continued to play with the pension fund in subsequent years. In the 1993 city budget, the pension contribution was cut $27 million thanks to increased earnings. To confirm the uselessness of official watchdogs, city comptroller Elizabeth Holtzman criticized the city administration for not making the cut larger. Ms. Holtzman was a trustee of the city pension funds, but she was also a perennial candidate for high office.

In a "fiscal crisis" in 1992, New Jersey changed its method of accounting, allowing the state to increase its assumed earnings on pension assets from 7 percent to 8.5 percent. The resulting increase in projected assets to pay future benefits allowed the state to cut its annual pension contribution from $900 million to $600 million.

Bart Naylor, an economist and a keen judge of political character at the American Federation of State, County and Municipal Employees, comments: "We're concerned not only because we believe that money is ours, but it's a dishonest and politically problematic way to solve a budget crisis that will usually result in a tax increase. . . . Then we'll probably get blamed."

FIGHTING BACK

Some pension raids have gone to court. Wisconsin's Retired Teachers Association and the State Engineering Association won a case against the state, which had tried to finance a retirement supplement with funds that were set aside for basic pensions. Illinois public employee unions have sued the state because the legislature reneged on a promise to repay some deferred contributions to five pension funds, but the case remained unresolved in early 1994.

There are a few other rays of hope for public pensions, such as the reform administration in Philadelphia: Mayor Ed Rendell focused his administration on renewing economic growth in the city rather than taxing its way out of its almost overwhelming slump. Things had gotten so desperate that a state-sponsored agency had to bail the city out of its deficit. Of taxes, city finance director Steven P. Mullen said: "The facts sort of speak for themselves. We've raised tax rates nineteen times in the last decade . . . all [tax increases] do is help erode the tax base."[7] Rendell drove a hard bargain with nonuniformed city workers to reduce benefits by $100 million. This cut the promise to workers, but made the promise more secure.

5

DEFINED CONTRIBUTION PLANS

GTE CORP.'s $16.5 BILLION defined benefit pension fund had long been considered one of the best managed in the country. Other funds watched it in particular for investment sophistication, because John Carroll, head of the pension department, was a pension trend-setter. He was among the first American plan sponsors to put a heavy emphasis on overseas stocks; he put money managers on a fee schedule based on their performance; most recently, he applied the principles of Total Quality Management to pension fund management.

Total Quality Management is the updated management advice "The customer is always right." It means that an enterprise and all of its workers focus their total attention on improving their product or service to satisfy the customer. It puts pressure on an organization for continuous improvement, so much pressure that workers sometimes say it means "Time to Quit and Move."

The basic application of Total Quality Management to finance is simple: maximize returns for participants. But that requires managers to have a good idea of the risk-adjusted rate of return produced by various investment advisers and to have a real handle on costs of running investments inside the company.

GTE found that its in-house managers outperformed its external managers and market indexes, while incurring one-tenth the cost.

The company adopted a principle of quality management by reducing the number of suppliers and then establishing close relationships with the survivors. Instead of dealing with forty brokers, the fund decided to work closely with fewer than ten, and allocate their volume based on their performance for the fund. It seemed to bring more attentive service. GTE also developed computerized evaluation of portfolios managed by outside advisers, being careful to show the managers how they were judged and rewarded. In general, GTE pension managers declared all their service providers as each other's customers, so that brokers, computer specialists, investment analysts, and portfolio managers reported on each other's performance, made their needs explicit, and offered suggestions on how their colleagues could meet those needs.

Most important, GTE treated its pensioners like customers. The company interviewed employees around the country in focus groups, permitting people to reinforce each other's observations and brainstorm their ideas for improvement. They found that GTE's supplementary savings plan did not live up to the high standard set by the defined benefit plan. The employees said they wanted more investment options than the four items offered: Guaranteed Investment Contracts issued by insurance companies, a stock index fund, a short-term bond fund, and company stock. They also wanted more help in making their choices. About half voiced anxiety about investing.

GTE management asked for proposals from many benefit consulting firms and investment management companies. Two independent teams evaluated the proposers; one looked at administration and the other at asset management. Though the two groups did not collaborate, they both gave Fidelity Investments their top grade and Fidelity was hired.

Now GTE employees have ten options for their savings plan. The only one remaining from the old plan is company stock. Fidelity provides investment opportunities in four of its regular mutual funds—the Magellan stock fund, biggest in the country, a growth and income fund; a U.S. stock index fund; an overseas stock fund; and a money market portfolio. Considering the $3 billion size of the account, Fidelity was also happy to create four "strategy funds" for GTE that invest in portfolios of regular Fidelity bond and stock funds. One is 100 percent bond funds, another is 75 percent bond funds and 25 percent stock funds, another is fifty-fifty, and the fourth is 75 percent stocks and 25 percent bonds. Employees can switch between their investment options as often as they desire, just by calling an 800 phone number.

Fidelity and GTE also shared responsibility for a continuing education project to teach participants about retirement finance, investments, and their choices.

Since the launch in January 1993, participation has climbed from 70 percent in the old plans to 80 percent for the new one. The participants number 95,000 workers.

The company even made out financially: GTE had paid all recordkeeping costs and investment fees in its old savings plan; now participants pay investment fees plus five dollars a year for accounting.

PROMISES OR PROPERTY

A *defined contribution plan* can address the retirement needs of employees at least as well as, and probably better than, a defined benefit plan. In a defined benefit pension system, workers must live with a system of promises, all too often hollow promises, about their future. They need a system of property. Some Americans are fortunate enough to be working under such a system already, if they are covered under a defined contribution pension plan. In a defined contribution plan, the employer cannot make empty promises; what the employer makes are real cash contributions, which immediately become the property of the employee, to be paid after retirement.

All defined contribution plans share certain characteristics. Every worker has an individual account in which annual contributions are deposited, with the amount depending on a percentage of salary or on a portion of profits, or a combination of the two. Benefits at retirement depend on the amount accumulated in an individual account, plus investment earnings. Each employee receives the entire value of his account at retirement as a lump-sum distribution, though he may buy an annuity to pay a monthly benefit. In an important difference for workers who change jobs frequently, employees also receive the full balance of their accounts if they leave the company before retirement. When the employee receives a lump sum, either at retirement or on leaving his job, he can pay taxes on it and do whatever he wants with it or he can roll it over into another tax-sheltered plan, usually an Individual Retirement Account.

About half of defined contribution plan participants make their own contributions to their accounts to add to the contributions of their employers, either voluntarily or as a requirement of participation. These contributions, which are not tax-deductible, remain unequivocally the property of the participant.

More than a third of U.S. workers with pension plans now have a defined contribution plan as their primary plan, which is an increase from 13 percent as recently as 1975. About 39 percent of workers have two pension plans, and the second is almost invariably some form of defined contribution plan, even if the first one is a defined benefit plan.[1]

Most analysts acknowledge that the government's regulatory complexity and tax hostility have pushed employers away from defined benefit plans. By the Labor Department's count, 5.3 million workers participated in defined benefit plans that were terminated between 1975 and 1988.[2] Defined contribution plans added more than 11 million participants.

The fastest-growing defined contribution plan is the newest. The 401(k) plan, which got started in 1980 under a provision of the 1978 tax law, is named for the section of federal tax law that authorizes employers to create plans in which employees can make voluntary contributions to savings from pretax income. Employers can add to the employee contribution if they wish, and their contribution can be in the form of company stock. By 1988 24 percent of all U.S. workers were offered a 401(k) plan and 14 percent were participating, more than half of all those eligible.[3]

Because all 401(k) plans require an affirmative contribution by the employee, some analysts worry that people who have trouble making ends meet won't contribute enough to assure a decent benefit. Indeed, only 35 percent of people at minimum wage or nearly minimum contribute to 401(k) plans when they are offered, while it's 80 percent for people who make more than twenty dollars an hour. But this is a question of whether the glass is 35 percent full or 65 percent empty. Although it is true that most people will not put much into a 401(k) while they are making five dollars an hour, it is equally true that encouraging such workers to form habits of thrift and planning for the future may be an important way of educating them to rise out of minimum-wage jobs. Some studies also suggest that most of the people who don't contribute are young, and that they will eventually get around to contributing later on in their careers when they make more money. Also, Social Security benefits are more generous to the lowest-paid workers.

ADVANTAGES TO BOTH SIDES

The defined contribution plan carries the advantage to the employer of being completely predictable. A contribution once made is invested, and that's the end of it. There's no risk that a sudden reversal in the investment portfolio will require the employer to make up a pension shortfall, because the employee is only entitled to what's in his account, for better or for worse.

The defined contribution plan is also an honest deal with the employee because there's no risk that the employer will sneak money out of the plan or make rash promises that aren't backed up with hard assets. It's advantageous for any employee who changes jobs several times during a career, because the ultimate value of the retirement fund is not tied to the length of continuous service with one employer. Even a worker who has two jobs at successive companies with equally generous pay and defined benefit plans will receive a lesser pension than if he had stayed at the first job for an entire career. At the extreme, the worker who moves around a lot and never stays anywhere for as long as five years may earn no pension at all, even if every one of his employers had a defined benefit pension plan.

Honesty and portability aside, there are problems for the participants in defined contribution plans, mostly problems born of ignorance.

Many participants in defined contribution plans don't sock away enough to produce adequate retirement income. And most beneficiaries who control their investments are too conservative—they invest in fixed-income securities like Treasury bills and Guaranteed Investment Contracts, which don't yield enough earnings to provide all that they expect from their pension plan.

The Wyatt Company consulting firm compared rates of return for defined contribution plans with investments selected by participants—usually a range of mutual funds—with defined benefit investments handled by professionals. The company also compared returns of individual investors, gathered from mutual fund companies, to retirement plans as a whole. The returns for plans where the individual had a choice were 2.5 percentage points to 3 percentage points lower than those of the defined benefit plans. In other words, individuals are so concerned with safety that they are willing to sacrifice 2.5 to 3 percentage points of yield compared to professional managers. They need more information about what they are giving up in the long run.

Many employees apparently do not want to become knowledgeable about investments. Says Morgan Yeates of the Wyatt Company: "We've gradually migrated to giving employees all these choices. Now many of them are wanting to simplify them and are saying, 'I don't care what the funds are. I don't really care what the overall return is. Here is where I am on the risk spectrum, and here is where I want to be on the long-term return. Now you pick the fund combination that will meet those needs for me. Don't make me become an expert in investments.' "[4]

Current regulation of defined contribution plans makes it difficult to satisfy the worker who is determined to stay ignorant. Employers are afraid to manage workers' investment decisions for fear that they will be held responsible for any adverse investment results. That would take away the certainty that is the main advantage of a defined contribution plan.

UNHERALDED RISK

One investment the most risk-averse members of defined contribution plans employ may, in fact, be among the most risky. Guaranteed Investment Contracts issued by insurance companies are riskier than the name implies, since the guarantee is simply the insurance company's promise to pay. A 1991 General

Accounting Office study of 174 large pension plans found that 28 percent of defined contribution plan assets were held in Guaranteed Investment Contracts. Defined benefit plans only held 2 percent of their assets in GICs on average, although some individual plans have been loaded with them.

Only fifteen state insurance guaranty funds explicitly guarantee all GICs, and even these limit the amount of the guarantee regardless of the number of employees involved. Guaranty funds in California, Idaho, Kansas, Kentucky, Louisiana, and Missouri exclude all GICs. GICs that are not clearly allocated to specific individuals or groups are excluded from protection in Florida, Hawaii, Massachusetts, Nevada, Oklahoma, South Dakota, Virginia, and Wyoming. Twenty other states have various other eligibility limits.

Another kind of guarantee frequently employed by defined contribution plans is found only in the imaginations of some participants. A growing share of defined contribution wealth is invested in mutual funds, which are pooled investments of stocks or bonds or a combination. As we shall see in Part Four, mutual funds are an excellent investment vehicle for informed investors. But many people who own mutual funds imagine that they are backed or insured by the government, either as if they were banks insured by the Federal Deposit Insurance Corp., or as if regulation by the Securities and Exchange Commission conferred some special government backing on them. Neither is the case.

Mutual funds stand on their own feet. The value of each fund goes up and down with the price of the securities in each fund's portfolio. No two of the thousands of mutual funds are exactly alike, any more than two companies or two communities are exactly alike. An investor should put the same care into selecting mutual funds as into deciding where to live or where to work. The federal government does not insure your job or the quality of your schools; it also does not insure your mutual fund.

SELF-DESTRUCTION

Defined contribution plans are also open to a group of predators: the beneficiaries themselves. If they change jobs, they can get their retirement fund in cash and keep it after paying taxes on it.

At least $12 billion a year leaves the defined contribution retirement system this way. Too often this means that the worker exchanges some part of his retirement security for a car or a trip or, at best, some college tuition. The employee sacrifices not only the money withdrawn, but also the tax-free buildup of the withdrawn investment. That $12 billion would quintuple into $60 billion in retirement assets if it were invested at 10 percent and held for seventeen years. Younger workers are most likely to miss this opportunity if they fail to recognize that even small sums grow dramatically if they compound for a long time.

Plan participants are also allowed to borrow from defined contribution plans, which means they supply their own return on investment and thus diminish their equity working within the plan. Still, it seems logical—the money belongs to the worker and he should be able to borrow from his fund, just as he could use it for collateral or flat-out withdraw it if the money were in a regular bank or securities account. Logical it is. Fair it is. Sensible may be another story, though it depends on the rate of interest the pension account charges. The rate may be above or below the market at the time of the loan, and thus may be a good or bad deal for the beneficiary.

Suppose new car loans at a bank or credit union are at 12 percent, and the pension account charges 10 percent. Looks like a great way to finance a car, and so it would be, except that the borrower is really also the lender. If bank interest rates stay at 12 percent for the life of the loan, the pension account earns at least two percentage points less on that money than it might have earned by investing in a debt security of similar term and risk. (Actually, the loss will be greater than the nominal difference in interest rates because the single car loan is riskier than a same-sized share of a securitized portfolio of car loans.)

If car loans are at 10 percent and the pension account charges 12 percent, it's such a good deal for the pension account that the worker won't borrow from his account. So every time a worker borrows from his pension account, it's a safe bet he's crediting the present with a debit on the future.

Such transactions are popular, of course, especially when they are cloaked with confusion. And the company that allows and encourages borrowing from defined contribution plans will be popular with its workers, even though it is encouraging them to do something foolish. Such a company is Steelcase, the office furniture company based in Grand Rapids, Michigan. Steelcase offers loans from its profit-sharing retirement plan and just to make it easier, the company offers its 10,000 employees the convenience of a toll-free 800 telephone number and an automated voice response system.

"On the first day of operation, the phone system received 1,295 loan inquiries, followed by 450 in the next week," the company's supervisor of retirement program administration told the newsletter of Hewitt Associates, the benefits consulting firm that provided the phone system. "During the first month of operation, 2,000 loans were processed. If we had handled that level of volume manually, it would have taken months," said the supervisor, Rosemary Klackle.[5]

Ms. Klackle and Hewitt were proud of the way they satisfied their clients, but their pride was deeply misplaced. Making it easier for employees to borrow from the retirement accounts is like running a liquor store in a dry-out clinic.

Some 401(k) savings plans allow withdrawals after a few years. Again, it seems only fair, since the employees made voluntary contributions, that they should be allowed to reverse their decision. But some 401(k) plans seem to have developed a pattern in which money stays in just long enough to attract an employer match. Then the money is withdrawn. It becomes a twisted form of current pay.

GOVERNMENT HELP

In 1992 Congress enacted a law that purported to help pension plan participants by giving them an incentive to roll any lump-sum distributions over into a new retirement vehicle. The basic idea was that if a person leaves a job and gets a cash settlement from a pension plan, it should go into an Individual Retirement Account where it will likely stay until retirement, not just be taken and spent. Tax law already reflected the basic idea, imposing income tax and a penalty on any money that was not rolled over. Congress imposed 20 percent withholding on the money not rolled over, adding an immediate out-of-pocket penalty to the basic tax.

Congress was displaying a good grasp of human nature by adding the out-of-pocket penalty, but the change cost pension plan sponsors an estimated $4.5 billion just to rewrite their rules and plan documents.[6] And the cost fell most heavily on the smallest plans. The legal and financial cost of amending plans and changing accounting was about $1,500 per plan, large or small, and the continuing costs of compliance are about $1,000 a year. Net results are also likely to be less than estimated, because some plan sponsors will throw in the towel and shift to some less regulated way of compensating their employees.

It's not hard to invest for yourself, or to think for yourself, but it's not that common either. A lump-sum distribution from a retirement plan can be an invitation to act stupidly. For example, the Senate Special Committee on Aging heard the sad testimony of a sixty-two-year-old toolmaker from Fairfield, Connecticut, named John Us.[7]

Somehow, this gentleman entrusted $50,000 of savings and money from a retirement plan to the hands of a stockbroker. Us believed he was investing in a "no-risk, safe government fund." Instead, the broker put his money into penny stocks and lost it all in three years.

The broker may not have been a crook, merely incompetent, because he could have misappropriated the money in a much shorter time if he had put his mind to it. The North American Securities Administrators Association reports that many consumer complaints about investments concern well-meaning, licensed, trained advisers and brokers who had little more knowledge than their customers, and passed on whatever information or misinformation their bosses told them.

Us had to go back to work with his retirement dreams shattered, and he felt so betrayed that he was willing to tell his sad story to a Senate committee. But truly, Us betrayed himself. He had no idea what he was doing with his money.

At the same hearing, we met Minnie Lou Parr of Walls, Mississippi, a retired court reporter. She and her husband, Ezekiel, a retired postal clerk, were looking for a higher yield on their savings. A mutual fund salesman told them about an investment that was "as safe as a bank certificate of deposit." It was a junk bond fund, and this was 1990, when the junk bond market went into the tank. Mr. and Mrs. Parr never really understood their fund statements and they aren't really sure how much they lost. But they know they never would have invested in junk bonds if they had known what they were.

Senator William E. Cohen, Republican from Maine, a member of the Senate Special Committee on Aging, concluded, "With lump-sum retirement benefits and other assets to invest from a lifetime of work and savings, older persons are especially attractive for fraudulent and abusive advisers or salespeople." No kidding. Old people have always been targets for snake oil salesmen. They prey on their fears and sell patent medicine for the bank account.

Unfortunately, Senator Cohen and many state securities regulators believe they can save such people from themselves with a nice helping of rules and regulations. It's not so. Only you can save yourself.

Almost every financial misstep begins the same way: a person with a large check, from the sale of a house or a pension distribution or a legacy, entrusts the whole thing to someone else, in an investment that the trusting person does not understand. If you can't sit down and write your brother or your daughter or your mother a hundred-word letter explaining it, this investment is not for you. Any good financial adviser will take the time to explain everything to you, until you can understand it. If not, take your money somewhere else.

Part Two

REGULATING THE PENSION INDUSTRY

THE PENSION INDUSTRY

Managing money for pensions in the vast and efficient American securities markets has become one of the biggest businesses in America. In fact, pension investing has become the dominant force in the securities markets. Whether actively managed or indexed to follow the markets passively, pension assets account for more than $4.7 trillion in a $9 trillion investment market. About $2.34 trillion is in private pension funds and $1.01 trillion of private pension assets are on insurance company general accounts. State and local government funds have investments of $1.1 trillion and federal plans account for $331 billion.[1]

Pension assets are greater than the $1.8 trillion held by life insurance companies, greater than the $1.3 trillion deposited in thrift institutions, greater than the $1.4 trillion in mutual funds and money market funds, greater than all three combined.

Pension assets are widely dispersed: the 1,000 largest U.S. pension funds hold $2.3 trillion, just over half the total.

Pension fund management is highly competitive; plan sponsors can choose among hundreds of managers. They can pick among dozens of styles of investing and shift their picks within days. For every firm managing assets of more than $10 billion there are half a dozen firms managing less than $500 million.

With $4.4 trillion in assets to control, there's something for everybody.

Pensions & Investments magazine's annual survey of pension managers turned up 674 investment counseling firms, plus 107 banks and eighty-six insurance companies, employing 7,432 portfolio managers and 5,723 security analysts. The ten largest pension managers at the end of 1992, according to the magazine, were Wells Fargo Nikko, managing $113 billion; Bankers Trust, managing $109 billion; State Street Bank, managing $84 billion; J.P. Morgan, managing $59 billion; Metropolitan Life, managing $59 billion; Fidelity Investments, managing $58 billion; Prudential Asset, managing $49 billion; Northern Trust, managing $41 billion; Pacific Investment, managing $38 billion; and Alliance Capital, managing $36 billion.[2]

The efficiency and diversity of securities markets create problems for pension fund sponsors. With every promising investment strategy thoroughly covered, it has become harder and harder to find one that beats the average market performance over the long term. For multibillion-dollar portfolios, it has become a truism, at least in some circles, that a portfolio that beats the market is riskier than the market and will eventually be done in by the market.

The market here does not mean the stock market, the bond market, the real estate market, or the futures market; it means the total market for investment assets. A good deal of economic research suggests that being in the right assets at the right time is a more important factor in overall performance than picking the right investments within an asset class. That is, being in stocks in a rising stock market is better than picking the best-performing stock. Careful examination of market history suggests that at least two-thirds of the return of a portfolio depends on the allocation of assets, while investment selection, market timing, and other factors account for only one-third.

This observation, so rich with hindsight, does little to help a forward-looking portfolio manager. So researchers have concentrated on finding the most effective diversified portfolio of assets to maximize the long-term total return for the lowest risk. The Nobel Prize–winning work of Harry M. Markowitz and William Sharpe established the idea of an "efficient frontier" of portfolios of assets. There is, at least in theory and at any given time, one best portfolio for each individual combination of desired return and tolerance of risk. They range from the lowest-risk portfolio, made up entirely of Treasury bills, to the highest-reward portfolio, made up entirely of equities.

There are a lot of portfolios in between, of course, and the relationships among asset classes constantly change with the markets. An entire subindustry of pension advisers has grown up offering to reallocate assets to increase return without increasing risk—so many, indeed, that asset allocation has become as competitive an industry as stock-picking.

MANAGEMENT STYLES

Many plan sponsors change managers frequently as market fashions change. New managers pick new asset allocation models, new stocks, and new bonds. The resulting turnover of investments gives rise to the oft-heard complaint of industrial managers that Wall Street investors are too shortsighted, too unwilling to wait for long-range strategies to pay off. In the aggregate, though, industrial managers are the ones who hire the pension investment strategists and press them for speedy returns.

In the late 1970s, a few pension funds put some money into venture investing, in which the investor puts equity into newly formed companies. Pension funds, with their longtime horizons and tax-free status, are almost ideally suited to make such investments with adequate patience and with an ironclad tax shelter for the profits.

Too much money rushed into a small market, however, creating a big market of weak investments. Gresham's Law, which says that bad money drives out the good, was formulated in the days of gold coins. Coins alloyed with base metal would be put into circulation while the heaviest coins with the highest proportion of gold would be hoarded. Much the same thing is true in investing: the provision of ample capital to an investment sector calls weak investments out into the open market while those who know about companies with strong prospects hoard them in private placements.

Pension money was also caught up in the real estate debacle of the late 1980s and early 1990s, but real estate is a far bigger sector of the economy than start-up companies in fragile industries. Also, more capital was thrown at the real estate industry by other financial intermediaries beyond pension funds. Banks, savings and loans, broker-sponsored private partnerships, and the capital of individuals all went rushing into the real estate market in search of the next great high-rise and financing the fourth big mall in a one-horse town. It took all of them flooding the market together to construct so many see-through office buildings, vacant retail strips, and unoccupied condos.

One problem for pension funds that invest in real estate is liquidity, the ability to convert an investment to cash whenever desired. Real estate properties are all unique. Although there is a real estate market, there is not a single market where every investment is continually priced. Liquidity is not a problem in a rising market because there are always new investors ready to buy. But falling markets fall because of an absence of buyers, and because sellers want to or must cash out.

The only thing more predictable than real estate cycles is that many people forget that real estate moves in cycles. They will buy anything in an up cycle and nothing in a down cycle; the investor who goes against the crowd can make out very well.

The real estate down cycle of the late 1980s and early 1990s was driven in part by something irrelevant to pension investing. It was driven by the Tax Reform Act of 1986, which took away some substantial tax incentives for private real estate investors. But even though it took some of these buyers out of the market, that law did nothing to change real estate investment finance for tax-exempt investors. Another way of looking at the real estate market was to say that pension investors would encounter less competition for attractive properties.

In a law enacted in 1993, Congress cleared away a couple of barriers to pension fund investments in real estate, hoping the change would inject new capital into Real Estate Investment Trusts. REITs are the equivalent of mutual funds investing in properties or mortgages, and the market for REIT shares is more liquid and efficient than the market for individual properties. But their ability to troll for pension fund money had been limited by a requirement that the five largest investors in a REIT could not own more than 50 percent of its shares. The new law took effect January 1, 1994, and more pension fund money was expected to enter the real estate marketplace through REITs.[3]

INVESTMENT CYCLES

When pension funds rushed headlong into junk bonds and take-over financing in 1986 and 1987, the market meltdown of October 1987 followed naturally. More recently, pension funds have turned their attention to other forms of private placements, such as hybrid stock and debt offerings. The $20 billion Pennsylvania Public School Employees Retirement System was featured in a 1991 *Wall Street Journal* article on private placements, and the chief of investments, John Lane, was quoted as saying he expected to average 25 percent annual returns from private deals over five years. The five years are not up and anything could happen, but one of Lane's three big private deals was a $100 million investment in convertible preferred stock issued by GPA Group, an Irish aircraft leasing firm. A tailspin in the airline industry brought GPA to the brink of bankruptcy, driving down prices of all its securities.

Some pension specialists ask how a pension fund should select its comfortable level of risk. Naturally, different analysts produce different answers.

One way to look at a defined benefit pension fund is to say that the pension fund is an obligation of the firm to the workers, and that it's backed, more or less, by the assets of the plan and by all the assets of the firm. If this is true, then plan assets should be managed aggressively to make them grow as rapidly as possible. Growth relieves funding pressure on the firm, but a growth strategy also means accepting some risk that the plan will at times be underfunded and at other times be overfunded.

Another way to look at a defined benefit pension plan is that the pension fund is a separate legal entity with claims and obligations of its own. The pension plan makes promises to the workers and receives promises from the employer. If this is true, then the employer should see to it that the pension fund's obligations are matched with defined assets, that is, with bonds selected to pay interest and mature on a schedule that delivers cash as the benefits must be paid. This eliminates the risk that an employer will have to make up a funding shortfall.

People in the real world try to fudge this difficult choice. And so pension assets are usually divided among equity and fixed-income investments. The currently fashionable proportion is 65 percent stocks and 35 percent fixed-income. Although economists have consumed thousands of pages of scholarly journals attempting to prove that this or some other proportion is exactly correct for maximizing the risk-reward ratio, most professionals are convinced that intelligent investing—their intelligence, of course—is superior to any cold ratio. Thus pension fund managers are always looking for a new gimmick or a new way to beat the averages.

Unfortunately, most portfolio managers don't beat the market. They share the same values, objectives, and legal constraints, and they move markets when they move assets. The average return on individually managed portfolios in *Pensions & Investments* magazine's annual performance evaluation report lagged the Standard & Poor's 500 stock average in seven of the ten years in the 1980s. Although the median total return for the decade exceeded the S&P 500, 19.09 percent to 17.57 percent, much of the difference was consumed in higher fees and trading costs.[4]

This performance costs more than it's worth: In the United States, active management costs nine times as much as passive management following an index.[5] In general, the money management industry takes about 2 percent of all financial assets as fees each year. Passive management would leave most of that 2 percent in funds as earnings.

BEATING THE MARKET

Do money managers earn their fees? Most are judged on performance, measured as percentage points above or below the market rate of return. But many analysts question whether institutional managers really can beat the market, except by luck. If markets efficiently translate information into prices, investors cannot consistently acquire information the markets do not have. And if investors act on new information by buying or selling stocks, their actions move prices in the market, resetting the price to incorporate even secret information.

Study after study shows that pension fund managers as a group do not beat the market, even though they enjoy the advantage of very low transaction costs, such as commissions. In a study of pension managers in the bull market of the 1980s, three economists, Josef Lakonishok, Andrei Shleifer, and Robert W. Vishny, found that the average annualized returns of 769 equity pension funds with more than $120 billion in assets lagged the Standard & Poor's 500 stock index by one percentage point, not counting management fees and transaction costs worth at least another half a percentage point.[6] When the returns were adjusted for the size of the funds, the average performance lagged the index by 2.1 percentage points. This study even gave fund managers the benefit of the doubt by measuring performance over three-year periods, so that a year's fluke results would not overwhelm a good performance over a longer term. The only possible conclusion is that pension fund managers live in a place that's the mirror image of Garrison Keillor's Lake Wobegon. In the village of pensions, all the managers are below average.

The Lakonishok-Shleifer-Vishny study also found, as others have, that a manager's doing well in any three-year period did not accurately predict superior performance in the next period. So how and why do pension fund sponsors pick managers? How and why do they switch from one to another? There are no sensible economic answers to these questions. It's not that one strategy isn't better than another at a particular time, and it's not that some people don't have good runs picking individual stocks. It's that you can't predict who's who and what's what. It's like the product manager who confessed that he knew that half of the money he spent on advertising was wasted—he just didn't know which half.

The three economists who ran this study, published in 1992 in the *Brookings Papers on Economic Activity*, hypothesized that marketing and other branches of psychology are what make the difference in the selection of pension fund managers. Money managers stroke their clients, providing constant reports and reassurance. (They may also offer less ethical stroking, such as access to inside information or to nonpublic investments.) Pension fund sponsors enjoy the feeling of power that comes from picking managers from a crowd of supplicants, and the constant change of managers lets treasurers and executives demonstrate the illusion of responsible activity. Having outside managers, after all, means one need never blame oneself. One merely fires the underperforming managers.

The most sophisticated investment managers pursue the simplest strategy. Because the penalties for not beating the market are greater than the rewards for beating the market, many investment managers reduce their personal risk and invest to match widely followed market indexes. Index-fund investing is a buy-and-hold strategy applied to the Standard & Poor's 500 stock index or some other index. A manager who buys the stocks in the S&P 500 can't help but match the index. Even if he never beats it, it will never beat him. By the end of 1992, index funds accounted for 30 percent of U.S. pension assets invested in equities, or 14 percent of total equity market capitalization.

Similarly, Morningstar Inc. reports that over the past ten years, the average bond mutual fund returned 10.76 percent a year. That was 122 basis points below that of the Salomon Brothers Broad Investment Grade Bond Index. And three out of four professional bond portfolio managers had total returns lower than the index, according to the SEI investment research firm.[7]

Here are some benchmarks for investing in the 1980s. Did your pension managers do this well?

The table opposite presents index results for the 1980s.

RETURN ON MANAGEMENT

Even the California Public Employees Retirement System, which some believe is the best-managed public pension system in the country, is finding that its investment managers aren't earning their keep. Earnings on CALPERS' $75 billion portfolio, which covers benefits for nearly a million current and retired workers in state and local government agencies, have been pushed down by losses, and its five-year record lags the average public fund. "We just haven't cut the mustard," CALPERS trustee and state controller Gray Davis admitted to the *Los An-*

Year	S & P 500 Stock Index	Lehman Bond Index	90-day T-bills	60/40 Equity/Bonds
1980	32.50%	-2.94%	12.02%	18.32%
1981	4.92	0.37	13.07	3.10
1982	21.55	41.76	11.12	29.63
1983	22.56	1.99	8.94	14.33
1984	6.27	14.79	9.94	9.68
1985	31.73	31.56	7.73	31.66
1986	18.66	24.09	6.15	20.83
1987	5.25	-2.67	5.91	2.08
1988	16.56	9.19	6.86	13.61
1989	31.63	18.94	8.43	26.55
1990	-3.11	6.30	7.74	0.65
1991	30.40	18.49	5.48	25.64
1992	7.61	7.96	3.48	7.75
1993	10.06	17.25	3.04	12.94
Average	**16.90%**	**13.36%**	**7.85%**	**15.48%**

Source: Lipper Analytical Services

geles Times in April 1993.[8] Over 1990, 1991 and 1992, CALPERS produced an average annual return of 9 percent—not bad compared to inflation but below the 12 percent average return for all public pension funds.

CALPERS pays average benefits of $784 a month to about 270,000 beneficiaries. It takes in more than $4 billion a year from government and employee contributions and from the earnings of the portfolio. By the year 2000, the CALPERS portfolio may hit $200 billion.

CALPERS' performance seems odd because the big fund spends so much on money managers. The 1992 management bill was $53 million paid to forty firms—three times the fees paid as recently as 1989.

The CALPERS fees drew objections from the California Legislative Analysts Office, which reported in early 1993 that CALPERS was spending about as much for investment advice as it spent on all other administrative expenses. Worse, CALPERS' own inside investment managers did better than the combined performance of the outside advisers. The report concluded, "What appears on the surface to be a runaway spending situation might be justified if the PERS could demonstrate that the significant expenditures for investment advisers were resulting in higher returns on investments than reasonably could have been achieved without such spending. The record, however, does not demonstrate this case."[9]

On the other side of the nation, New York State also has an inverse relationship between advice and performance, adding advisers and seeing returns on investment decline. And all over the country there are scandalous relationships between government pension funds and the firms that are paid to take care of workers' money:

- Massachusetts pension fund officials hired former colleagues and political associates to be financial advisers, and created false documentation to hide the faults in the selection process. The outside actuarial consultant helped officials wire the selection process.
- The Virginia Retirement System attracted attention to itself when its custodians agreed to finance a football stadium for the owner of the Washington Redskins. All the members of the retirement board are appointed by the governor, and the legislature finally decided in 1993 to look at the way outside managers are selected and its stewardship of land it owns all over the state.
- Texas pension officials had close relationships with hired advisers, and some staff took free trips from investment firms.
- The state of Washington lost hundreds of millions of dollars on real estate and venture capital deals that were hardly researched at all before the fund plunged in on the advice of outside consultants.
- The District of Columbia Retirement Board pays dozens of advisers to produce mediocre results for a plan that only has $2.5 billion to cover $7.5 billion in liabilities.

The city of Chicago has a lesson to teach about the multiplicity of investment managers. Treasurer Miriam Santos studied the investment management of the four pension funds for city police, firefighters, laborers, and other municipal employees and found that the total $5.9 billion of assets had been given to so many managers that virtually every investment strategy was covered. There were sixty-nine investment management contracts, although some management firms worked for more than one of the four plans.

The result, Santos reported, was an inadvertent index fund, with fees that were high even for managed funds. Chicago political tradition suggests that many of the sixty-nine contracts were won the old-fashioned way, as political patronage, but Santos said firing most of the managers and intentionally indexing most of the assets could increase fund earnings by six-tenths of a percentage point a year or more. That would represent $35 million a year to funds that need the money. The four funds combined are 32 percent shy of covering $8.6 billion in accrued liabilities.

PITFALLS

Even though the highly competitive market in pension management offers an investment style for any taste, and even though plan sponsors are responsible to beneficiaries for their stewardship, things often go wrong. But it's usually hard to pin blame on a manager or an adviser or a sponsor, because markets are full of unexpected events—who can say that some loss was the result of incompetence or malevolence when it might as easily have been the result of unforeseeable factors?

That doesn't stop lawmakers from trying to pin blame on the nearest victim. In 1993, for example, Senator Howard Metzenbaum, Democrat from Ohio, tried to work an amendment on the tax bill that would have made employers and benefit advisers jointly and severally liable for any breach of fiduciary responsibility. Actuaries, accountants, investment advisers, and employers would have been open to suit any time something went wrong in a pension plan that harmed beneficiaries. It's fair to hold professionals responsible, but Metzenbaum went further: if the individual or firm actually responsible for a real breach of trust were no longer in business, any or all of the remaining responsible firms would be made to bear the cost and restore the "full economic value" of any losses to beneficiaries, even if they had no responsibility for the losses. The amendment also allowed for punitive damages, which was an open invitation to lawyers to take cases on a contingency basis.

While this might be desirable from the point of view of the beneficiaries, it was intolerable from the point of view of the employers and advisers, who could not imagine being held responsible for someone else's wrongdoing. They lobbied heavily and Metzenbaum was forced to delete his amendment.

7

THE INSURANCE GAME

Pension management is a specialized form of insurance management, the financial practice of commingling money from the members of a group, investing it temporarily, and paying it out when certain conditions are met. In the case of life insurance, the condition is death; in the case of health insurance, the condition is hospital or doctor bills; in the case of liability insurance, it is being at fault for damages to another; in the case of pensions, it is retirement.

Insurance companies make their money on the spread between the receipt of premiums and the need to pay out benefits. On the front end, they adjust the size of the premium and the risks they will underwrite, attempting to be sure that enough money comes in to cover the eventual payment of benefits. On the back end, they scrutinize claims to be sure that all conditions are met. In the middle, they maximize investment returns.

As long as there are enough people in the group being insured, running a sound insurance company is a very simple financial proposition. Actuaries can estimate very well how many people in a given large group will die, or be injured, or have car wrecks, or retire. Assuming a particular rate of return on investment, they can set premiums with precision.

The two problematic details are at the beginning and the middle. Operating an insurance company is a constant scramble to keep the book of business big enough to let the actuaries do their job with precision. Too few customers in the group means too much unpredictable variability in the group's claims rate. A company may have a stellar year, followed by a disastrous year of unforeseen claims. In a competitive market, of course, a constant scramble for customers means a constant temptation to cut prices, and make it up on volume.

And the way an insurance company makes it up on volume is to increase the book of business rapidly, receiving premiums at the front end and investing them for profit before the benefits must be paid. There is, therefore, a constant temptation to reach for a little more yield on investment.

In the early 1980s, inflation delivered a lot more yield on investment. Insurance companies registered record profits based on the 12 percent nominal earnings of recent years, and then they began factoring continuation of those yields into the prices of their insurance products. In other words, they assumed that 12 percent interest rates would last well into the twenty-first century. Life insurance, annuities, and any other product requiring the client to pay money now to receive dividends in the future got cheaper. Cheaper products naturally mean that more products can be sold, whether we are talking about lettuce or life insurance.

The price of lettuce in the grocery store quickly reflects the cost of producing lettuce, but the market for insurance is not so quick to respond to changing economic signals. Just as it had taken several years for companies to lower prices—they had preferred to make larger profits, build reserves, and expand sales forces—it is taking companies a long time to reflect changes in costs that should drive prices up. Those long-run 12 percent interest rate projections were clearly wrong by 1991, but companies did not reduce them. Those that did found that they priced themselves out of the market. Aggressive insurance companies were able to find high-yield investments, such as junk bonds, that allowed at least a tenuous justification for low prices. Of course the nature of the business—taking in money now and paying benefits later—allows a growing insurance company to defer the day of reckoning.

EXECUTIVE LIFE

First Executive chairman Fred Carr built his insurance company on junk bonds. At the end of 1987, its main Executive Life subsidiaries had 54.1 percent of their investment portfolio in junk bonds, most floated with Drexel Burnham Lambert as the lead investment banker. The company next most heavily into junk bonds at that time, according to a Moody's survey, was Southwestern Life, at 11.7 percent. No other major insurance carrier of the thirty-six on the Moody's list of junk bond investors among life insurance companies had even 10 percent of its portfolio in junk bonds.

Fred Carr and his companies were among the best customers for Drexel's junk bond king, Michael Milken. Their businesses interlocked many times, as they did in the 1986 takeover of Pacific Lumber, a northern California timber company, by Maxxam Group.

According to testimony before the House Energy and Commerce Committee's Oversight and Investigations subcommittee, Executive Life of California was the main purchaser of junk bonds issued to finance the takeover of Pacific Lumber. Then Maxxam, to liquefy Pacific Lumber's hidden assets, terminated Pacific Lumber's pension funds to capture about $60 million in excess assets not required to pay vested benefits. Federal law permits this kind of raid as long as the beneficiaries are given annuities to cover their vested benefits.

For the annuity, Maxxam executives instructed the Pacific Lumber pension consultant to get a bid from an affiliate of Executive Life. The bid was late, delivered to the wrong place, and lacked conclusive proof that Executive Life had proper financial backing. Pacific Lumber officials objected strongly, but in vain: Executive Life defeated nine other bidders on the annuity contract. Even some Maxxam people had qualms about the deal: one official urged giving the annuity to the second bidder even if the second bidder was $800,000 higher than Executive Life. Executive Life's bid, however, was the winner by $2.5 million.

The price of an annuity varies inversely with the interest-rate assumption made by the insurance company providing the annuity. A high interest-rate assumption makes an annuity cheaper. Thus First Executive's high-yielding junk bond portfolio—including the Pacific Lumber takeover bonds—backed the high-interest-rate assumption and the cheap annuities offered by its subsidiaries.

Another Executive Life customer and client was Cannon Mills, sold in 1982 to California financier David Murdock. The new owner raided a $38 million surplus in a pension plan in 1985 by terminating the plan and buying annuities from Executive Life. Then he resold the company to rival Fieldcrest and went home.

The Amalgamated Clothing and Textile Workers Union, which was trying to organize Cannon Mills, charged that Murdock had done more than make a legal raid on the pension surplus. The union claimed he had also used the Cannon pension fund to buy stock in an unsuccessful run at Occidental Petroleum in which the pension fund purchased $197 million of stock and facilitated a $60 million profit for Murdock. The case was settled out of court in 1989 for a reported $1 million. The pension fund was also involved in Murdock's successful bid for Castle & Cook, the Hawaiian fruit company.

First Executive came to a bad end in April 1991, when California and New York regulators questioned its solvency, seized its assets, and put it out of business. Executive Life annuity payments were cut 30 percent to reflect the lack of assets to back up its liabilities.

About 13,000 retirees and workers at Cannon and its Fieldcrest affiliate were affected, as were about 10,000 at Pacific Lumber, and more at other companies. All told, about 84,000 people's pension benefits were "guaranteed" by Executive Life annuities.

Among the worst losers were about a hundred Louisiana residents who were retired employees of Strachan Shipping Co. of Savannah, Georgia, whose pension plan was terminated in 1987 with the substitution of Executive Life annuities. Their case left them with reduced pensions and set a terrible precedent for any future cases. There was no Louisiana guaranty fund coverage for them so they sued the company to recover their lost benefits. A federal judge in Louisiana rejected all their claims, holding that a statute of limitations in ERISA barred them from making any claim more than three years after the plan was terminated—

even though they had no problem with benefits until four years after the termination. Also, the judge held that the retirees had no standing to sue, because ERISA allows only participants to seek relief from plan sponsors, and the retirees ceased to be participants when the plan was terminated.[1]

Though First Executive was reorganized and many annuity payments were covered by guaranty funds, the whole episode should serve as a warning that nobody should ever again consider an insurance company's word to be an ironclad, guaranteed promise.

INSURANCE VULNERABILITY

The year 1991 was a lousy one in the insurance business. In addition to the Executive Life failure, New Jersey closed down Mutual Benefit Life and New Jersey Life Insurance; real estate losses caused rating agencies to downgrade such strongholds as John Hancock and Aetna.

The strains on insurance companies created concern about much more than just their annuities. Insurance companies also provide pension funds with instruments called Guaranteed Investment Contracts. As we saw in Chapter 5, a GIC resembles a bank certificate of deposit, running at a fixed interest rate for a fixed term. Insurance companies issued them to compete with bank certificates of deposit, and they were very successful.

The guarantee is just the company's promise, nothing more, and that fact was driven home when Executive Life stopped paying interest on its GICs in 1991. Some companies volunteered to buy the frozen GICs out of the pension plans they had sponsored, but others with less secure finances, such as Honeywell and Unisys, did not. Placing a large percentage of pension assets in the GICs of one firm would seem an obvious violation of a plan sponsor's fiduciary obligation to keep a fund's investments prudently diversified. But the Labor Department kept its hands off. Beneficiaries had to go to court to do the policeman's job.

The only thing the Labor Department succeeded in doing was obstructing those plan sponsors that were willing to bail out their pension funds. They ran afoul of Labor Department regulations that prohibit sponsors from having financial dealings with their funds.

The Labor Department embarked on a tedious process of giving individual waivers to plan sponsors, even as it moved slowly to investigate whether sponsors or managers should be held responsible for buying GICs and annuities from First Executive companies in the first place. ERISA requires that a plan sponsor act prudently in the selection of an annuity, as with any other investment decision. The department said it had more than 350 formal complaints in 1991, but only a few lawsuits and settlements ever came of the investigations, and the Labor Department also never made good on a 1991 promise to write rules governing the selection of annuity providers.

The whole Executive Life episode called into question the usefulness of state guaranty funds, which purportedly stand behind insurance companies to protect policyholders who would suffer if their insurance carrier fails. Just as federal officials were forced by the thrift industry to avoid early and decisive action in the savings-and-loan crisis because they feared being blamed for forcing thrifts into bankruptcy, the insurance industry has bullied state regulators and Congress into keeping hands off the guaranty funds on the grounds that they might panic the public and cause companies to fail.

Even if guaranty funds live up to their name, they may offer inadequate benefits. The national association of state insurance regulators has set up a "model," adopted in fifteen states, that offers maximum benefits of $100,000 cash value for annuity benefits, $300,000 for death benefits, $100,000 in health insurance benefits, and a $300,000 maximum for all benefits, regardless of the number of policies. The other thirty-five states vary widely in their payment limits. New York and Washington, for example, have benefits up to $500,000. Kansas limits guaranty fund coverage to $100,000.

The states also impose residency requirements on policyholders and insurance companies. Some cover resident policyholders, some cover all policyholders of resident companies, some split the difference. When Executive Life went down, many New York policyholders had no protection from their state guaranty fund because their benefits had been written by the California subsidiary, which was not licensed in New York, and their particular type of policy was not covered by the California fund.

Similarly, Executive Life had been barred from doing business in Connecticut in 1974, but the California company had subsequently sold annuity policies to firms terminating the pension plans of employees located in Connecticut. California cut the value of the annuities by 30 percent, but Connecticut retirees had no recourse from their state insurance guaranty fund.

LOCKING THE BARN

The Labor Department and the PBGC issued notices of proposed rulemaking in 1991, asking whether there should be firm guides to cover the selection of annuity providers to replace defined benefit pension plans after termination.

A classic response came from all eight members of Congress from Connecticut, home of many major insurers. While claiming to support consumer protection, they warned against "blanket, draconian prohibitions" that might disrupt the industry. "If the department sets minimum financial standards for providers of termination annuities—which we believe is a good idea—it should avoid a narrow, bright line test based on ratings by national rating services," the eight lawmakers said, advising instead that the department should use a "flexible, multifactor approach."

Though they would never have said so, they clearly had in mind the same kind of protection without pain that the thrift industry wanted for its members in the early 1980s. The hint was strong enough that the Labor Department dropped the whole issue.

Another possibility was that the federal Pension Benefit Guaranty Corp. would back annuities because the annuities merely replaced insured pension benefits. California insurance commissioner Raymond Garamendi, whose state guaranty fund would have to come to the rescue of Executive Life if it could not be hung on another hook, was a leading proponent of this view.

The spirit of ERISA "would lead any layman to believe that it was the pension benefits that were guaranteed," no matter what entity had been paying them, Garamendi argued. "I invite you to imagine having to explain to the widow of a retired pensioner that she is out of luck because the elaborate pension benefit guarantee system we set up for her does not in fact guarantee her pension because her pension is not the exact kind of pension we guarantee," he told a subcommittee of the House Ways and Means Committee after the shutdown of Executive Life. In particular, he added, "Surely companies that did reversion raids in the '80s should be held accountable" and "make up any losses to people with annuities."

But in fact the PBGC did tell thousands of widows that they had the wrong kind of benefits, and Congress let the PBGC get away with it because the alternative was too expensive to contemplate.

Until the first big failures of life insurance companies writing annuities, federal officials were cheerily blind to the dangers of annuitizing pension benefits. "We don't deal with fly-by-night outfits," said the spokeswoman for the Pension Benefit Guaranty Corp. But it turned out that the PBGC rarely considered the strength of insurance companies providing annuities for terminations. If it did anything, it checked to see that the company was rated A or better by the A. M. Best rating service. Executive Life enjoyed an AA rating, for what that was worth. PBGC never turned down any company's plan to convert a pension to an annuity and could not organize the data on its reporting forms to find out which insurance companies were getting the bulk of the annuity business.[2] Similarly, the Pension and Welfare Benefits Administration at the Labor Department neglected most of the cases in which companies terminating pensions were charged with abusing their responsibility to pick sound insurance companies.

After thousands of terminations had gone through without a complaint, the failures of Executive Life and Mutual Benefit Life started Garamendi and others asking if the PBGC stood behind the substitute promise of the insurance companies. James Lockhart, PBGC executive director from 1989 through 1992, adamantly refused to back the annuity policies. To do so would expose the PBGC to $50 billion of added risk, he said, blithely ignoring the key point that all that risk had been on the PBGC before it allowed the plans to be terminated.

Growing awareness that some insurance companies are riskier than others also led to other questions. Had the PBGC approved the soundness of the insurance companies before letting the employer substitute annuities for pensions? It had not.

"Our reading of ERISA," said Lockhart, "is that Congress didn't say we were supposed to. Our function is to make sure people get their pension benefits and when that passes to an insurance company we are off the hook. The selection of the insurance company is an ERISA decision, a fiduciary decision."

Lockhart realized that if the PBGC were put back on the hook to back all the annuities that have been used to replace pension benefits, the agency would have to add several billion dollars a year to the premiums it charges every American company with a defined benefit pension plan. Lockhart urged Congress in the strongest possible terms not to change the rules so far downstream. The PBGC has no premiums to cover annuities and has no authority to regulate insurance companies, he said.

"We have a good defense: that Congress did not require us to insure annuities, and that our legislation on approving terminations does not speak to the quality of the insurance company. It just has to be an insurance company."

In an announcement of the policy decision, PBGC said, "We have concluded that the statute does not authorize PBGC to guarantee benefits distributed in the form of irrevocable annuity contracts from insurance companies." ERISA required PBGC to guarantee the payment of basic pension benefits when a covered single-employer pension plan terminates with insufficient assets to pay for those benefits, PBGC wrote. "Nowhere in the statute is PBGC authorized to pay benefits upon the occurrence of any other event, such as the failure of an insurance company." The agency declared, "Had Congress intended for PBGC to insure against the failure of insurance companies from which annuities have been purchased, it surely would have also addressed the liabilities to which this would expose the PBGC." It took a Washington lawyer to read that with a straight face—Congress hardly ever addresses hidden liabilities or expenses when it promises to protect the innocent.

Perhaps the most appalling point of all was that PBGC had acknowledged its responsibility to protect pension benefits paid through annuities in the preamble to a 1981 regulation. Ten years later, the agency waved its hand and made that promise disappear: "We have searched PBGC records and found no legal memoranda or other document to support this statement," said general counsel Carol Conner Flowe. "The statement in the preamble was made without legal analysis, and was simply incorrect."

Just as it had allowed employers to make off with surplus pension assets, PBGC took leave of its responsibilities to protect more than three million beneficiaries who lost PBGC coverage when their benefits were converted to annuities.[3] The reason was not legality, but cost. Lockhart estimated that PBGC would face new liabilities of $50 billion at a time when the agency's long-term deficit was being estimated at $1.8 billion, and he had the easy job of convincing Congress that it should not have to come up with the money for a bailout. The point ignored the significant fact that PBGC would have faced few if any liabilities if it had reviewed the providers of annuities and forced companies terminating pensions to spend more to buy more safety.

Congress passed the buck to Garamendi's department. But the blame belonged squarely on PBGC, on the officials that had never tried to stop asset reversions, never set useful rules for fund terminations, and never reviewed the security that replaced a terminated pension fund. Congress certainly deserved some blame for not giving the PBGC tougher laws to enforce, but PBGC never tried to use the power it had. The government agency that was so concerned with preserving the voluntary private pension system wound up accelerating its demise.

The PBGC under Lockhart somehow did find the power to require employers who terminate plans to identify the insurance company that will provide the annuity, and it eventually proposed a rule to set standards for the companies. This amounted to trying to bolt the barn door after horses worth $50 billion had escaped. As even Lockhart, a veteran of the Alexander & Alexander insurance brokerage, said, "Perhaps people should have been aware a little quicker that there have been changes in the insurance market. There didn't used to be risky insurance companies and now there are."

The problem went deeper than that. PBGC and the Department of Labor never should have permitted employers to capture pension surpluses immediately. Any surplus should be maintained in trust for the covered employees until the last beneficiary dies and the replacement annuity expires. Only then should the employer receive the surplus.

The Clinton administration came into office attuned to the problems of pension finance, but a commission that studied the situation in 1993 quickly decided not to reopen the question of insuring pension replacement annuities. The members concluded, as Lockhart had, that the government just couldn't afford the liability. They also decided that the Executive Life experience was unlikely to be repeated.

THE NEXT MINEFIELD

The pension regulatory system cannot cope at the margin where pension issues meet insurance issues, and this is a relatively simple area of conflict. The next big conflict is likely to come where pension funds meet the arcane world of derivatives.

Derivatives are financial instruments such as futures and options that depend on the price of fundamental securities such as stocks and bonds. A perfect example, and one becoming more and more popular with pension fund managers, is an interest-only "strip," which confers upon a holder the right to receive interest from a bond, while some other holder retains the right to receive the principal. This is a fairly simple annuity in the case of a Treasury bond and pricing it is also a simple matter. The Treasury strip goes up in price when interest rates fall, and vice versa. But the situation can be set on its head if the underlying bond is itself a derivative, such as a mortgage-backed security. In that case, the term of interest payments is indefinite, and depends on the number of mortgages that are prepaid. The interest payment to the "strip" will fall with the number of mortgages that are prepaid, and of course mortgages are prepaid rapidly in a time when general interest rates are falling. So instead of becoming more valuable, the market value of a strip on a mortgage-backed security will fall rapidly when interest rates fall.

If that sounds dangerously confusing, add the fact that trillions (no, that is not a misprint) of dollars of derivatives are traded worldwide by telephone, on the honor system, so that no money actually changes hands until the delivery date. Even when there are deposits, down payments, and collateral requirements, they are usually very small.

Some derivatives are so complex that it seems very unlikely that anybody trading them really understands them. With derivatives, a bank or a mutual fund or a pension fund or a corporate treasurer's office can protect its core investments against changes in international currency values, commodity prices, stock prices, interest rates, or all of them at once. A company doing business all over Europe may find that it needs to borrow in Spain this month and pay off debt in Switzerland next month, so it buys derivatives to freeze the relative price of pesetas and francs for a month. The same institutions can also make bets on price swings in any of these areas.

The market meltdown of 1987—when the Dow Jones Industrial Average lost five hundred points in one day—was attributable in large part to trading in stock derivatives in a manner known as portfolio insurance. Large funds that bought futures and options to protect themselves against a decline in the market had to sell them when the market actually took a sharp drop. The fall in the derivatives market then dragged down the stock market, which then forced the sale of more derivatives, and so on for five hundred points on the Dow Jones Industrial Average. Portfolio managers now use other forms of "dynamic hedging," but they still rely on derivative markets to provide protection against big moves in fundamental markets and to squeeze a little extra performance out of their portfolios. Another market meltdown is still possible.

Derivatives bring with them all the elements required for a financial crisis: high leverage, novelty, ignorance, and uncertainty. Hopefully, the crisis will be as educational and no more damaging than the collapse of First Executive and its annuities.

CHAPTER

8

DANGEROUS INVESTING

Until the late 1970s, most government pension funds were managed out of an antique textbook. They put most of their funds in bonds, attempting to match the maturity schedule of their assets with the retirement schedule of their participants. While responsible, the strategy was expensive—indeed, disastrously expensive during the period of high inflation and interest rates that prevailed in the 1970s and early 1980s. Governments found that cost-of-living increases and pay hikes for workers outpaced the earning capacity of their bond portfolios. To improve total yield, they switched to stocks, and the great bull market that began in 1982 obliged them.

In 1980 public pension funds had $44 billion in stocks in their portfolio, which represented 22 percent of their assets and 3.9 percent of the total market value of the stocks on the New York Stock Exchange.

By 1990 things had changed: most state legislatures had given their pension managers a freer hand to invest in stocks, the growth of public payrolls and benefits had increased annual contributions, and the stock market had tripled in price. Public pension funds held $293.2 billion in stocks, 39 percent of their total assets of $752 billion and 9.6 percent of the market capitalization of the NYSE. Private pension funds of course were still larger, holding $691.4 billion in stocks. Together, all pension funds owned 32.4 percent of the market capitalization on the exchange.

On the grounds that he who pays the piper calls the tune, some pension funds grew dissatisfied with the music and started looking for ways to replace the fiddle player.

Relationship investing means that American pension funds have begun to believe that they should influence the companies in which they invest. The old rule was that the way to express disapproval of management was simply to sell the stock, nothing more. Now investment counselors are trying to meet with corporate managers and influence them.

They and their spokesmen argue that their very size has rendered them helpless giants. Wall Street's tradition that institutional owners sell their stock if they are unhappy with management had become a variation on the old Street joke, whose punch line is "Sell to whom?"

Writing in the *Harvard Business Review*, management consultant Peter Drucker said, "The shareholdings of even a midsize pension fund are already so large that they are not easily sold." Anybody who holds 1 percent of a company's stock will find it hard to dispose of, he said, adding, "And the 40 percent holder [of all stock], that is, the pension fund community at large, cannot sell at all."

Drucker claimed, in effect, that pension funds are forced by their size to be in the market and are forced by their place in the market to control management.

The result has been a movement by pension fund managers to intervene in the corporate affairs of the companies they own. When the board of directors throws out the chairman of General Motors or demands a shakeup in the business strategy of IBM, the directors are speaking for and empowered by pension fund investors. The result is a curious daisy chain: fund managers work for the companies they wish to control, while the performance of the companies determines the income of the funds and the power of the managers.

INVESTORS OR BOSSES?

Pension funds are becoming the American equivalent of European merchant banks and Japanese *keiretsu*—participants in the management of the companies whose stock they own. Many Americans think that this consolidated structure is the secret of Japanese success and that it's the underpinning of the European welfare state.

Former New York City comptroller Elizabeth Holtzman speaks for this view: "When there is stagnation in the company or when it's not performing well, we want to see what can be done to change the structures, to bring in new energy, new vision, new strategizing," she says. "For instance, when the board of directors is made up of cronies of the CEO, there isn't the opportunity for the monitoring that has to come into place or the new ideas that are necessary."

Jack Sheinkman, president of the Amalgamated Clothing and Textile Workers, agrees: "We must never forget that we are the major owners of corporate America, with untapped power to affect the way this nation conducts its business. We are positioned to support corporate strategies that will lead to long-term value."[1]

Even if this is true, politicians and union leaders are the last people we should want as enforcers.

Really, it's fascism with a human face. The American economy is energized by freedom—freedom to leave the company and start a new one, freedom to move capital unhindered by politics, freedom to take a chance. America is still far ahead of the countries with corporate giants directed by benevolent bankers and bureaucrats.

Sheinkman's clothing union is pretty far down the road: it already owns a bank in New York, and it has created a stock investment fund called the Longview Fund that Sheinkman intends as a Trojan horse for union activism. "The Longview Fund is the opposite of a social investment fund," says Sheinkman. "Social funds screen out bad corporate citizens and often place noneconomic issues ahead of investment return. We will put investors in the largest, ugliest, and potentially most profitable companies, and engage in active shareholder advocacy."

In an extreme form, relationship investors give up on the relationship and challenge management directly. Wall Street calls this a proxy contest, because contenders attempt to round up supporters among shareholders and bind them to their cause by obtaining a proxy authorizing the contender to vote the owners' shares at the annual meeting.

The proxy contest is the ultimate expression of shareholder democracy. It also became an expression of the bare-knuckles market of the 1980s, since most takeover bids required a shareholder vote to approve selling the company.

It's curious that many shareholder activists hold that proxy contests are so difficult, and that so many managers hold them to be so unduly threatening. Actually, the odds are pretty even. Georgeson & Co., a leading proxy solicitation specialist, covered proxy activity between October 1984 and September 1990. Their study found that the challenger won 29.4 percent of the time and was defeated 23.9 percent. The challenger gained minority representation on the board of directors 14.1 percent of the time and received other concessions in 1.8 percent of the cases. In 13.5 percent of the votes the company was sold. In 7.4 percent of the cases the challenger sold his shares, but at a profit. In 1.2 percent of the cases the challenger sold at a loss. In 3.7 percent the company was restructured.

Recently, some groups have been advocating changes that would make the challenger's chance far better than roughly even. T. Boone Pickens's United Shareholders Association claimed credit for inducing about fifty corporations to institute confidential proxy voting and removing antitakeover provisions such as "poison pills" in corporate rules. (United Shareholders Association went out of business at the end of 1993 but the movement lives on.)

Not all companies roll over; some play hardball, reducing the number of directors, requiring supermajorities to elect directors, and otherwise raising the hurdle for insurgent investors.

TURNCOAT COMPANY

In the summer of 1993, Campbell Soup Company became one of the first corporate converts to relationship investing, or, as the company put it in its press release, voting the stock in its billion-dollar pension fund "according to Campbell's own progressive practices of shareowner-sensitive governance." The company said its shares of other companies will be voted to oppose election of boards of directors that include more than three representatives of management. Campbell itself has an unusually independent board, with fifteen outsiders and only one insider. Earlier in the year, Campbell announced that it would require executives to own Campbell shares in proportion to their salary, and the company said its pension fund will vote in favor of "pay for performance" ideas at other companies. Some companies, however, have stock options and other ways of linking share prices or profits to executive pay, but then play "heads you win, tails they lose" by repricing the options if they don't pay off for top managers. Campbell said its pension fund shares will be voted against such deals.[2]

Relationship investors in the United States have even tried to export the idea to Japan, home of the interlocking *keiretsu* structure that so impresses many Americans. Several major American pension funds with large holdings in Japan tried to send messages to some two hundred Japanese companies by voting against management at the 1993 annual meetings.[3] Those sending the messages included CALPERS, State Street Global Advisers, and J.P. Morgan Investment Management; Global Proxy Services Corp. of Boston coordinated their voting. They objected, for example, to Mitsubishi Heavy Industries and Aoyama Trading paying too small a dividend and to Nissan Motors and Daiwa Securities making too large a payout. They also voted against making large boards of directors even larger and more unwieldy at Furukawa Electric and Nomura Securities, on the theory that large boards are too easily manipulated by top management.

Oddly enough, none of the targeted Japanese companies reported receiving any negative votes, which may highlight the difference between relationship investing from the inside and relationship investing from the outside. Relationship investing Japanese-style means a long-term relationship among suppliers, customers, financiers, and related industries. Relationship investing American-style means kibitzing, meddling, and sticking one's nose into somebody else's business.

Relationship investing paves the way for another philosophy that moves some public pension fund managers to try to rule corporate America in pursuit of their own political agenda. They complain about executive salaries, they jawboned companies to pull investments out of South Africa, and they push companies to one side or the other of many social controversies.

The South African disinvestment movement cost the State of New Jersey pension fund $500 million in divesting itself of $4 billion in politically undesirable investments.

The counterboycott of the Arab boycott of Israel has forced many U.S. companies to avoid doing business with the boycotters. In 1991 Baxter International explicitly acknowledged the power of the New York City pension funds in forcing it to abandon plans to build a plant in Syria. City comptroller Holtzman had introduced a shareholder resolution on behalf of city pension funds, which held two million Baxter shares, that would have required the medical equipment company to make public an internal report about Baxter's sale of a plant in Israel before announcing the venture in Syria. The actual resolution drew a small percentage of the vote, but the public embarrassment drove the company out of the deal with Syria.

Holtzman declared with satisfaction that pension fund managers "cannot stand idly by while corporations and their managers take actions that harm the long-term interests of our investments."[4] But the real issue is whether Holtzman is more competent to define the long-term interests of a company like Baxter International than Baxter's managers and board.

Holtzman had a clear-cut conflict of interest. She is a perennial candidate for city and state office in races where the Jewish vote is crucial to her chances of election. Her determination to block Baxter's moves in the Middle East appealed to voters while its benefit to pension fund members was not so clear.

SOCIAL-INVESTING SOCIETY

In 1985 the California Public Employees Retirement System rounded up some other state and municipal pension officials and formed the Council of Institutional Investors to push the agenda of the fund managers. The council was instrumental in pushing Roger Smith out as chairman of General Motors, and participated in the changing of the guard at IBM, Eastman Kodak, Westinghouse, and other big corporations.

The Council of Institutional Investors campaigns against companies that try to institute takeover defenses, winning victories at Honeywell, Kmart, Champion International, and other companies. Sarah Teslik, the council's executive director, has become a gray eminence behind corporate boards because she speaks for funds that own $400 billion in stock. "We are nowhere near dictating," she claims. "We still have to say 'Please.' " But the united public pension funds, even if they do have to say "Please," form one of the most formidable powers in the business community, and anyone who has ever worried about the power of large corporations ought to worry about the power that influences them.

More directly dangerous is the use of pension fund clout to enlist corporations in supposedly public investments, such as small-business loans, investments in industrial development, and single-family housing projects. This "economically targeted investing" (ETI) calls on pension funds to pay for public works projects that may not appeal to investors on the open market.

Pension fund assets "represent roughly half of all the available equity in the country and it should be used," says Steven J. Nesbitt, a senior vice president at Wilshire Associates. He adds, "The use of ETI allows state and local pension funds to do something other than simply provide for its beneficiaries' retirement. Now they will both protect and advance the investments of their members."[5]

Nesbitt, who advises state pension funds in California, Massachusetts, Pennsylvania, Washington, and Oregon, really should know better. Pension funds cannot serve two masters. The money, $4.4 trillion as of the end of 1992, is already invested. Somebody is already using it, although perhaps not to "advance the investments" of Nesbitt's favorite groups. Providing for beneficiaries' retirements is not simple, and will not be simple as long as there are people like Nesbitt trying to advance a political agenda with the beneficiaries' money.

There are many such people. The Maine State Retirement System, which handles all public pensions in the state, has lent $10 million to the state's finance authority for economically targeted investments, even though the pension fund has one of the worst rates of return on its investments of all public funds in the nation. Bills are pending in several states, including California, Illinois, and Connecticut, to require state pension funds to invest in the infrastructure. Some funds in Arizona, Arkansas, California, Iowa, Missouri, Ohio, Pennsylvania, and Texas are already required to make various kinds of economically targeted investments.

Funds in Massachusetts, California, and Connecticut make direct investments in "affordable" multifamily housing, while about a dozen states invest in mortgage-backed securities providing capital to first-time homebuyers in their states. Outrageously, housing received 64 percent of the $20 billion of economically targeted investments tallied in a 1993 survey by the Institute for Fiduciary Education.[6] Other real estate took another 20 percent, while 13 percent went to bank deposits, providing capital to real estate lending. If there's anything in the national economy that's overbuilt and overnourished already, it's housing. These investments are very unlikely to be less risky or more profitable than loans to business, and they certainly won't stimulate the economy the way a successful business loan would. Yet less than 4 percent of the economically targeted investments in the survey went to small-business and venture capital investments.

INSUFFICIENT PROFIT

ETI supporters say they can support their social goals without sacrificing return on investment, but it should be obvious that these deals would not be worth doing from a political point of view unless the investors thought they were providing capital at a concessionary price.

Returns are mixed. New York City's ETI investments, from small-business loans to rehabilitation of housing for the poor, averaged 13 percent return from 1988 to 1992, compared to 10 percent on all other investments, according to Carol O'Claireacain, then commissioner of the New York City Department of Finance.

Alabama state pension funds invested $100 million to buy a one-third share of a venture building eighteen municipal golf courses, on the dubious promise of 12 percent of the profits earned by private developers. The state claims the economic targets are corporate executives, retirees, and tourists who might come to the state if there were better golf courses.

Connecticut invested $25 million in pension money with the Colt Manufacturing Co., whose major claim to fame was its location in the state capital. The firearms company promptly went bankrupt.

The Kansas Employees Retirement System lost $236 million on its targeted investments, primarily from support of a savings and loan that went into federal receivership. The state legislature rescinded its ETI law.

MISSING THE TARGET

If economically targeted investments have any purpose, they must provide a return on investment. State pension funds do not belong to the state economy, nor do they owe any duty to a state's citizens, no matter how hard-pressed its farmers, bankers, real estate developers, or steel mill magnates may be. Their sole obligation is to the beneficiaries.

The California Public Employees Retirement System missed this point in 1993 when its board adopted a policy favoring investment in real estate projects that hire union labor, or at least provide "fair wages." The managers of the state's real estate funds warned that favoring the highest-wage contractors would probably reduce income or increase risk, but the board went right ahead.

A spokeswoman for state controller Gray Davis explained, "It makes more sense to pay a decent living wage so that they don't have to draw welfare and medical assistance from the state." This amounts to the suggestion that pensioners should risk their money to hold down expenses for the state.

Although most public officials acknowledge the idea that pension funds must not accept unwarranted risk or submarket returns, it often turns out to be the barest lip service. For example, Carol O'Claireacain of New York City acknowledged, "We cannot allow our funds to have investments with a questionable rate of return." But her real interest was in infrastructure, so she sought a middle way. Her suggestion was a federal guarantee so pension funds can invest with impunity. "We have a huge pool of savings from the nation's workers and a huge amount of projects to invest in," she said at a 1993 conference of the association of state treasurers. "If the Congress would implement a federal guarantee, then pension funds could bridge that investment gap."

O'Claireacain, of course, was simply calling for national taxes and borrowing to fix local problems. If she thinks a federal subsidy is warranted, she should seek a direct appropriation from Congress.

The state of Oklahoma did something honest like that when its legislature conceived a need for making economically targeted investments. The state created an Oklahoma Capital Investment Board and gave it a $50 million backing for its bond issues. The board sold bonds to the public—not to pension funds—and put its money to work with established venture firms who made commitments to work with companies in Oklahoma.

One influential advocate of social investing is the AFL-CIO. One of its consultants, Randy Barber, complains that the shareholder democracy movement is too limited because it merely attempts to maximize pension fund wealth by putting takeover candidates in play. The AFL-CIO wants to use pension funds to maximize the wealth of workers. Barber proposes that funds make investments that preserve jobs and lift up struggling communities. If groups like the Council of Institutional Investors really have managements listening to them, he adds, they should push managers not to move union jobs to nonunion states or out of the country entirely.

This proposition highlights the most dangerous problem with pension funds' actively participating in management. Pension funds are masses of wealth accumulated in the past as deferred income for work done in the past. Their obligation is to preserve the deferred income that workers have earned so that it can be paid in the future. It's wrong for them to look to the present to employ more workers, or to fight against economic change if the change is good for the American economy and good for the balance sheets of the pension funds. It is hard enough to keep corporate managers' hands off the investment policies of private pension funds; it's virtually impossible to keep government and union managers from being more responsive to their constituencies than to their financial responsibilities.

One example is the movement to control executive pay, an issue with plenty of political importance and practically no economic relevance. The studies that show that executive pay is not reasonably related to corporate performance should not be used to prescribe that institutional shareholders should set the pay of executives. If pay makes no difference, the political pension managers should stay out of it entirely. Nevertheless ITT and Avon, among others, have invited their institutional owners to help them set executive pay, and companies that do not want any help get it anyway.

JOINING THE PARTY

The most predictably dangerous thing about social investing and economically targeted investing is the near certainty that the well-intentioned movement will be perverted and captured by political corruption. In Washington there is a whole industry of supporters of social investing. Their proposals usually require a federal guarantee or a federal tax subsidy to make them attractive to responsible pension managers. For example, Congress could require pension funds to make infrastructure investments to qualify for tax exemption. That would be politically easy and financially dangerous, a combination Congress often chooses.

The Infrastructure Investment Commission, created in 1992 as an election-year gimmick, put forward a report in February 1993 that called for creation of a structure of guarantees and partnerships so that $5 billion in federal money could lure $95 billion in pension money into infrastructure investments. Fortunately for the nation's pension beneficiaries, it's hard to dress up a twenty-to-one leveraged expenditure on a pork barrel project as a secure investment any fiduciary would be pleased to make. The report contained such baffling flow charts and grimly bureaucratic terminology that pension industry lobbyists openly mocked it and compared it to a report from the agency that sells the depleted assets of failed savings and loans.

The Clinton administration is hungry for investment capital, and it's drooling over pension plans. As a candidate, Clinton talked about obtaining pension money from both private industry and public employment plans to fund a $20 billion-a-year investment in national infrastructure.

Clinton had led Arkansas pension plans into social investing, which produced such luminous investments in the state infrastructure as a mortgage loan on the Kappa Kappa Gamma sorority house at the University of Arkansas. (The executive director of the Arkansas Teachers Retirement System explained, "I know the daddies of those girls and there is no way they would have let that loan go bad."][7]

In the first one hundred days of his administration, HUD Secretary Henry Cisneros entered a "partnership" with the AFL-CIO's Housing Investment Trust, intending to use $500 million in union pension money for low-income housing. The administration has also floated ideas for taxing the assets of plans or—as six states including Arkansas do—demanding that 5 percent of assets be invested where the government directs.

President Clinton's appointee as Assistant Secretary of Labor for pension and welfare benefits was Olena Berg, a former chief deputy treasurer of California whose principal interest was in economically targeted investment, steering pension funds to make investments that would stimulate the economy.

"We will be asking pension plans to change their thinking," Berg told *The New York Times* on taking office. "Instead of thinking only about beating the market by another increment, we want them to think about how their investments are contributing to the long-run health of the economy."[8]

Perhaps reflecting the interest of Labor Secretary Robert Reich in promoting job training and education, Berg urged pension fund managers to invest in companies with effective training programs. She claimed that there will be a high return on investment for those who follow her advice. "A company that invests in developing the value of its human capital should, over the long term, perform better than its competitors, and this superior performance will be reflected in the growth of its stock prices. If this is indeed the case, pension fund managers should be looking to invest in companies with such characteristics."[9]

But is it the case that companies investing in training always perform better in competition and in the stock market? Reich's Labor Department is studying that. Other related questions include whether such things as workplace safety, employee participation in management, profit-sharing, and flexible work schedules affect company performance. According to Berg, the department is trying to convince corporations to develop a "high-performance workplace" and to convince investors to give them the capital they need to do it.

One can't help but be skeptical about a study that's designed to prove what the boss already believes. And even if there are links between labor policies and company performance, there's no proof that one caused the other. The Labor Department would serve workers far better if it kept its eye on financial responsibility of pension funds, rather than trying to push managers to invest according to the latest official's latest theory.

Social investing always fails to answer two simple questions: If this is such a good investment, why hasn't somebody already put money in without government pressure? And if it's not such a great investment, why does the government want to use retirement savings—the property of workers—to finance it? Unfortunately, there are no sound answers to these questions.

PENSION REGULATORS

PENSION PROBLEMS ARISE because defined benefit trusts are pools of money from which individual benefits are withdrawn. As with any community property, there's an incentive for each individual to increase his own wealth at the expense of the total trust.

All too often, defined pension plans are set up with the best intentions to be too equal. Sometimes at the behest of a union and sometimes on their own motion, employers often agree to give credits for past service that wasn't funded at the time. This can happen when a pension plan is newly created and the employer decides to let a sixty-three-year-old worker retire with the benefits he would have earned if the plan had been in effect his whole time with the company. It can happen when a company wants to close a plant with a minimum of pain, granting full pension benefits to anyone over a certain age. However it happens, the result is always to push the pension plan's obligations past its funding. Federal law allows underfunded pension plans to be brought up to snuff over forty years, but while they creep along, slowly curing past defects, they can pile new unfunded promises on top of the old ones.

Problems also arise because management is in charge of the pension fund. The law designates employers and the people they select to run a pension fund as fiduciaries, meaning they are financially responsible for their actions to the beneficiaries of the plan. Everything they do must be for the exclusive benefit of the participants. Unfortunately, lawyers finely parse the fiduciary responsibilities, which can only be applied and enforced after the fact, after a long song and dance in civil court according to arcane, infinitely debatable standards.

One of the toughest arguments about defined benefit plans concerns the size and fairness of plans as they apply to highly compensated people and rank-and-file employees. The government has been unwilling to grant companies the right to allocate any sums they please as tax-deductible pension contributions. That would create a potentially infinite tax shelter. So Congress has created a panoply of laws and the Internal Revenue Service has followed up with an even greater array of rules, all designed to limit pension contributions to some "reasonable" amount.

In 1982 the Tax Equity and Fiscal Responsibility Act (the huge tax increase that undid some of the Reagan tax cut of 1981) limited "top-heavy" pension plans in which most contributions went to the accounts of owners, managers, and highly paid employees. This limited tax-deductible contributions in general, whether or not the whole plan was well-funded. It also worked against pension savings for small family businesses, because it introduced the practice of aggregating all members of the family of a highly compensated employee for determination of tax deductibility.

The Retirement Equity Act of 1984, incorporating a 1983 Supreme Court decision, equalized annual benefits for women (women live longer and so had been receiving lower benefits per year for the same contribution) and lowered the worker eligibility age for pension plan participation from twenty-five to twenty-one. It also provided for undiminished pensions for people with a break in service of five years or more, up to the number of years of service before the interruption began. These changes increased prospective benefits without changing funding rules.

In 1986 Congress stuck a provision into the budget reconciliation bill that reduced the vesting period from ten years to five years (seven years in some cases) and required pension plans to continue accruing pension benefits for anyone working past the normal retirement age. Again, these changes increased prospective benefits without changing funding rules.

Also in 1986, the Tax Reform Act reduced tax rates, which reduced the benefits of any tax deduction, including pension contributions. And Congress further limited top-heavy plans by mandating that at least 70 percent of a firm's employees had to participate in its pension plan.

The 1987 Budget Reconciliation Act limited tax-deductible contributions to defined benefit plans. No contribution is tax-deductible if it would raise the funding ratio above 150 percent of termination benefits.

A perfect example of the way the legislative road to ruin is paved with good intentions is found in the rules about pension vesting. Vesting, remember, is the term for the right to receive a pension, even if the vested worker leaves the company. ERISA and follow-on laws tightened controls on vesting and required companies to vest their employees' benefits more quickly. The first result was to increase the proportion of workers who had some vested rights to a future pension, from 48 percent of workers at places where there was a pension plan in 1979 to 64 percent in 1988. But in the same period, the percentage of workers who actually worked at places where there was a pension plan fell, from 43 percent in 1979 to 38 percent in 1988.[1]

Even some reformers worried about going too far with regulation of the pension system. "I hate to sound like the Chamber of Commerce," Phyllis C. Borzi, the pension counsel to the House Education and Labor Subcommittee on Labor-Management Relations, told the *National Journal*, but acknowledged: "Highly compensated individuals in decision-making positions in companies always start with the question 'What's in it for me?' Take away pension plan incentives for the highly paid, and upper management will take less interest in them, finding other means of ensuring that top executives get rewarded." Borzi observed that, for example, managers can pay themselves bonuses, insightfully anticipating the brouhaha over allegedly excessive executive compensation that would erupt in the early 1990s.[2]

But other pension reformers who are focused on fairness want to go further. One Clinton administration official, Assistant Treasury Secretary Alicia Munnell, advocated a 15 percent tax on pension contributions and on the annual capital gains within a fund, on the grounds that too much of the tax benefit goes to high-paid individuals. She went still further, holding that since such a tax would be fair, then capturing 15 percent of all existing pension assets would serve to levy the tax on past contributions and earnings—that is, on the balances of every U.S. pension fund. Such a seizure of an estimated $450 billion would be the biggest confiscation in American history, but Munnell merely observed that it would have "intriguing" possibilities for balancing the budget. Munnell made her proposal in a paper in 1992, and critics thoroughly aired the issue before her Senate confirmation, yet neither the Clinton administration nor the Senate seemed to think it was out of bounds.[3]

No Cops to Call

A pension plan is just a big pot of money, and pots of money draw crooks the way pots of honey draw bears. Sadly, there are no effective cops in the pension system. The U.S. Labor Department's Pension and Welfare Benefits Administration is supposed to police the whole benefits area with a staff of 600 and a budget of $67 million. That's only enough to provide the illusion of protection for pension investments and beneficiaries.

To substitute for real protection, Congress has enacted volumes of laws to tie the hands of pension plan sponsors and managers. Regulations require employers to treat their workers more generously than themselves, to file reports that no regulator will ever read, to comply with arcane details that even an actuary can't comprehend.

Employers and their advisers are responding by eliminating pension plans altogether. A study by the American Academy of Actuaries reported that more than 30,000 employers terminated defined benefit pension plans in 1990 and 1991. More than a third did not replace them with some other kind of retirement plan; nearly half offered a new plan that was less generous.

The crowning blow is that all the regulations driving employers out of the pension system can't be trusted to protect beneficiaries. Raymond Maria, former acting inspector general of the Department of Labor, issued clear warnings in 1989 and 1990. He reported that private pension and welfare funds receive only the most cursory examination from the Pension and Welfare Benefits Administration. His last report before he left office in 1990 compared the agency's regulatory effectiveness to that of savings and loan regulation before the S&L crisis came to public attention.

Maria's report noted that fewer than three hundred federal workers are assigned to supervise five million pension and welfare plans. Naturally, they really depend on auditors to turn up problems. But when the inspector general inspected the quality of private audits, his investigators found that 64 percent of plan reports did not meet disclosure requirements, that nearly half the audits did not test assets held by financial institutions, and that 22 percent of the reports and audits did not meet Generally Accepted Auditing Standards.

From that, Maria concluded, "These vulnerabilities do not reveal a system currently in crisis; but they do demonstrate it to be at risk."

The IG's office studied 168 pension plans that contained $6.7 billion in trust for 500,000 participants in which the Office of Labor Racketeering and the Pension and Welfare Benefit Administration already had turned up evidence of wrongdoing. The point was to see how well independent auditors had done in discovering problems in problem-ridden plans. It turned out they had failed to find or disclose seventeen cases of criminal violations involving misuses of funds ranging from $7,000 to $5 million. There were also procedural violations that had cost the funds another $16.4 million.

More than half the audits failed to comply with at least one ERISA disclosure requirement—the audit reports weren't turned in to the Labor Department until about two years after the year of the report being audited. The IG's conclusion: "Sufficient enforcement and reporting safeguards are not in place to deter or expose fund misuses."

Like Cassandra, Maria found that his fate was to be disbelieved. The most significant Labor Department response to Maria's warning was to remove most of the power of his Office of Investigations.

The pension establishment, in the government, academia, and trade groups, said Maria was just tooting his horn to get publicity. The Deputy Secretary of Labor at the time, Roderick A.

DeArment, told Congress, "Neither the inspector general's reports nor the Department of Labor's enforcement experience demonstrates that the nation's private pension system is unsound. In fact, it has never been healthier."[4] DeArment also inadvertently drew attention to some of the system's weaknesses by pointing out the laudable if tardy steps the department was taking. He announced creation of a computer system to review annual reports (because no human or machine was doing it), new regulations to penalize filers of inadequate reports (because cheaters had nothing to fear), and a system of referring accountants who perform substandard work to professional organizations for disciplinary action (because there were no sanctions in place).

The executive director of the Employee Benefits Research Institute said Maria ought to lose his job, and one of the leading ERISA lawyers in Washington, former representative John Erlenborn, questioned Maria's sanity. Georgetown University professor Roy A. Shotland was comparatively civil when he merely called Maria a "bomb thrower." Shotland said, "The really big money is by and large in places where someone is watching: actuaries, lawyers or major unions. . . . Criminal [violations] are on the fringe."

It would be more accurate to say that virtually all known criminal violations have occurred in small plans. That once could have been said of savings and loans, as well. Maria's point was that the government's protection of pension plans could not be trusted, that the henhouse door was open.

Here's a sample of a "small" abuse from St. Louis that Maria and his investigators highlighted. A well-connected lawyer induced administrators of the $300 million St. Louis police and firefighters' pension fund to engage friends of his as investment counselors. They then ran their stock and bond purchases through a broker who charged double the normal commission rate and kicked back 70 percent of the excess commissions to the counselors and the lawyer. The group took thousands of dollars over three years, and were caught and convicted only because the IRS stumbled onto the illicit cash flow quite by chance.

"There is a new generation of racketeers that has evolved from the ethnic stereotype," said Maria. "Racketeers disguised as attorneys, bankers, accountants, beneficiary plan administrators, portfolio managers, doctors, and dentists—everyone wants to think that it's just Teamsters who pillage their members' benefit plans. That clearly is not the case."

Maria, a former FBI agent, complained that even when violations, big or small, were discovered, it was hard to get a criminal prosecution rolling because the Labor Department's tradition favored civil action. "Civil process doesn't cover the problem," Maria argued. "State-by-state efforts don't work. We recommend criminal investigation and criminal prosecution." But a Labor Department advisory council working group emphatically opposed giving the IG criminal enforcement power. "The Labor Department's current emphasis on civil enforcement is consistent with a deliberate policy choice made by Congress," its report said.

As Maria said: "The department sees itself as social service oriented, and it doesn't see vigorous criminal enforcement as consistent with its social service goals. When you rely on fines and administrative actions, you foster a climate in which crimes are worth committing. The benefits are so high and the risks so low that the question is, 'Can I afford the fine?' "

Efforts to increase the power of civil action failed anyway. The administrator of the Pension and Welfare Benefits Administration—a family friend of President Bush named George Ball—did propose a change in procedure at the agency that would make it easier for pension plan participants to sue plan managers. At least if the federal watchdog could not enforce the law, victims could try for restitution. The pension industry compared it to "dropping a nuclear bomb on the administration of plan benefits" and Ball put it "on hold" permanently.

The Bush administration proposed a series of changes in the law to increase protection, but nearly all of the Labor Department's proposals were designed to encourage whistle-blowing, not true enforcement. Anyone reporting pension fund shenanigans would get a bounty of 10 percent of anything collected in fines or restitution; trustees found to have misused funds would be required to pay court costs of those who brought suit against them. Even these mild reforms never passed in Congress. The henhouse door is still wide open.

TAXING PENSIONS

Unlike the Department of Labor, the Internal Revenue Service is not underfunded, not understaffed, and it zealously regulates pension fund affairs. Unfortunately for beneficiaries, the IRS is almost entirely interested in maximizing revenue for the U.S. Treasury. That means that the IRS zeal is directed to reducing the tax deductions that employers can take for pension contributions. In other words, the IRS works to hold down pension contributions.

The Internal Revenue Service reflexively questions large deductions of all kinds, and every so often goes on a nationwide crusade against certain types of deductions. For example, the IRS undertook a sweeping enforcement action on small pension plans to review the actuarial assumptions undergirding pension contributions. Although actuarial assumptions can be and are used by struggling companies to hold down their contributions in an effort to conserve cash, the IRS was only interested in cases with the opposite problem, in which companies deflated their estimates of the earnings of pension assets and inflated their estimates of pension liabilities.

It was as if the IRS were confronted with a lot of water glasses and tried to find the ones that were half empty while ignoring the ones that were half full.

Such small pension plans were popular until the Tax Reform Act of 1986 made them unattractive, but the IRS thought they were too easy to manipulate with questionable actuarial assumptions. The IRS had thought its Small Plan Actuarial Program could capture $666 million in back taxes and it undertook about 15,000 audits, but after nearly four years of work it collected only about $38 million in unpaid taxes. In 1992 the effort pretty much collapsed when a judge told the IRS it could not question actuarial assumptions in retirement plans.

Among the targets of the IRS were a couple of the savviest—and most profitable—law firms in the country. Wachtell, Lipton, Rosen & Katz of New York and Vinson & Elkins of Houston became the lead cases in Tax Court, and both firms won judgments that the IRS could not move to question their actuarial assumptions or force them to make changes retroactively.

Both firms had used 5 percent interest rates to value assets and estimated that their partners would retire at age fifty-five in one case and age sixty-two in the other. Prevailing interest rates in the years covered by the cases were much higher than 5 percent and the IRS quite reasonably claimed that the partners were just using their retirement plan as a tax shelter. The judge in the case, however, respected the actuaries' decision and said the rates and retirement ages were within the bounds of reasonableness because actuaries had approved them.[5]

Since it was a case of defeating the tax collector, Judge Charles Clapp's decision was widely hailed as a blow for freedom and individual rights. But by granting wide latitude to actuaries and those who hire them to set nearly any assumptions they choose, Judge Clapp opened the door to the henhouse much wider.

The U.S. Supreme Court upheld the ruling, saying in effect that one man's retirement account is another man's tax shelter; that big law firms can defend themselves against the IRS; that pension law and pension regulations can suddenly change back and forth; and that actuaries can be found to support both sides of most mathematical propositions. All true, but the court wound up establishing legal precedents that will make it easier for plan sponsors to fiddle with actuarial assumptions in the future.

In 1993 the IRS announced its enforcement priorities for the future. "The key phrase in our audit initiatives is balance," declared Preston Butcher, a district chief based in Los Angeles. "You will never, never see again a program like Small Plan Actuarial, where so many of our resources were tied up in one narrow area."[6] Particularly important areas from the beneficiaries' point of view will be plan valuation and prohibited transactions.

RAISING REVENUE

The impulse to recoup taxes lost on deductible pension contributions runs through the entire government. Despite a whole series of laws, rules, and budget cuts, all designed to limit the pension tax shelter, the $52.6 billion in taxes that were not paid on employer contributions to pension plans was still the largest tax expenditure in the federal budget for fiscal 1994. Other pension exclusions are worth nearly $8 billion in forgone taxes. These will be tempting targets as long as the federal government tries to reduce the deficit without making major policy changes. They will be especially tempting because a change takes so long to work an effect that an ordinary person might notice.

In the 1993 debate over President Clinton's first budget reconciliation bill, the increase of the tax rate on the rich from 31 percent to 39 percent was hotly debated. Such major issues as a gas tax were aired over and over again. Retirees were generally aware of the increase in the taxable portion of Social Security, from 50 percent of benefits to 85 percent, applying to married taxpayers with $44,000 in income. They may not have grasped the full subtlety of the tax increase, failing to note that since the income threshold is not indexed for inflation, more and more retirees will join the 13 percent of Social Security beneficiaries who pay tax on the full 85 percent of benefits.

But a measure to pare back the tax deductibility of pension contributions was scarcely considered before passage, and most affected persons will never notice what happened to them. The bill cut the ceilings on income from which tax-deductible pension contributions are figured and it reduced the projected benefit that could be funded. Both measures would reduce the amount of plan assets to be accumulated without tax, putting future payment of defined benefits more in doubt and reducing the buildup of savings in defined contribution plans.

These changes were part of President Clinton's emphasis on raising tax rates for the rich, and indeed, they only affected persons with individual incomes above $150,000 and projected benefits of more than $115,000 a year. But these are not benefits for the rich; a thirty-five-year-old earning $35,000 a year will be affected. Projecting his earnings out thirty years at an average annual growth rate of 5.5 percent produces an estimate of his final compensation of $165,342 a year. Discounting the excess back to the present means our thirty-five-year-old would find that $3,200 of his $35,000 salary could not be considered for funding a pension.[7] Higher salaries would mean higher exclusions, of course. The ceiling was indexed so that the tax-deductible contribution can grow with the employee's income, but it will never push the final benefit back to what it would have been. Even worse, the IRS has disguised this sleight-of-hand cut in pension benefits by ruling that employers don't have to notify participants when they amend the plan to comply with the new cap. Normally, sponsors must notify participants of any significant reduction in the way future benefits are accrued.[8]

It's very hard to understand how an administration that talks so much about long-term investment ever adopted an idea so well-tailored to reduce the pool of long-term patient capital. But an equally distressing effect of this limitation is that attacking pensions this way thoroughly disconnects really high-paid people from the interests of the middle-class people the Clinton administration was trying to help when it proposed the change. Executives, managers, and owners who make the decisions regarding benefit plans will have their stake in the success of such plans reduced. They will feel less personal interest in their plans and they may neglect them or decide to terminate them. That could affect every covered employee, no matter how low-paid.

Overall, federal regulation has become too burdensome for the taste of many employers, even though it does not adequately protect beneficiaries. For example, the pension law reforms contained in the Tax Reform Act of 1986 are still working through the legal system. Just that one law produced regulations taking effect in 1989, 1992, 1993, and 1995. And, of course, new pension laws in subsequent years added new changes, new rules, and new effective dates. It seems to many pension experts impossible to comply with every feature of federal pension law.

At the very least, the flood of laws and regulations forces pension advisers and sponsors to modify their legal documentation every year. Eventually, our lawmakers must realize that every change that brings in federal revenue now reduces pension benefits in the future.

VALUING PENSION PLANS

At the end of 1993, the Securities and Exchange Commission took a first faltering step toward fuller and more accurate disclosure of the value of pension funds. Not previously noted for its interest in protecting workers, the SEC suggested that shareholders needed to be protected from misleading valuations of pension fund liabilities.

As we have seen, valuation of pension plan funding is very sensitive to the interest rates a sponsor selects to estimate the future earnings on plan assets and to estimate the future pay rates and service lives on which benefits will be based.

SEC chief economist Walter Schuetze declared that he was very unhappy about the high discount rates that some pension plan sponsors were employing to reduce the present value of their pension liabilities. He strongly suggested that companies use a discount rate in line with the yield on AA-rated corporate bonds—7 percent at the time of his warning.

Gabrielle Napolitano, an analyst at Goldman Sachs, was one of the first people on Wall Street to call attention to what she called "the miracle of compound interest in reverse." She examined data for 366 companies out of the Standard & Poor's 500 and found that only eleven had used a discount rate as low as 7 percent in 1992. There were 307 that used discount rates of 8 percent or more, of which forty-five used discount rates of 9 percent or more. On the earning side, 350 assumed long-term investment returns of at least 8 percent, of which 273 were assuming at least 9 percent and 104 were assuming returns of at least 10 percent.

Schuetze's warning was no idle threat. The SEC must approve the financial disclosures of publicly traded companies, or they cannot have access to public capital markets. And his warning came at a time when long-term interest rates were falling anyway, so that companies with overgenerous discount rates would have a large adjustment to make and a large new liability to recognize.

A one-percentage-point cut in a discount rate would normally produce a 10 percent increase in liabilities, so it was clear that some companies that had been cheerily reporting pension surpluses would be forced to report underfunding. In turn, that report could lead to unexpected writeoffs against corporate net worth, and increases in federal pension insurance premiums.

GUARDING THE GUARDIANS

The professionals who regulate pension funds from the inside are hired by management, not by workers. Sponsors are fiduciaries, but their advisers are not. So when a company wants to fiddle with its pension plan, it can easily say that the move was approved by the actuaries and accountants. After all, if they don't approve, they're out of a job.

The U.S. Supreme Court upheld this system in June 1993,[9] holding that federal pension law does not allow individual beneficiaries to sue for damages against pension advisers, such as actuaries and accountants, who were not actually fiduciaries of a plan. A fiduciary has financial responsibilities to the beneficiaries, but the court held that nonfiduciaries doing business with a plan—even corrupt business—do not share the fiduciary's responsibilities.

Retirees argued that Hewitt Associates, a consulting firm, had failed to change the actuarial assumptions in a Kaiser Steel pension plan to account for the drain on the plan as the company phased out steel operations in the 1980s. Plant closings produced early retirements for which no contributions had been made. The plan became underfunded and was eventually terminated in 1987. Federal pension insurance kicked in, but those early-retirement benefits and other pensions in excess of the PBGC guarantee were reduced.

In a callous 5–4 decision, the Supreme Court said, in effect, that actuaries have no fiduciary duty to plan members. Justice Antonin Scalia wrote for the majority that if service providers were exposed to liability there would be "high insurance costs on persons who regularly deal with and offer advice to ERISA plans and hence upon ERISA plans themselves."

Scalia was right to point out that there is no such thing as a free lunch and that all beneficiaries of all plans would eventually bear the burden of their own protection. But that is no reason to allow a few beneficiaries to bear the whole burden of the collapse of a pension plan. It's a lot like requiring people who live near the Gulf of Mexico to buy hurricane insurance: anybody who can't afford the insurance shouldn't live there at all.

Not only did this decision relieve advisers of much responsibility to keep plans straight; it also cut off the chance of beneficiaries to receive direct damages from crooked advisers. Only the plan can receive restitution. The Department of Labor said it would try to get Congress to amend ERISA, but that could take a long time.

Follow-up decisions in lower courts came quickly. For example, the Labor Department lost an action against a foreign bank that sold insurance to a union health plan. The bank refused to honor its claims but a trial court following the Supreme Court held that only the plan managers could be sued, not the bank that knowingly participated in their scheme. About three hundred plan participants lost out on insurance for $200,000 in unpaid medical expenses.[10] The Labor Department also reported that its decision might destroy cases for recovery from Executive Life companies that wrote annuities in a corrupt arrangement with companies terminating pension plans.

10

PENSION INSURANCE

THE FEDERAL PENSION Benefit Guaranty Corp. insures more than $900 billion in private pension liabilities of defined benefit plans. It collects premiums (a tax, really) from employers on the number of their employees participating in defined benefit pension plans. The PBGC was set up under the Employee Retirement Income Security Act of 1974 and modeled on the Federal Deposit Insurance Corp. and the Federal Savings and Loan Insurance Corp.

Until the savings and loan collapses of the 1980s, this was considered a compliment, but now it is clear that these agencies insure risks they do not regulate, and that these are risks that feckless or corrupt managers can easily make more threatening in a time of crisis.

In truth, the only difference between the PBGC and the late, lamented FSLIC is that savings and loans were always required to have reserves on hand and to maintain a positive net worth; there is no such requirement for pension funds. Also, bank and thrift regulators are supposed to monitor the condition of financial institutions, require them to keep their reserves up, and close those that cannot liquidate at one hundred cents on the dollar. The wave of S&L closures cost the taxpayers so many billions of dollars because the regulators didn't close troubled institutions quickly enough. There is virtually no effective regulation of defined benefit pension funds, and the strongest regulatory authority, the Internal Revenue Service, works primarily to hold pension funding to a minimum level.

Savings and loans collapsed because they became more like pension funds: underfunded, underregulated, and underwater. The crisis of the pension system has not arrived, but we should be concerned about the public liability of the agency that insures pension funds.

As Brian A. Jones, a New Jersey actuary, has observed: "Sponsors can largely control both the size of the gap between the value of benefit expectations and assets and the timing of plan termination. It is hard to imagine a better example of an uninsurable risk."

The original PBGC premium for defined benefit pension plans was set in 1974 at one dollar per covered employee per year. This figure was based on pious hope and a love of round numbers, not on fact. The PBGC has been forced to ask Congress for several premium increases, and now has a risk-based premium that runs from nineteen dollars per employee per year for healthy plans to seventy-two dollars per employee per year for those that are seriously underfunded. And even this is not enough.

The PBGC estimated in 1993 that the insured private system is about $51 billion underfunded, but this is pitifully short of the real problem. For years, the General Accounting Office threw up its hands in disgust when asked to audit the agency, because the auditors had no way of estimating the liabilities that might be thrown on the agency in the future. Neither the PBGC nor anyone else can guess how rapidly troubled companies will suck wealth out of their pension funds. There are many legal ways to turn soundly funded pension funds into worthless husks.

Starting in 1990, PBGC has annually published a list of the fifty most underfunded plans. The PBGC executive director at the time, James Lockhart, was trying to embarrass companies into tightening up their funding, but most of the companies that should have been embarrassed were outraged instead.

Some said they were outraged at being held up as bad citizens endangering their workers, because they would never, ever default on the obligations. Some companies complained that they were funding the plans right up to the limit of the tax deduction allowed by law. Some were annoyed that the PBGC had made their bad situation look worse by reducing optimistic interest-rate assumptions and by adjusting for the fact that PBGC does not insure all benefits. Others pointed to other plans that they had overfunded and said Lockhart should have published their net position.

"Well, I'd be glad if they shifted some of their overfunding to their underfunded plans, but I don't think they're going to do that," Lockhart said, noting that the participants in the over-funded plans, primarily plans covering management and salaried workers, might object.

The list and the responses to it highlighted the fact that vir-tually all companies with underfunded plans have made the minimum contributions and that many have made the maxi-mum tax-deductible contributions—an excellent argument for a change in the funding standards.

While some observers thought using intimidation and public embarrassment against companies with underfunded plans was a neat idea, others sharply disagreed. "The PBGC is shouting 'Fire!' in a crowded room when no fire exists," said *Pensions & Investments* magazine in an editorial. "It is irresponsible and fear-mongering." But if publishing the list of fifty is fear-mongering, then a fire inspector is fear-mongering when he points out open containers of fuel and the absence of fire extin-guishers.

CREATING THE DANGER

The most important point about the PBGC is that the very ex-istence of federal pension insurance increases the chance of a collapse of the pension system, just as deposit insurance did to the savings and loan system.

"Few of the many risks that S&L operators took could have been financed had deposits not been guaranteed by the federal government," observed Robert Litan of the Brookings Institu-tion, a member of the National Commission on Financial Insti-tution Reform, Recovery and Enforcement.[1] "Truly uninsured depositors would have been far more careful with their money. They would have insisted on accurate financial data from the institutions, not the phony financial statements encouraged by federal regulatory policy. Simply put, in the absence of insurance, high-risk S&Ls could not have grown."

All this is equally true of the defined benefit pension system: uninsured beneficiaries would not be so complacent about their pension plans. As a group, they would insist on better information about their pension plan. They would recognize that the underfunding of a pension plan is an involuntary loan from them to their employer and they would be more concerned about their employers' credit-worthiness.

Instead, pension insurance leaves beneficiaries happy to accept the assurances of their employers and their unions that they were winners in the last negotiation. Employers are left equally happy to make promises. Some even calculate the value of the option to throw a pension onto the PBGC as a hidden asset of the corporation.

If the pension system follows the path of the S&L system, we can expect more and more corporate obligations to be thrown onto the shoulders of the pension system, while federal regulators work to conceal the system's problems and responsible people leave the system entirely. That is, indeed, what we see today. The only question is whether pensioners will be bailed out the way S&L depositors were bailed out. If they are not—and the ground is being prepared for the government to turn its back on its obligations—then the pension collapse will be even more painful than the S&L debacle.

Defenders of the system say that the PBGC has the power to claim the assets of the sponsors of underfunded plans. True enough on paper, but as demonstrated in the so-called reorganization of TWA, the PBGC's power is actually very limited by political reality. In theory, the PBGC could have terminated the bankrupt airline's pension plans and gone after everything chairman Carl Icahn owned to satisfy more than $1 billion of unfunded TWA pension liabilities. In real life, everything had to be negotiated while Senators Robert Dole and Nancy Kassebaum of Kansas and Christopher Bond and John Danforth of Missouri put huge pressure on Labor Secretary Lynn Martin and other Bush administration officials to save the jobs of 25,000 TWA employees, many in the senators' states.

Bond called it "nuclear warfare," and it really was mutually assured destruction. Either jobs would be destroyed to save the jobholders' future pensions, or the jobs would be saved and the pensions would be thrown on the PBGC and on the healthy companies that pay taxes to support the agency.

The political choice was easy. The lame duck Bush administration declared, "The jobs, stupid." The PBGC negotiators could not make a credible threat to shut down the airline. The result: Icahn contributed a stack of paper guarantees and pledges of dubious TWA assets. He walked free of any further liability.

The PBGC had intended to use its power to demand support for an underfunded terminated plan from any member of a controlled group of companies that included the plan sponsor. Icahn controlled a wide range of operating and holding companies with many billions of dollars; all PBGC had to do was order that the underfunded plans be terminated and it could tap the riches of Icahn's other companies.

Instead, the PBGC embarked on long negotiations with Icahn, one of the toughest negotiators in American business, and the agency came away with no shirt and only a raggedy pair of pants. Ultimately, Icahn agreed to freeze the two underfunded plans so they would not accrue any new benefits, to provide $80 million in direct funding, and to guarantee payments of $240 million over eight years if the airline terminated the plans. He also agreed to let TWA pay $15 million to support a new defined contribution plan that would supplant the two underfunded defined benefit plans. And he paid $200 million to TWA, not to the pension plan. The underfunded plans received $80 million, not $1 billion, plus an allegedly improved chance of receiving more in the future.

On that improved chance, PBGC's then–general counsel, Carol Connor Flowe, commented, "TWA's pension plans remain ongoing, which means that neither the PBGC nor plan participants have suffered a loss. Equally important, TWA continues to fly and its 25,000 employees continue to work. . . . As part of this settlement, Mr. Icahn provided TWA with $200 million of financing that it could not obtain elsewhere. TWA could not have continued to operate without this financing."

The comment shows how close to the edge of the world TWA was sailing. In addition, some other details in the deal show that benefit accruals have not really been frozen, that TWA will have greater liabilities and less chance of funding them than if the deal had never been made. Flowe's concern for the 25,000 workers is understandable, but ignores the interests of TWA's 15,000 retirees.

In effect, the PBGC allowed Icahn and TWA to get away with a promise to provide the same minimum funding the man and his company would have been required to make if they had never negotiated at all. The agency also allowed most of the money wrested from Icahn to be used to support the airline and not the pension plan.

As David Langer, a consulting actuary from New York, observed in a critique of the settlement, nobody involved, from Icahn to TWA's creditors to the workers and retirees and their unions, had any reason to defend the solvency of the PBGC. All of them "would clearly not be averse to the use of PBGC's assets as a solution to TWA's financial problems." Langer complained that PBGC had hinged its settlement on the assumption that the troubled airline could keep flying and return to health. "Is PBGC taking on the role of keeping TWA going?" he asked rhetorically, asserting that the deal was equivalent to a back-door bailout of TWA, off the books and out of the public eye.

"It would be ironical indeed if Mr. Lockhart, who has been issuing dire warnings that the PBGC faces a savings and loan type of debacle, were to be responsible for the impairment of PBGC's solvency," Langer said.[2]

Another practical limit on the PBGC's power to protect pensions is the fact that pension sponsors have the right to terminate their plans. As Lockhart observed, "We don't want to have the government create so much hardship and hassle that they discourage creation of new defined benefit plans and encourage termination. Ultimately, it could mean we'd be left with only the sick puppies."

PRICE OF PROTECTION

One thing that comes out of any examination of the PBGC is that the agency needs to charge a realistic premium. Those sick puppies are getting an indirect subsidy from the federal government: "For the financially weak companies, the PBGC is not

being adequately compensated for the risk we are assuming,"
said Lockhart. "A severely underfunded plan is paying less than
three cents per hour per worker for this protection."

But it may be problematic to charge a realistic premium. Conventional estimates of an economic premium for pension insurance range up to about $100 per employee per year. That would
quintuple the current rate on the best-financed plans.

James Smalhout, a pension analyst who once worked at the
PBGC, has produced an unconventional but compelling estimate of a proper risk-adjusted premium. Instead of following the
typical insurance practice of using past experience to predict
future claims, he used an economist's method from his corporate finance textbook. He noted that in today's markets, financial guarantees are priced according to the spread between the
guarantor's cost of funds and that of the borrower. Thus we have
insured mortgages, insured municipal bonds and so forth, and a
market for the insurance based on the spreads.

Since sponsors of underfunded pension plans are, in effect,
borrowing from their employees on the strength of the PBGC
guarantee, Smalhout figured that the value of the guarantee is
related to the difference between the plan sponsor's corporate
cost of funds and the government's cost of funds. Using this
differential to amortize the guarantee over an average duration
of about eight years produces enormous economic premiums
even for the soundest of companies.

Thus Smalhout figured that a shaky steelmaker with a very
high cost of funds ought to be paying the PBGC more than $4,000
per participant per year. Even an extremely sound concern in a
growing industry such as electronics, with a cost of funds only a
percentage point or two above Treasuries, should be paying more
than $1,000 per participant per year, he calculated. Not today's
maximum seventy-two dollars or today's average twenty-three
dollars or today's minimum nineteen dollars, but more than
$1,000 per participant per year for healthy companies and more
than $4,000 a year for sick ones.

If this is the real cost of pension insurance, it indicates the size
of the problem the nation has accepted by embracing pension
insurance. It means the bill that eventually will come due will
be far bigger than the S&L disaster.

A NEW ADMINISTRATION

The new executive director of the PBGC, Martin Slate, is not inclined to perform radical surgery. Speaking in July 1993, soon after taking office, Slate declared that the Clinton administration wants to make sure it considers the financial burden on companies that may be forced to beef up their pension funding.

He told the United Steelworkers Union, "We want to give businesses the opportunity to meet their cash-flow requirements and at the same time want pension plans to be better funded." Although he said he was talking about the need for people to have jobs as well as pensions, he did not grasp that pension funding has to come out of business cash flow.

On taking office, the Clinton administration formed a task force to consider pension funding and pension policy. According to Slate, one of its first decisions was to focus pension reform only on those companies that are in trouble now. "If people have well-funded plans, they would be reassured that we won't come after them, that we'll go after the bad actors."

Unfortunately, the essence of the pension finance crisis is that pension funds can appear to be well financed, reporting positive net worth and taking in more money than they pay out, while they sow the seeds of their own collapse. Any pension reform that does not address the supposedly healthy plans will have to be repeated over and over again. The closest that the Clinton administration legislation comes to recognizing this is to tighten up the amortization schedule for funding newly created obligations from fifteen years to no more than eight years. This will help, but not enough. In the first five years after creating a new unfunded obligation, a company will not be required to raise its total pension contribution by more than 3 percent.

The sorry track record of some of the underfunded companies does strike the right note on Slate's moral sense. Speaking of the seventy underfunded plans sponsored by the fifty most underfunded companies, Slate said in January 1994, "In 40 percent of them, they didn't even contribute enough to cover the interest that was owed on their delayed contributions."

Slate defended the decision to go after currently troubled plans, noting that plans with 80 percent of the underfunding in the system now pay only 25 percent of the PBGC premiums. The administration's proposal would increase that to 50 percent, but it ignores the underlying problem that healthy plans are not paying an economic premium for the risk they bring to the pension insurance system.

The administration's task force also decided to try to improve the PBGC's bargaining position in bankruptcy proceedings, proving once again that those who do not learn from history are condemned to repeat it. Congress has done that twice in twelve years, and the PBGC still gets less than fifteen cents for every dollar of benefits owed by bankrupt firms.

Slate also promised to increase enforcement efforts to be sure that companies with underfunded plans don't make matters worse. Close monitoring would allow the agency to terminate plans and claim corporate assets before the company goes into bankruptcy, he said. The administration's pension bill would allow PBGC to ask a court to bar financial transactions and corporate restructurings that would increase the danger of a claim against the PBGC. For example, if a company spun off a subsidiary that had a troubled pension plan, PBGC would be able to ask a court to order that the old company keep on funding the plan for a certain period.

PBGC has been stretching its reach into court for years, but the problem continues to grow. And it seems unlikely that Slate or any other federal pension official can overcome the enormous pressure to keep endangered companies from failing.

The government's record of protecting pensions is sadly deficient. The stories of the valuation of the Republic Steel salaried workers plan and of the decade-long dissolution of Pan American World Airways and its pension fund are classic cases of government failure to recognize false valuations and prohibited transactions. General Motors is clearly on its way down the same path. Pension participants should not trust the government to protect them until the government has some success stories to balance its long record of failure.

Part Three

REFORMING
THE
PENSION
SYSTEM

FROM BENEFITS TO CONTRIBUTIONS

CONFRONTING BURDENSOME REGULATION and the responsibility for benefits, sensible companies no longer sponsor new defined benefit plans. Too many unfunded benefits must be created in order to make a defined benefit pension a really attractive part of the compensation package. A properly funded defined benefit plan just isn't very attractive to employers or employees. In particular, more than one in five small employers has dropped out of the defined benefit system.[1] A defined contribution plan looks better.

Big companies in mature industries are probably locked into their defined benefit plans by union contracts and the weight of tradition, but that won't stop them from trying to change their situation. In the 1993 contract talks with the United Auto Workers, Ford Motor Co. proposed a step toward a defined contribution system. The company offered to leave current workers in the existing defined benefit plan, but put new workers in a defined contribution plan where they would receive only 2 percent of pay for their retirement accounts.

Unlike General Motors and Chrysler, which have very large underfunded pension plans for union workers, Ford has only a

$300 million underfunding of a $9.7 billion accrued liability for union workers. The company was clearly feeling the pinch of the pension plan anyway. Unhappily for Ford and its workers, the union didn't agree to the proposal.

THE RIGHT CHOICE

For workers, the advantages of a defined contribution plan include:

- Immediate vesting. Workers own the sums contributed to their pension accounts.
- Portability. Workers who leave the company at any age can take their pension accounts with them.
- Flexibility. Workers can usually designate their own mix of investments and design their own benefit payment schedule.
- Responsibility. There can be no such thing as an underfunded defined contribution plan; no promises are made to be paid off with future dollars.

For employers, the advantages of a defined contribution plan include:

- Certainty. A contributed dollar is gone forever and nobody can later come back to make a claim for another dollar to support some expected benefit.
- Simplicity. The burden of government regulation is lighter and the cost of plan administration is lower.
- Responsibility. There can be no such thing as an underfunded defined contribution plan; no promises are made to be paid off with future dollars.

Thus the growing popularity of defined contribution plans. From 1975 to 1989, the number of total participants in defined contribution programs tripled, to 36 million from 12 million, according to the U.S. Labor Department's Pension and Welfare Benefits Administration and the Employee Benefits Research

Institute.[2] Participation in defined benefit programs grew only 21 percent, to 40 million from 33 million.

The number of active working participants with a defined benefit plan as their primary plan held at 27 million during the fourteen-year period and never rose above 30 million during that time. The number of participants who had defined contribution plans as their primary plan increased from 4 million in 1975 to 15 million in 1989.

The total number of defined benefit plans was 103,000 in 1975, rose to 175,000 in 1983, but fell back to 113,000 by 1990. The American Academy of Actuaries surveyed its members in 1993 and projected that the number of defined benefit plans may have fallen by another 30,000 since 1990. The actuaries reported that about a third of the plans, covering more than a fifth of the affected workers, were not replaced at all and about half were replaced with a less generous plan.

The total number of defined contribution plans has risen steadily, from 208,000 in 1975 to 428,000 in 1983 to 600,000 in 1990. Most of the action, both the shrinkage in defined benefit plans and the growth in defined contribution plans, took place in very small plans. But even among publicly traded firms with 100 to 10,000 employees, the percentage of firms sponsoring a defined benefit plan is dropping, and the percentage sponsoring a defined contribution plan is rising. Only at firms with more than 10,000 employees is the number of defined benefit plans rising along with the number of defined contribution plans.[3]

While defined benefit assets of the top 1,000 pension plans in *Pensions & Investments* magazine's annual survey grew 7.3 percent in 1992 to $1.812 trillion, defined contribution assets rose 20.9 percent to $572 billion.[4] Defined benefit contributions have been falling short of benefit payments for five years, in part because some plans were more than 50 percent overfunded—the level at which sponsors no longer get a tax deduction—and in part because many funds retained high investment earnings assumptions dating back to the early and mid-1980s. Cash flow may be a better measure of the real condition of defined benefit plans. *Pensions & Investments* reported that the two hundred largest funds had negative cash flow of $20.6 billion in 1992. That compared with $12.9 billion in 1990 and $2.8 billion in 1988.

WARNING SIGN

Some pension analysts take a casual attitude toward the negative cash flow statistics that show more money being paid out than being paid in. They point to the rising market value of assets in plans—from $104.2 billion in 1987 to $365.9 billion in 1992 in the two hundred largest plans—and say that contributions are declining because many plans have no need for them. They overlook the fact that need is defined by Congress and the IRS, not by pension managers. Almost every pension plan stops making contributions when a plan is overfunded by 50 percent, because there's no more tax benefit for making contributions. It would be much safer to keep making contributions to build up reserves against the day when markets fall, corporate profits sink, and early retirements make demands on pension funds that were never funded. If that day never comes, the pension could be increased to cover beneficiaries' losses from inflation.

It may be too much to say that a defined benefit pension plan can kill a company, but it sure can't aid the fortunes of a company that is facing a decline into old age. A defined benefit plan creates loyalty in workers the company would be better off without. It sucks money out of cash flow whether the company is profitable or not. It gives workers a false sense that job performance will have no effect on their security.

Businesses also recognize that defined benefit plans cost a lot to administer. A small plan with fifteen participants averages $805.45 per participant to administer, compared to an average $228 per employee for a defined contribution plan, according to a 1990 study by Hay Huggins Co., a benefits consulting firm in Philadelphia, for the Pension Benefit Guaranty Corp. Administrative costs for a bigger plan of five hundred participants run $161.73 per participant for defined benefit plans and $85 per participant per year for defined contribution plans. For a plan with 10,000 participants the administrative cost of a defined benefit plan was $55.50 and $40.96 for a defined contribution plan.

Most of the actuaries surveyed by their association in 1993 said their clients who terminated defined benefit plans cited several reasons, but the burden of federal regulation was most often cited, with 30 percent of the actuaries mentioning it as a reason. The cost of the plan was a close second, at 22 percent.

A defined contribution plan gives workers what they earn and no more. It makes them responsible for their actions at work and in the investment of their retirement assets. Its existence constantly reminds them of their other options, good and bad, as free agents on the labor market. For the time being, at least until Congress catches up, it eases the employers' burden of complying with ERISA regulations.

DANGERS OF DEFINED CONTRIBUTION PLANS

Defined contribution plan participants gravitate toward fixed-income investments and insurance companies' Guaranteed Investment Contracts, in preference to equity investments, even though equity investments provide a greater long-term rate of return. It is also true that the average rate of return to the average dollar in a defined contribution plan with investments directed by participants was lower during the 1980s than the average rate of return for professionally managed defined benefit plans. Moreover, some workers take their defined contribution balances as lump sums and spend the proceeds without adequate provision for future income in the form of annuities or income-producing investments.

But to declare these facts to be problems Congress should cure is to say that workers don't know what they are doing and can't learn. It is to say that employers and government have the best interests of plan participants at heart, and will look after them more effectively than the workers themselves.

The sums invested in defined contribution pension plans are not crying out for professional management; they are tucked away in a form that satisfies the hopes and fears of individual workers. Sums withdrawn and spent are disposed of in a manner that satisfies the beneficiary, especially in view of the fact that the tax collector will take 20 percent or more to remind him of the tax-free option of continuing to hold his money.

Quite possibly workers' preferences will change as their portfolios expand and loom as a greater share of their total wealth. Just as people learned about creative financing of home mortgages in the 1980s and about refinancing for lower rates in the

1990s, people of any age and income and education can learn about retirement finance. They are better off having learned these lessons for themselves, surely better off than if the national government had tried to control rates or force them to change.

Sooner or later, though, Congress is likely to listen to the paternalistic plaint of pension analysts who worry that workers are making bad investment and withdrawal choices in their defined contribution plans. There will come a day when those who believe in financial liberty will have to fight in the halls of Congress for the right to control their own pension assets.

GOVERNMENT MIGRATION

Even public-employee pension systems, which are not suffering from an excess of ERISA regulation, are starting to shift from defined benefit to defined contribution plans. In 1996 they will become subject to nondiscrimination rules like those governing corporate pensions, requiring all employees to receive the same type of benefit. That could cause problems for many cities that have different plans for different jobs, such as the earlier retirements given to the uniformed services in preference to clerical workers.

Defined contribution plans may help states and municipalities comply with the new regulations. But most state plans changing over to defined contribution are merely suffering from an excess of liabilities and a shortage of assets; they are trying to get out from under heavy financial responsibilities.

Donna Arduin, the chief deputy director of the Michigan Department of Management and Budgets, proclaims that the new state and public school defined contribution system will save $80 million in the first year just from the savings on new employees, without shifting any current employees over from the old system.

The new Michigan plan submitted for legislative approval in 1993 provides for the state to pay just 4 percent of gross salary for pension and 1 percent of retiree health benefits, nothing more. Workers are free to add after-tax contributions, but they will get no tax incentive. The state's contribution alone will, of course, produce much less retirement pay than the old system. And the state can't offer the corporate stock and other side benefits that make private defined contribution plans so attractive.

Alaska's proposed defined contribution plan calls for a contribution of 9.65 percent, which sounds generous until it's noted that Alaska opted out of Social Security for its state workers. The new system is a lot cheaper for the state, which has underfunded the existing defined benefit system by $600 million.

The IRS short-circuited some state and municipal moves toward defined contribution plans. Just as 401(k) savings plans were becoming vastly widespread in the private sector, the IRS issued a rule blocking new 401(k) plans in the public sector. But there are other defined contribution plans that are still available, and Congress is considering reopening the 401(k) to public employees.

THE AGING OF AMERICA

THE GOOD NEWS for individual Americans is that we are living longer. The bad news for American society is that we are living longer. Old people are unproductive. Retirement is a luxury that only a wealthy society can enjoy. We will all grow old, we will all want to retire. We will all be unproductive. Who will earn the wealth to support us in the manner to which we have become accustomed?

This question intensifies such problems as pension regulation, funding requirements, and investment strategies. The natural life cycle of the baby-boom generation is leading to a collapse of the American pension system.

The baby boom began at the end of World War II. There were almost a million more births in 1947 than in 1945. Then the baby boom lasted and lasted, for longer than anything that could be explained by the lusty homecoming of 10 million men. The annual birth rate rose for more than a decade, to a peak in 1958, and the rate stayed high until 1964.

Among the measurable demographic changes that created the baby boom were more marriages, earlier marriages, and larger average family size. The baby boom produced 76 million Americans—about 17 million more than would have been born during the period if the birth rate of the early 1940s had continued.

It's well to remember that the baby boom is not one generation with one universal experience. Some were high school juniors when President Kennedy was assassinated; some were infants. Some fought in Vietnam; some fought against the war in the streets; some watched the war on television; some studied it in history class. Some were packed into schools stretched to the point of double sessions and learned by rote; some had the newest of everything, from new carpeted classrooms to New Math.

As important as the baby boom is the birth dearth that followed. The annual birth rate suddenly fell by nearly a third, and stayed there for more than two decades. Women put off having children, and had fewer. In 1960 the total fertility rate was 3.6 children born to the average American woman. By 1975 the average American woman was bearing 1.7 children over her lifetime. Since then, the fertility rate has rebounded, but only a little, to 1.85 children per woman as of 1990.

The baby boom was set off by the return of American soldiers from the war, although that event does not fully explain it. In the same way, the birth dearth was set off by the advent of the birth control pill, although that event does not fully explain it. Another factor surely was increased opportunities for women in the cash economy, but that also may not fully explain this wild demographic swing.

Whatever the reasons for nineteen years of baby boom and twenty-nine years of birth dearth, this demographic roller coaster has thrown American society and the American economy out of balance. "Rock and Roll Is Here to Stay," as the song says. More than 1,150 U.S. radio stations, 12 percent of the total, have adopted the classic rock format, playing the Top 40 tunes of the baby boomers' youth. Very few stations in the 1960s played Benny Goodman and the great bands of the swing era.

Many baby boomers never even notice that the world around them tailors itself to their preferences. Americans glorified children and the parental model of the organization man when the boomers in their millions were kids; the country accepted long hair, a defiant attitude, and low productivity in honor of the boomers' mass adolescence; business and family became interesting just as the boomers wanted to make their pile and settle down; health care and physical fitness have become national concerns just when the boomers are starting to worry about getting sick and growing old.

Economically, American society remade itself to accommodate the baby-boom generation, although not without difficulty. The baby boom entered the economy from 1965 to 1985, pushing the labor force from 74.5 million to 115.5 million. For the net increase of 41 million new workers, 36 million new jobs were created. It was a record of job creation unmatched in the world, and yet the competition to fill those jobs grew stiffer and added 6 million people to the unemployment rolls. Among the other economic impacts were low productivity growth, a virtual stagnation of real wages after 1973, and a widening gap between the income of well-educated people and the income of those with a high school education or less.

MEDICAL MIRACLE

Baby boom and birth dearth combine with a third great American demographic factor, increased life expectancy for adults. Advances in medicine are prolonging life, so that more people live to a ripe old age.

Great advances in life expectancy at birth occurred in the first half of the twentieth century because of dramatic decreases in infant and child mortality. The average number of years a randomly selected infant born in 1900 might expect to live was forty-seven years. By 1950 an infant's life expectancy was sixty-eight years and for an infant born in 1990 it was seventy-five years. Only about 41 percent of persons born in 1900 survived to age sixty-five, while 60 percent of those born in 1940 are expected to live to age sixty-five and 80 percent of those born in 1990 are expected to live to age sixty-five.

In the second half of the twentieth century, medical advances prolonged the lives of elderly people. In 1900 the average person who was age sixty-five could expect to live another twelve years. That had increased to fourteen years for a sixty-five-year-old in 1950. In 1990 an average sixty-five-year-old could expect to live to age eighty-two—seventeen more years of life.

Combining the increased number of people living to age sixty-five with their improved prospects for longer life thereafter is drastically changing the American demographic profile as the nation moves into the twenty-first century.

- In 1900 3 million people, about 4 percent of the population, were over age sixty-five.
- In 1950 12 million people, about 8 percent of the population, were over age sixty-five.
- In 1990 31 million people, about 12.5 percent of the population, were over age sixty-five.

Making assumptions about future mortality rates, fertility rates, and immigration rates, the Census Bureau projects:

- In 2010, as the baby-boom generation begins to retire, about 39 million Americans, about 14 percent of the population, will be over age sixty-five.
- In 2030, after the baby boom has retired, about 65 million Americans will be over age sixty-five, and they will constitute 21.8 percent of the population.[1]

These estimates assume moderate lengthening of life expectancy, moderate immigration, and no change in fertility rates over the next sixty years. The Census Bureau's high estimate of the future elderly population assumes longer life, higher immigration, and higher fertility, and its low estimate assumes the reverse. Using these different assumptions, the bureau produces these ranges:

In 2010 we can be pretty sure that there will be between 38 million and 42 million people over age sixty-five, about 14 percent to 15 percent of the population. In 2030 there will probably be between 59 million and 75 million people over age sixty-five, accounting for between 21 percent and 23 percent of the population. By 2050 there are likely to be between 57 million and 87 million people over age sixty-five, constituting 21 percent to 25 percent of the population.

For some purposes, such as forecasting the burden on hospitals and other service institutions, the number of people over age eighty-five is more important. People over eighty-five are more likely to be frail, dependent, and needy. From 122,000 people, 0.2 percent of the population, in 1900, the number of people over age eighty-five grew to 577,000, 0.4 percent of the population, by 1950, and to 3 million people, 1.2 percent of the population, by 1990. The number of people over eighty-five is expected to grow to 6.1 million, 2.2 percent of the population, in 2010. That would increase to 8.1 million people, 2.7 percent of the population, in 2030 and 15.2 million, 5.1 percent of the population, in 2050, the year that all baby-boom survivors will be over eighty-five. In 2050, the percentage of Americans over age eighty-five will be about what the percentage of Americans over age sixty-five was in the 1920s.

Here's a table to help keep the numbers straight. It shows how the concentration of people in the baby boom, the subsequent birth dearth, the increase in life expectancy, and the general decrease in fertility are combining to age the American population.

Year	Population (000)	Over 65	(%)	Over 85	(%)
1900	75,995	3,080	4.3	122	0.2
1950	150,697	12,269	8.1	577	0.4
1990	248,710	31,079	12.5	3,021	1.2
2010	282,575	39,362	13.9	6,116	2.2
2030	300,629	65,604	21.8	8,129	2.7
2050	299,849	68,532	22.9	15,287	5.1

DEPENDENCY

The American economy is always divided into producers and beneficiaries. Producers are the people who earn; beneficiaries include those who live on charity and welfare and those who live on interest, dividends, and capital gains. Retired people, even those who met their savings goals and retire independently wealthy, are as much beneficiaries of the U.S. economy as the most destitute welfare recipient. The only difference is that the wealthy person has a property right to his benefits. Though this is a large social difference in our society, it is not an important economic difference. The economy—the aggregate organization of capital, labor, resources, and technology into business—must create sufficient value to support the beneficiaries.

So far we have been looking at people over sixty-five as a percentage of the whole U.S. population. In economic terms, it is more important to look at what the Census Bureau calls dependency ratios—the proportion of retirees to people of working age. During the 1990s, there were five Americans of working age for each retired member of the older generation. Each retiree in 2030, however, will have to be supported by only 2.6 younger people.

Look at the following table to see this dependency ratio grow.

Year	Pop. Over 65 (millions)	Persons Over 65 as Percent of Those Aged 18–64
1960	16.6	16.8%
1970	20.1	17.5%
1980	25.7	18.6%
1990	31.5	20.4%
2000	34.8	20.8%
2010	39.3	21.8%
2020	52.1	29.0%
2030	65.6	38.0%
2040	68.1	39.3%
2050	68.5	39.9%

Even the Census Bureau's dependency ratio is misleading. Some percentage of the people aged 18–64 will not be producers. There will be disabled people and other people outside the cash economy, by choice or through inability to get jobs. In 1990 the workforce was estimated to be 122.6 million people, compared to a working-age population of 154.8 million. The Census Bureau and the Labor Department's Bureau of Labor Statistics try to estimate changes in the age and composition of the workforce, but their crystal balls don't reach beyond a few years.

DEMOGRAPHIC TRENDS

Most forecasts are really just extrapolations of what is already happening. Here are some of the widely recognized current trends about age and employment:[2]

- Older men are retiring earlier. In 1950 two-thirds of men over age fifty-five were in the labor force; in 1990 the proportion was down to two-fifths. Based on life expectancy, the average fifty-five-year-old working man will end his career in less than nine years and spend more than twelve years in retirement.
- Older women are participating more in the workforce, but they also retire early. Because today's older women grew up in an era when most women were not expected to work outside the home, there are fewer of them in the cash economy now. But the female share of the older workforce is growing rapidly and 45 percent of women aged fifty-five to sixty-four are in the workforce, compared to 27 percent in 1950. But 8.7 percent of women over sixty-five are in the workforce—not much different from the 9.7 percent that worked in 1950.
- Professionals, managers, and salespeople retain their jobs longer; factory workers and laborers are more likely to retire early. Self-employed people stay in the workforce the longest.
- Older workers are concentrated in declining industries, such as manufacturing.

Every one of these trends makes it harder to achieve proper funding of a pension system.

13

THE SOCIAL SECURITY
CRISIS

THE AMERICAN DEMOGRAPHIC crisis is most clearly documented in the annual reports of the Social Security Administration. By studying Social Security, we can see the demographic dangers in the whole economic system.

Social Security is the American government's most loved and least understood social program. Together, the love and the misunderstanding make it "the third rail of American politics: touch it and you die."

The love is easy to explain: Social Security pays monthly checks to 41.5 million Americans and promises to protect all Americans from destitution in old age or disability. Without Social Security, 44 percent of the elderly population would live below the poverty line. With Social Security, the elderly poverty rate is just 11 percent, the lowest of any major age segment of the population.

The misunderstanding arises from the way Americans pay for this security. Since the program began, Americans have been told they are not really paying a tax, but rather making contributions to a retirement program, or paying insurance premiums. They have been told their money is in a trust fund, and that they will be withdrawing their money when at last they retire and begin to collect Social Security.

It's a lie. It has always been a lie. From the day they paid the first check, Social Security has been paying today's beneficiaries with the contributions of tomorrow's retirees.

Social Security was designed to be the "responsible" alternative to several really crackpot schemes circulating in the crisis years of the Depression. There was the plan of Dr. Francis Townsend, a California physician who wanted to pay two hundred dollars a month to every American over sixty. (The average working wage in those Depression days was seventy-five dollars a month.) Townsend clubs across the country had 5 million members pushing the pension and a sales tax to pay for it. Apparently none of them ever sat down to figure out how steep the sales tax would have to be. There was the "share the wealth" plan of Senator Huey Long. Long's slogan was "Every Man a King," and he wanted pension and unemployment benefits paid for out of a tax on assets above $1 million. Wealth over $8 million would be taxed at 99 percent. Long did not say how he would pay for the program in the second year.

In the crisis atmosphere of the Depression, Social Security was enacted in 1935 as a government savings vehicle, in which workers and their employers would be taxed to make deposits to their own accounts and withdraw them after retirement. The tax started in 1937 at a rate of 2 percent of the first $3,000 of annual earnings—1 percent paid by the worker and 1 percent paid by the employer. The original U.S. Social Security plan also had a welfare component, intended to pay minimum benefits to people who had not really earned them.

POLITICAL CRISIS

In 1939 the Great Depression seemed to be coming back—the economy had sunk into a tailspin in 1938—and economists believed that savings and investment did not stimulate the economy as much as consumer spending. Some of them even blamed the downturn of 1938 on the imposition of the Social Security tax. Also, the Democratic Party faced the election of 1940. It was politically imperative that people begin to benefit from the new program right away.

Social Security was transformed into a "pay-as-you-go" system in 1939, with extended coverage, more generous benefits, and easier eligibility. "Pay-as-you-go" normally denotes a responsible financing scheme, the opposite of "fly-now-pay-later." But in retirement finance, America could go more rapidly than it had to pay. The Social Security tax applied to about 30 million workers, but only a few of them would become eligible to receive benefits.

The name for a system that uses receipts to pay off early investors, while leaving little or nothing for later investors, is a Ponzi scheme, named after a notorious investment fraud in the 1920s. It's a fraud because none of the receipts are invested outside the scheme, to grow and pay dividends to all investors. As currently structured, Social Security is an enormous intergenerational Ponzi scheme, set in motion in 1940 to pay early benefits with massive tax receipts from those who were promised benefits later.

In addition, those benefits were decoupled from the amounts people had paid in, so that low-wage workers received a greater share of their former income while high-wage workers received a lesser share. Social Security to this day toils to keep elaborate records of each American's wage history, and pays different benefits to different workers based on that history, but it's almost entirely symbolic busywork, conducted to maintain the fiction that citizens earn their benefits.

The result, however, is not merely symbolic: actually, the more they earn, the less of their earnings they receive as benefits. A person who retired in 1993 after a lifetime of high-income jobs and a final income above $57,600 a year would receive $1,128 a month in Social Security. A person retiring after a lifetime of minimum-wage jobs, ending with a $12,000-a-year job, would receive $529 a month. With four times the income and four times the taxes, the better-off person would receive only twice the benefits.

LUCKIEST BENEFICIARY

Probably no one in the history of Social Security could have fared better than the woman the Social Security Board's publicists designated in January 1940 as the first beneficiary. She was Ida Mae Fuller, a legal secretary from Ludlow, Vermont. Her first check of $22.54 was fifty-four cents more than she had paid in taxes; her employer had paid in $22 on her behalf, so she really started profiting from the system on her second check. She lived to be a hundred years old, and her last monthly check, in January 1975, was for $112.60. In her life, for $44 in taxes paid, she received $20,944.

Even today, after more than fifty years, the Ponzi scheme is still in its early, attractive stage. Today's typical retiree recouped all he paid into the system inside of two years. The average sixty-five-year-old man has fourteen years more to live, and a woman eighteen years.

A 1993 study by the Congressional Research Service of the Library of Congress reported that a person retiring that year at age sixty-five (born in 1928, he's one of the winners) would get back in benefits all his Social Security taxes plus interest on those taxes at rates that prevailed during his working lifetime in just six years and five months. A worker retiring in 2000 would need eight years and two months to get back all he put in plus interest. Born in 1935, he's less of a winner. And a worker retiring in 2015 would need ten years and eight months of checks to receive all he put in plus interest. Born in 1950, this worker is still less of a winner.

Losers are the people who get to pay for the retirement of the baby boomers—anybody born after 1965. They will pay high Social Security taxes for their whole working lives, and when they retire the baby-boom generation will have so consumed the national wealth that benefits probably will have to be cut.

The payback periods must be doubled to account for employers' payroll taxes if we want to know if society gets its money's worth from Social Security. After doing that calculation, the answer is that high-income males retiring in the 1990s who earned more than the taxable wage limit already stand to get back less during their retired life expectancy than the total of their taxes, their employers' taxes, and the interest that would have been earned on those taxes in a bank account. High-income women, with their longer life spans, will reach that point soon, and average-wage workers will reach that point before 2005.

In other words, Social Security is becoming a dead-weight burden on the most productive people in the American economy.

Even former chief actuary Robert Myers, one of the system's most persistent and influential defenders, concedes, "In the very narrow and specific definition of 'money's worth' as being the return of at least the contributions plus appropriate interest in every single case—as is true for bank deposits—the program would fail to meet the test." He adds, however, "In the broad aggregate, the Social Security program does meet the money's-worth criterion, because almost all of the contributions collected are used to pay benefits, either currently or in the future."

The same is true of a Ponzi scheme. Myers ignores the point that the money will run out on many beneficiaries (or taxes will have to be increased on future workers) because Social Security paid too much to early beneficiaries and still promises to pay too much to beneficiaries in the twenty-first century.

No Worries

People like Myers dismiss any concern about financing Social Security in the future. They say economic growth will probably cure all its problems, and they point to the projections of the Social Security trustees that show the system in actuarial balance for decades to come.

Unfortunately, the annual reports of the trustees are constructed to mask the long-run problems of the Social Security system. Every year, Social Security trustees report the financial status of the three main Social Security programs—Old Age and Survivors Insurance, Disability Insurance, and the Hospital Insurance program known as Part A of Medicare. The trustees publish optimistic, intermediate, and pessimistic assumptions about demographics and economics. Optimistic economic factors include high growth of gross domestic product with low inflation, low unemployment, and low interest rates. Optimistic demographic factors include high fertility rates and very small increases in life expectancy. (Though it may seem perverse, increases in life expectancy are bad for Social Security or any kind of pension because the beneficiaries will live longer to collect more benefits.)

The trustees, and practically everyone who analyzes Social Security, emphasize the intermediate estimates, on the presumption that the extremes are untrustworthy and the truth lies somewhere in between. Not in this case.

The Social Security Administration's "pessimistic" assumptions for the future are more favorable than the reality of the past twenty years. Here are some of the so-called pessimistic assumptions: one recession in the 1990s and steady, moderate, real growth in the economy thereafter; inflation averaging 5 percent a year; wage growth to exceed inflation except in two years in the 1990s; no period in which interest rates rise above the average of the last fifteen years; unemployment a little greater than the 1980s but a little lower than the 1970s; a fertility rate a little below that of the past twenty years; improvements in life expectancy over the next fifty years at about the same rate as the past fifty years. It wouldn't be hard to imagine a future that would be worse for the solvency of the Social Security system.

For example, inflation could return just when we least expect it, and global competition means it would be less likely that wages could keep pace with the cost of living. If wages were increased beyond the limits imposed by world markets, economic growth would falter. Or the new science of biotechnology could deliver treatments for some of the diseases of old age. Cancer, heart disease, and Alzheimer's, to name just three killers of the aged, may be postponed, if not eliminated.

Of all the economic factors, the assumption that real wage growth will outpace inflation is the most powerful and the most problematic for Social Security. Because benefits are indexed to cover increases in the cost of living, the system falls into trouble whenever wages, and taxes, don't keep up. Social Security has experienced three such periods since benefits were first indexed in 1972. The first two produced immediate cash-flow crises and were dealt with in 1977 and 1983. A third period began in 1989 in which the growth of wages and taxes failed to keep up with the growth of benefits. Fortunately (short term) and unfortunately (long term), there has been no immediate cash-flow crisis and no threat that Social Security checks would start to bounce. Thus there has been no political crisis and no political need for another dose of reform.

Untrustworthy Fund

At the end of 1992, the Social Security trust fund contained assets of $331 billion, just over a year's worth of benefits. But these assets are all government bonds—IOUs from the rest of the federal government. The actual cash receipts from taxpayers that exceeded the amounts needed to pay for benefits were spent by the federal government, and the bonds that would otherwise have been sold to the public to pay for that federal spending were instead deposited in the Social Security trust fund.

The Treasury bonds in the Social Security trust fund pay interest like any other bond, and they are backed by the full faith and credit of the United States, like any other Treasury bond. So the trustees of the Social Security system call them assets of the system. As the FICA tax continues to bring in more than is paid out in Social Security benefits, the trust fund surplus will grow, and earn interest, which the Treasury will pay in the form of more bonds.

The Social Security reform of 1983 created this growing surplus. Some of those who designed the reform say it was deliberate, to save for the retirement of the baby-boom generation; others say the surplus is just an accidental artifact arising from the taxes that were needed to keep the checks coming. Probably both sides are telling the truth as they saw it then, but either way the fact remains that the system was supposed to pile up some $20 trillion in Treasury bonds by 2020. This allowed contemporary leaders to claim that the system was in "close actuarial balance" over seventy-five years, as required by law.

This $20 trillion savings scheme was always something of a fraud, since it amounted to nothing more than the left hand of the government promising to pay the right hand of the government. The real arrangement was a tax switch: while receipts exceeded benefits, from 1984 to 2035, the Social Security tax would accumulate a surplus, invested in Treasury bonds. Later, when the baby-boom generation would be receiving benefits, the rest of the government would have to raise taxes to run a surplus to pay back what it owed the Social Security system. Or it would have to borrow the money from other sources.

Stripped of all the decorations, the Social Security reform financed an income-tax cut with a Social Security tax increase, and practically required a large income-tax hike in the twenty-first century to redress the balance.

The size of the Social Security surplus is a matter of some interest to every baby boomer. In 1983 the Social Security Administration did estimate that the pile of cash would reach $20 trillion around 2035. But the ensuing years, in which the whole baby-boom generation would be retired but most of its members not yet dead, would be so expensive for the Social Security system that the whole $20 trillion would be drained by 2055.

By piling up those Treasury bonds, the government was promising that it would raise new cash from other sources to pay baby-boom benefits. What other sources? The government only has three ways to raise cash: cut other spending, raise taxes, and borrow money. Even now, when the excess of Social Security taxes over benefit payments generates a painless $50 billion a year, plus a painless paper interest payment of $25 billion a year, the government does not cut spending or raise taxes very well. Imagine how much harder it would be to cut spending or raise taxes if the Social Security system is a trillion-dollar-a-year drain on government finances.

Raising taxes, moreover, would surely cripple the economy and kill more businesses, adding to the problems of the future government.

Borrowing a trillion dollars a year, on top of other run-of-the-mill borrowing, to roll over the government's obligation to Social Security makes you wonder if the government still will be a good credit risk. By that time, will Treasury bonds still be sound as a dollar? And how sound will a dollar be? How much other Treasury debt will be outstanding?

Rolling over the debt is no solution anyway. It means that $20 trillion in bonds that paid interest in bonds will have to be converted into debt held by the public, paying interest in cash. If interest rates are as high as 7 percent, the government that borrows to pay for Social Security will still have to raise $1 trillion in cash per year to pay the interest.

If Americans let Social Security grow to a $20 trillion pile of obligations and bonded assets, we would have only three ways of dealing with it: huge economic growth, huge inflation, a huge bankruptcy. The first seems hard to imagine without reform of all the policies that are leading to that $20 trillion overhang. The second may not even work because Social Security benefits are indexed to grow with inflation. The third will wreck the Social Security system along with the national economy. A fourth option, huge tax increases, most likely would produce inflation and bankruptcy, and would certainly eliminate any chance for economic growth to solve the problem.

BITTER MEDICINE

Cutting benefits now is a better choice. It can be done. The U.S. Supreme Court established in 1960 that workers do not accrue property rights in their Social Security benefits. Congress can raise or lower Social Security benefits at will.

In fact, much of the problem of Social Security arose because a shortsighted Congress raised benefits during the 1960s and 1970s without corresponding tax increases. As the baby boom entered the workforce, its members began paying Social Security taxes in amounts that were more than enough to pay current benefits. The obvious thing for a politician to do in such circumstances is raise the benefits to consume the revenue.

In 1971 Congress received a report that predicted a $1 trillion surplus by 2025. The lawmakers' response was to cut taxes, increase benefits 20 percent, and make future benefit increases automatic through indexing to the cost of living. Billed as a responsible way of holding Congress back from legislating even bigger increases, the COLA kicked in just as the nation started a decade of substantial inflation. Worse, the COLA index provision had been miswritten, so that the effective COLA was twice what it should have been. This mistake was repaired in 1977, but the political price was locking in the higher benefit levels accumulated from 1972 to 1977.

Congress also lowered Social Security benefits by 20 percent in 1983, without raising any serious outcry. It did it in a subtle way, to people who did not have Social Security on their minds. Instead of cutting benefits for people who were already receiving Social Security checks, Congress extended the retirement age schedule for people born after 1937—people who were less than forty-six years old at the time. The bill was crafted by a Social Security reform commission whose chairman was Alan

Greenspan, later to become chairman of the Federal Reserve System.

For these people, the "normal" retirement age will not be sixty-five, but will be according to the following table:

Year of Birth	"Normal" Retirement Age
1937 or earlier	65
1938	65 years, 2 months
1939	65 years, 4 months
1940	65 years, 6 months
1941	65 years, 8 months
1942	65 years, 10 months
1943–54	66
1955	66 years, 2 months
1956	66 years, 4 months
1957	66 years, 6 months
1958	66 years, 8 months
1959	66 years, 10 months
1960 or later	67

Deftly, the Congress never said you can't retire at age sixty-five, or even at sixty-two, the early-retirement age that many people use. The change simply redefined the "normal" retirement age. That transformed a normal retirement at age sixty-five into an early retirement, with lowered benefits. Early retirees at today's typical age of sixty-two get 80 percent of the Social Security benefits they would receive at age sixty-five, today's normal retirement age. By stretching out the normal retirement age, the person who retires at age sixty-two in 2022 will receive only 70 percent of a normal benefit.[1]

So far, this was a successful way to cut Social Security benefits, because there has been no outcry. But we shall have to see what happens after the turn of the century, when people find that their benefits are a little less than their older neighbors' or that they must work a little longer to increase their benefits.

Finding a fairly acceptable way to cut Social Security benefits further should be one of our highest national priorities. But the government should not cut benefits like a thief in the night, lest it be treated like a thief when the loss is discovered.

Some people advise that Social Security taxes be increased on the rich, since no Social Security tax is levied on income above about $58,000 a year. The first objection to this advice is that it would raise trivial sums of money compared to the problem facing the system. The second objection is that Social Security benefits are already much more generous to low-income workers and repay a relatively small part of the taxes paid by upper-income people.

Meanwhile, the $20 trillion surplus is shrinking rapidly. After several years of subpar economic performance, it had turned into a projected $12 trillion surplus by 1992. In the 1994 report, the Social Security Administration acknowledged that there may not be a surplus worth worrying about at all. The recession of 1990–91 and the slow recovery have diminished the take on the payroll tax and pushed people into early retirement. According to the latest trustees' report, Social Security outgo will surpass income as early as 2001, on the pessimistic projection. Rather than reaching mammoth surpluses, the trust fund may be depleted in 2014—only four years into the retirement of the baby boomers. That's using the pessimistic projection of the Social Security Trustees' Report of 1994. Their intermediate projection puts the bankruptcy of the Old Age and Survivors program trust fund at the year 2029.[2]

Among the reasons for the reduction of the projected surplus are that the Disability Insurance program of Social Security has suddenly turned into a black hole. The trustees have asked Congress to allow the Disability Insurance program to cover its losses by sucking in money from the surplus in the much larger Old Age and Survivors Insurance program. Otherwise, the Disability Insurance trust fund balance will fall to zero between 1995 and 1997. By 2002, however, the Disability Insurance program will be consuming between $100 billion and $200 billion as the baby boom reaches its peak years of incurring disability and more victims of AIDS become eligible for disability payments.

The result of combining the two programs is that they will, by the pessimistic projections, have positive cash flow only through 1997, and the combined trust funds will be exhausted in 2014. The intermediate projection extends the period of positive cash flow to last until 2013 and puts the bankrupty of the combined funds at the year 2029.[3]

In addition, the actuaries at the Social Security Administration have tightened up some of their assumptions, moving the intermediate assumptions a little toward the former pessimistic guesses and getting a little more realistic about some of their alleged pessimism. This is a process, however, that still has a long way to go. We can expect to see the surplus continue to shrink.

The major reason for the disappearance of the Social Security surplus is the fundamental unreality of the program. Social Security benefits are indexed to rise with inflation while Social Security taxes increase with the size and compensation of the labor force. Whenever wage increases fall behind inflation, Social Security gets in trouble. It happened in the mid-1970s, requiring reform in 1977. It happened in the early 1980s, requiring reform in 1983. And it happened in the early 1990s.[4] A close reading of the trustees' reports shows that the 1994 actuarial estimate of the long-run deficit of the system was more severe than in the "crisis" year of 1982.

Critically Important

Social Security is the biggest source of income for retired people today. More than 90 percent of elderly families receive a Social Security check. The median (half above, half below) size of the annual benefit is $7,590.

For some, Social Security is very important: 38 percent of elderly households rely on Social Security for at least 80 percent of their income. Only 28 percent of couples rely on Social Security for as much as four-fifths of their income, but 45 percent of single people (and this means mostly widows) are that reliant on Social Security.

There's little authoritative information about the sources of retirement income, so the Advisory Council on Social Security that was set up during the Bush administration commissioned a computer simulation from Lewin/ICF, an economic consulting firm. The results of the Pension and Retirement Income Simulation Model (PRISM), based on 1988 data, were published in a paper, *Future Financial Resources of the Elderly*.[5] Though it's only a model, not a poll or other form of real-life study, it's the best indicator available, and here are some findings:

Only 40 percent of elderly households have income from private or government workers' pensions and the median annual income is $4,730; 19 percent have job earnings and the median income is $11,940; 73 percent have income from assets (meaning investments, bank accounts, and property), but the median from this source is $890. Other income, paid to 11 percent of elderly households, accounts for a median $2,000, but this is largely income from Supplemental Security Income, a welfare program for the poorest of the poor, such as persons who don't receive Social Security.

For the readers of this book, the most important categories are pensions and assets. Here are three daunting statistics:

- Only 7 percent of elderly families in 1988 had pensions that provided as much as half their income.
- Only 40 percent of elderly families in 1988 had as much as $67,000 in financial assets, including bank accounts.
- Only 20 percent of elderly families in 1988 had as much as $25,000 a year in income.

How will elderly income change in the future? That is, how will changes in society, public policy, and corporate finance affect people in their thirties and forties? Almost every occupation is now covered by Social Security. The Lewin/ICF model suggests pension income may increase substantially by 2018, with 76 percent of elderly families receiving some income from pensions and similar benefits. There are several reasons for this increase:

- In 1940 only 15 percent of workers were covered by pension plans, but that figure rose to more than 40 percent by 1960 and more than 50 percent by 1970. Now, as workers retire who were covered for a whole career, the values of pension payments are really starting to increase. (Unfortunately, the percentage of people covered by a pension plan hasn't risen much since 1970.)
- There are more types of employer-sponsored retirement

plans—meaning that employers and individuals have a better chance of funding a retirement finance plan.

- Since 1974, Congress has enacted several important changes in pension law to give more workers more rights to receive pensions. These laws particularly forced employers to give workers pension rights much earlier than used to be the case. (The vesting period is the number of years a worker must be employed to have a right to receive a pension at retirement, even if he changes jobs, and recent law changed it to five years.) Legislation also made it more likely that spouses will receive survivors' benefits if the pensioner dies. So more people working at firms with pension plans will actually receive pensions when they retire.
- More women have been working, and more of them in companies with pensions. Thus many retired families have a better chance of receiving at least one pension check.

The PRISM model simulations indicated that average family income of the elderly would increase by nearly 50 percent in real (after inflation) terms, from $18,220 in 1988 to $26,780 in 2018. The median income would increase by nearly 60 percent. Pension income would account for 25 percent of the income of elderly families, up from 17 percent. The poverty rate of elderly people would be expected to decline from 12 percent in 1990 to about 7 percent by 2018, finishing triumphantly the job that began with the first major increases in Social Security benefits enacted in the late 1950s. Back then, more than 35 percent of elderly people lived in poverty.

THE TIGHTENING NOOSE

So what's the problem?

The problem is that the aging of America threatens the country's finances. The government is running up debts and obligations; the private economy is borrowing from a graying future. Benefit promises are simply expanding faster than the earnings to pay for them. It is a vicious circle that will get tighter and tighter, until it becomes a noose around the neck of the American economy.

Some economists are watching the noose tighten with a technique called generational accounting.[6] Generational accounting attempts to estimate the government's fiscal treatment of different generations by figuring the present value of a generation's tax payments over its whole life span, compared to its lifelong receipts of government benefits.

Birth Year	Tax Rate	Transfer Rate	Net Tax Rate
		(Percent of Lifetime Income)	
1900	24.8	3.3	21.5
1910	29.8	5.2	24.7
1920	32.5	6.2	26.3
1930	35.3	7.2	28.1
1940	37.5	8.0	29.3
1950	39.9	9.3	30.6
1960	42.3	10.2	32.1
1970	44.5	11.3	33.2
1980	45.5	11.7	33.8
1990	45.7	12.2	33.6[7]

This table from the Office of Management and Budget shows that the generation born in 1990 can expect that 12.2 percent of its members' lifetime income will come from government benefits—nearly four times as much government benefits as were paid to the members of the generation born in 1900. At the same time, the generation born in 1990 is slated to pay 45.7 percent of its lifetime income in taxes—less than double the 24.8 percent share of lifetime income paid by the members of the generation born in 1900.

According to the generation accountants at the OMB, the United States will need to double tax rates again to support the benefits already enacted into law. For generations born after 1990 the net tax rate—tax payments minus benefit receipts—will rise to 71 percent of lifetime income.

One generational accounting expert, Jagadeesh Gokhale of the Federal Reserve Bank of Cleveland, asked the right question in the title of a 1992 paper: "Has Someone Already Spent the Future?"[8]

He recognized the imbalance between current programs and

revenue sources: "Young and future generations cannot participate in choosing the level of [government programs] because
they are too young or not yet born when the decisions are made.
They must, however, make payments at a level chosen by earlier
generations."

And he recognized the imbalance between the large baby-
boom generation and its smaller successors: "The growing non-
working segment of the population will have to be supported by
output produced by a shrinking population of workers."

Gokhale warned that the situation cannot get better by itself.
"Unless corrective policies are undertaken now, [these imbal-
ances] will worsen over time. If future Americans perceive that
much of their income will be taxed away, their incentives to
work and save may be diminished, with obvious detrimental
effects on future U.S. living standards."

Can we muddle through without raising taxes and cutting
benefits? We would probably find the limit of the borrowing
power of the United States and even the limit to the U.S. ability
to inflate away the value of past debt. It is possible that some
technological or social innovation might push us into a new era
of vigorous economic growth, the way the railroad, the automobile, and the computer spurred previous eras of economic advance and paid for all our past mistakes. It is possible, but should
we bet on it? And if we are going to bet on it, we should at least
try to create an economic climate that fosters enterprise and
profits, rather than taxation and benefits.

14

FIXING PENSION POLICY

A FAMOUS, ALTHOUGH PROBABLY apocryphal, junior officer was reported to have declared in Vietnam, "We had to destroy the village in order to save it." The quotation resurfaces frequently, usually to illustrate the futility of violence. But if an officer actually said that, the point was that the physical village was destroyed to keep the people from being swallowed up by the Viet Cong. This point should be understood by everyone who tries to improve a structure for the benefit of those who use it. Whether the structure is political, legislative, or physical, something must be destroyed in order to create something better.

Surely the pension system is unsafe and full of empty promises, but how much of the present system do we have to destroy in order to save it?

The first choice for all pension reformers is to decide how voluntary the system should be.

Some reformers readily choose to replace the private pension system with a single national mandatory pension system like a more generous Social Security program. Few of them readily choose the steep taxes and economic stagnation required to put a mandatory system on a sound financial footing.

At the other extreme, some reformers facilely choose a voluntary, unregulated, unfunded system in which companies make promises and carry them out to the best of their ability. Few of these easily convince their neighbors to ignore the plight of workers who toiled all their lives only to be told that the company was in the wrong line of business and has no profits from which to pay pensions.

The United States has muddled its way to a system that is partly mandatory and partly voluntary, with every individual worker in the nation receiving a different combination of benefits, more or less protected by a panoply of private and government promises, many of which lack moral and financial conviction.

BROKEN PROMISES

If we weigh the contemporary pension abuses that warn us of the big crisis to come, we find that in each case a company turned its back on solemn promises to workers. However, if the employer had not walked away from the solemn promise to pensioners, he might have had to walk away from a solemn promise to bondholders or banks instead. Pension funds don't get into trouble until a firm is already in trouble and its managers look on the last remaining pot of money that might be available to save the business.

If Congress is to make sensible, effective pension policy, it must create a structure that guarantees benefits as they are promised, before a firm gets in trouble. And it must do it soon. Underfunding is still manageable, but economics and demographics are combining to make it worse every year. The next recession will put a whole new cohort of companies under financial pressure, and some of their managers will surely invent ways to tap their pension pools. And the national economy will never support the retirement of the baby boom unless the country's pension finances are repaired before the crunch comes in the twenty-first century.

Reforming the pension system can be accomplished on the asset side or on the liability side.

On the liability side, the simplest and most radical way to bring pension finance under control is to freeze the defined benefit pension system in its tracks. A meaningful reform might ordain that no new defined benefit plans be created or extended. Current minimum funding standards under ERISA and Pension Benefit Guaranty Corp. insurance probably would be adequate to fund and protect existing vested benefits. All future retirement finance would then be conducted on a defined contribution basis.

To a degree, this is being carried out by the marketplace now, as more and more defined benefit plan sponsors evade the burden of regulation by terminating them and substituting defined contribution plans. But if the government tries to hurry this process along with legislation, most benefit experts will fight it. They believe in the defined benefit system. They think that defined benefit plans protect workers because the employers do all the saving and assume all the risk. They refuse to recognize that something for nothing carries its own ultimate costs.

On the asset side, a little less radical proposition would be to require strict and immediate funding of any defined benefit pension promise, and to require that companies immediately make up any underfunding caused by investment market fluctuation. And still milder is the idea of tightening up the payment period from the current ERISA schedules. This is what the Clinton administration proposed at the end of 1993.

Tightening up funding for past mistakes, however, means putting intense pressure on the companies that made those mistakes. Many of the PBGC's Unthrifty Fifty companies—and even more of the underfunded plan sponsors who are too small to make the list—could not cope with tougher funding requirements. They would follow the example of Carl Icahn at TWA and start negotiating with the PBGC. Politically sensitive PBGC negotiators would cut the best deal they could to avert job losses and immediate increases in PBGC liability, and that would mean waivers of the tighter funding requirements, one way or another. Given the politics of the subject, ERISA probably reflects the best that can be done with funding standards until a real disaster comes much closer.

A better effort would be to take the PBGC out of the picture. Limit PBGC insurance coverage to those plans that have already collapsed. From there, reform could take the clear-cut but frightening step of leaving it to companies to convince their workers that their pension promises are secure. They could fund and overfund their pension plans and make such convincing disclosure of their funding that workers would have faith. Or they could purchase private insurance from reputable, well-rated insurance companies. Or they could let workers take their chances. In any such case, workers and managers alike would not fool themselves into relying on the unlimited but empty promise of federal pension insurance. That way leads to bankruptcy for us all.

Any proposal for reform also must address the effectiveness of pension regulation. One possibility is for the government to examine every pension plan regularly, like banks, and require each pension plan to be fully funded. Another way is to require companies to buy pension benefit contracts from independent financial institutions, rather than merely hiring investment managers to shepherd the assets.

CAN THE SYSTEM BE SAVED?

Reformers must face the coming crisis of the private pension system, the decline and fall of public employment pensions, the inadequacy of private savings, and the insolvency of Social Security, while meeting the needs of the aging population and preserving a strong economy.

Government officials responsible for the care and regulation of pensions, and most of the academics who advise them, say they want to preserve defined benefit pensions. Defined benefit pensions are more predictable; they require no brain work on the part of beneficiaries; their professional managers select better investments.

We should appreciate the irony of government officials' praising a system that government rules are pushing toward extinction. But there's a double irony because the officials are wrong. Defined contribution plans are better—they are fairer and more honest provisions for retirement.

Defined contribution plans are property rather than promises. What the employee has is his. Once a contribution is made, the money is placed with a custodian, but the employer has no further control over investment decisions and cannot exploit funding decisions.

Some analysts, however, think that savings plans already get too much tax sheltering. Phyllis C. Borzi, a key staffer on the House Labor Committee, has boosted the idea that no employer should be permitted to offer a tax-sheltered savings plan like a 401(k) until after he has created a "real" retirement plan. "Our government cannot simply expect people to take responsibility for themselves while continuing to pour tax expenditures into the black hole of our current employer pension system, if the result is that the only people with adequate pension income in retirement turn out to be those who would have had enough assets in retirement without the tax expenditure." She complains that the current system "subsidizes employers to create plans whose major benefits flow to the highly paid people."[1]

Karen Ferguson of the Pension Rights Center in Washington goes even further. She believes that savings plans are a threat to everybody who participates. Lower-income people cannot afford to save, and indeed often cash out anything they do manage to put in a 401(k). Upper-income people reap a disproportionate tax deduction "without providing any corresponding social benefit to the majority of taxpayers who support these plans either by receiving fewer government services or by paying higher taxes." And most people who do save put their money in Guaranteed Investment Contracts or other investment vehicles that are so risk-averse that they will not grow enough to provide a healthy retirement income.[2] Ferguson would outlaw 401(k) plans or, failing that, eliminate all favorable tax treatment for them.

At the other extreme of views on savings plans, William Gale and Robert Litan, writing in the magazine of the Brookings Institution, have offered a savings plan that most Americans would consider appropriate only in wartime. The two academics were worried primarily about the federal budget deficit, and they reasoned that if Congress cannot muster the will to reduce the deficit by raising taxes or cutting spending, the lawmakers could at least reduce the harm the deficit does by making it possible for the American public to finance it with their savings. They suggested that the government require everyone to save a substantial amount—4 percent of income for families making between $20,000 and $40,000 a year up to 10 percent of income for families earning more than $80,000.

This is one of those classic answers that seems simple to

execute, easy to understand, and is dead wrong. One can easily imagine, given the laws governing banking, securities, and pensions, that Congress and the Treasury would have a field day writing complex regulations to define savings, to set the holding period, to provide exceptions to the basic rules, and to steer the savings to approved investments. In addition, forced savings is little more than a tax by another name—it still deprives citizens of the right to choose how they use the fruit of their labor.

Changing Tax Incentives

A better idea is an unlimited income-tax deduction for savings and investment. Money put into any investment vehicle would be free of tax, as would reinvested earnings; money withdrawn would be taxed as ordinary income. (At the same time, if we really want to use the tax system to improve our economy, a parallel reform would bring borrowing under the same tax philosophy: money borrowed would be taxed like income; money repaid would be tax-deductible.)

Tax-deductible saving would require far less regulation than we have now because it would do away with the false distinctions between taxable investment and tax-sheltered investment, and among different types of investment vehicles. In terms of taxes, a contribution to a pension plan would be no different from a purchase of stock or a deposit to a savings account in a bank. Inside buildup in a brokerage account or a savings account would be as free of tax as the earnings in an insurance program. Complexity would only come in certain areas where a given expenditure combines elements of investment with elements of consumption. Chief among these is residential real estate, when the homeowner consumes by paying to live in the home and invests by building up equity in the home. It's not that hard to grasp and easy to justify, though most people probably would object to a sharp cut in the historic tax subsidy for home ownership.

An even more important tax reform on the road to solid pension finance is to end the tax deductibility of employer contributions to sponsored retirement plans. The right place for the tax deduction is with the individual, who should have an un-limited exemption from tax for any money that he puts away as savings.

This is a truly radical reform, because it gets at the root of the inescapable conflict of interest between the employer and the employee. No employer will put his workers' interests ahead of the firm's forever. When the firm reaches a crisis, as all firms eventually do, the employer will attempt to get cash out of work-ers by firing them, out of their pensions by terminating over-funded plans, out of the government by handing underfunded plans over to federal pension insurance. All too many employers don't even need a crisis to do these things; the business cycle will eventually make thieves of the rest.

Workers' money simply does not belong in the hands of the employer, and tax preferences that place it there in the name of retirement are misplaced.

At least we must take managers out of the business of han-dling pensions for their employees. Managers should not be asked to deal with the conflict between looking out for the in-terests of the firm and looking out for the interests of the em-ployees. It is a testament to the morality of American business managers—and the power of rules establishing fiduciaries' obli-gations to beneficiaries—that there have not been more pension horror stories, but that is no reason to test managers' morality to the point of destruction.

An independent pension management system should at least be a widely available, well-publicized option. It ought to be pos-sible for a company to hire a trust company that would manage every facet of a defined benefit plan, billing the company each year for the necessary contributions to keep it fully funded. This trust company would not really be much different from an hon-est insurance company, taking in pension premiums and paying out defined benefits, hiring actuaries to make sure the premi-ums and investment earnings cover the expenses, plus a profit.

Use of a pension trust company would stop companies from making unfunded promises, because the trust company would demand funding for every new promise, and give a full and hon-est report to workers every quarter. Or, if the employer and well-informed employees decided to allow unfunded promises, the trust company would report on the percentage of benefits that had been funded and reduce all projections of benefits by the same fraction.

The pension trust company would combine the best features of a defined benefit plan and a defined contribution plan. The defined benefit plan has professional management and it relieves the beneficiary from worrying about the value of his investments. The defined contribution plan has independent management and relieves the worker from worrying about the amount of his investment. The trust company could also receive contributions from workers, because every worker would have his own account.

Although the nation's insurance companies are frightened to death at the possibility of being drawn into ERISA's orbit, they could provide the intermediary trust relationship that workers and employers need to have an honest, well-funded, defined benefit pension system.

Insurance companies don't want the accounting burden of tracking assets for every beneficiary; they fear that ERISA will be in conflict with state insurance laws; and they say pension funds would lose the benefit of pooling assets into a large fund.

Insurance companies have been operating since 1975 under a Department of Labor exemption from ERISA for group annuity contract assets held in their general accounts, and a trade group estimates insurance companies held about $565 billion in general account assets backing annuities at the end of 1991.

The trouble with using insurance companies to back pension promises is that it raises the old question, Who will guard the guardians?

KEEPING PROMISES

With the pension trust idea and most other proposals to change the defined benefit system, reformers are saying that a defined benefit pension promise ought to be ironclad and irrevocable. Nobody forces a company to make a pension promise, but once made, it ought to be kept.

Like so many simple moral precepts, the irrevocable pension promise may be impractical. It may push financially troubled companies into bankruptcy before they ought to go and it will make it harder for them to work themselves out of trouble. And it will destroy pension benefits that would otherwise have been paid by companies that could have recovered from their financial problems.

Putting pensions first amounts to telling workers at a troubled company that they must sacrifice their job to assure their pension benefits. Losing their jobs means foreclosing the possibility that hard work and wage concessions could rescue the company, so that everybody could work until retirement and all benefits might be paid. Putting pensions first also amounts to telling bondholders and bankers that they should not lend money to any company with a defined benefit pension plan, and that they should certainly move to liquidate any company with an underfunded plan. If the pension liability does not strangle the company directly, its lenders will do the job.

A leader of pension reform in Congress is Representative J. J. Pickle of Texas, a senior member of the House Ways and Means Committee. He recognizes, "Many employees will be shocked to learn that their pension payments will be only a fraction of what was promised. Likewise, many taxpayers will be shocked to see their tax dollars used to pay for these pension shortfalls." And he doesn't fall for the idea that a few companies represent the whole problem: "About 15,000 businesses have a collective shortfall of $51 billion, and it's growing fast. . . .

"Responsible companies lose out, too. Premiums paid by federally insured plans have risen substantially in recent years to cover the collapse of a few irresponsible corporations. Companies with well-funded plans will not put up with this inequity much longer. Indeed, these companies are already pulling out of the system by converting their defined-benefit plans to defined-contribution plans, further endangering the federal system's financial soundness."[3]

Pickle would require sponsors of underfunded defined benefit pension plans to put up cash or collateral before promising more benefits. In effect, an underfunded pension plan would be frozen until the sponsor makes up the deficiency. "This bill won't solve the whole problem, but it will help keep it from getting worse," Pickle says.

FALSE PROMISE

The clearest danger to the pension system is the false promise of the Pension Benefit Guaranty Corp. It is inherently *more* dangerous than the Federal Deposit Insurance Corp. schemes it mimics.

The late, lamented Federal Savings and Loan Insurance Corp., which cost more than $100 billion to bail out, at least insured financial institutions that were required to have assets in excess of liabilities, and underwent periodic government inspections to assure that their heads were above water. So many savings and loans went under and their depositors had to be rescued in the FSLIC bailout because real estate assets lost value in the late 1980s faster than the thrift institutions could raise capital. This failure was compounded by the fact that many thrifts' real estate loans were not well-advised and some were the result of outright fraud. The failure was also compounded by a change in federal tax law that helped push down the value of commercial real estate. And it was compounded by the preference of the FSLIC to push thrifts into growing their way out of their troubles rather than to pay cash settlements of deposit insurance.

But at least thrift institutions are supposed to be solvent. And at least somebody comes and looks at the books every few years and tries to establish if they are solvent.

Defined benefit pension plans do not have to be solvent. In fact, there are regulatory and business incentives for even the most responsible managers to run them close to the edge of solvency. The IRS won't let a company overfund, raiders will use a target's overfunded plan to finance a takeover, and employees will demand that overfunding be used to increase benefits. So every time benefits are increased, or the capital markets take a dive, or the company needs money, pension plans slip into the netherworld of underfunding. Two of the three events in this list are entirely under the control of management, and the third, capital market risk, is somewhat under management's control because managers dictate the investment style and asset allocation of the pension fund.

Pension Benefit Guaranty Corp. insurance is like fire insurance in an uninspected dynamite factory, where the owner's son likes to play with matches, in a town without a fire department or a fire marshal or a police force arson squad. Would you guarantee to pay all the losses of such a business? All businesses with defined benefit pension plans, and therefore all their customers, pay taxes to the PBGC to make such a guarantee. And all taxpayers stand behind the PBGC when the direct taxes run out.

When former PBGC executive director James Lockhart declared, "If we were an insurance company, the state insurance commissioner would have put us out of business long ago," he revealed the biggest problem. The PBGC is not an insurance company. It's a social welfare agency that makes under-the-table loans to the most financially troubled and most mismanaged companies in the country.

Even if the PBGC were an insurance company, its safety would deserve serious question. The fifty state insurance guaranty funds are a slender reed of support.

Insuring Insurance

We have seen how pension annuities slipped through the federal safety net, to be caught, perhaps, by the uncertain hands of state guaranty funds. Also of particular importance for pension investors is the insufficient coverage of Guaranteed Investment Contracts, or GICs, those insurance company products tailored to resemble bank certificates of deposit and named to recall, though not to replicate, federal deposit insurance.

We must ask: who will insure the insurers?

The National Association of Insurance Commissioners and the National Conference of Insurance Legislators favor an interstate compact by which all states could agree on the same laws to regulate and guarantee insurance companies. Not all states would join, and many states would find it difficult to establish effective financial support for their guaranty funds.

The compact would create an interstate claim protection commission to even out the guaranty fund protections so they would be the same in every state. The national body would write laws and regulations binding on every state to govern insurance companies and would have the power to overrule any individual state's actions as a receiver of an insolvent company. But any state could reject any compact law so that it would not apply in the state.

Representative John Dingell, a Michigan Democrat who chairs the House Energy and Commerce Committee, wants to establish a federal charter for insurance companies so that those that qualify could participate in a national guaranty fund; Senator Howard Metzenbaum, an Ohio Democrat, proposes opening a national guaranty fund to all comers. These lawmakers apparently have not been taught anything by the woes of the former Federal Savings and Loan Insurance Corp. and the Federal Deposit Insurance Corp. Federal insurance, even when combined with federal regulation, cannot promise ultimate protection. It is more likely to protect people who take unreasonable risks with other people's money than it is to protect the innocents who gave that money over to crooks and charlatans.

One useful thing that Congress could do is establish uniform rules of coverage by state guaranty funds. Every person who imagines that he is entrusting his money to an institution protected by a state government should know which state government actually stands behind it. Whether the funds should cover all residents or all customers of a resident company could be decided by a flip of the coin; the point is to have reliable information about coverage.

Pension annuities, however, are another matter. When sponsors of defined benefit pension plans terminate their plans, the participants have a right to expect that the protection they enjoy has not deteriorated without their permission. When the Pension Benefit Guaranty Corp. allowed substitution of an insurance company's promise for a PBGC-insured pension promise, the PBGC had an obligation to satisfy itself that the two promises were equally likely to be paid.

This the PBGC did not do and still does not do. In satisfaction of participants' legitimate claims for protection, the PBGC ought to insure all annuities written in support of terminated pension plans, and Congress ought to back up that insurance with an adequate cash reserve fund. But this is only to make up for the PBGC's past ineptitude, not to provide a new entitlement so that every defined benefit sponsor can weasel out of its obligations. No new annuitized terminations should be allowed, unless the plan sponsor also deposits a reasonable reserve in cash and agrees to supplement that reserve if needed. The employer could recoup its reserve as the annuitants die off, but it would never be allowed to pass off its benefit promise.

Untrustworthy Funds

Like the Holy Roman Empire, which was neither holy nor Roman nor an empire, a federal government trust fund is not trustworthy and not a fund.

Even the federal budget contains this admission: "These programs are not trust funds in the private-sector meaning of assets held in a fiduciary capacity for someone else. The federal government owns the assets and, by enacting a law, can change the future receipts and the terms under which a fund's resources are spent."

The Social Security trust fund is Exhibit A. There, "assets" are "growing," although the projection grows more tenuous every year. The fund is completely unfunded and contains nothing but government IOUs. Exhibit B is the Federal Employees Trust Fund, which has the dubious honor of being the second-largest holder of government bonds.

Far too many people believe that these trust funds, and others like the ones for highways and airports, resemble huge piles of money, like Scrooge McDuck's money bin. This is as false as the even more common idea that Social Security is an insurance plan in which each beneficiary pays for his or her benefits. The truth is that surplus tax revenues are borrowed by the Treasury as fast as they come into the trust funds. Then, when the Treasury pays interest on its borrowings, it borrows the interest, too.

The Social Security trust fund has recently received some recognition as the accounting fiction it is, thanks to a politically astute proposal of Senator Daniel Patrick Moynihan. The New York Democrat suggested putting Social Security back on a pay-as-you-go basis, as it was before the system was refinanced in 1983 with a series of large tax increases. "We should not use the Social Security trust fund as general revenues," the senator correctly declared, adding that when he served on the 1983 Social Security reform commission the aim of higher taxes was to build up savings to pay for the twenty-first-century retirement of the baby-boom generation.

Moynihan acknowledged that there are only two ways to make real savings out of a government trust fund balance. These are to invest the balance in the private sector—which he rejected—or to have the whole government run a consolidated surplus, so that the trust funds repurchase previously issued bonds from the public, driving down the amount of government debt in private hands.

It is a measure of the peculiarity of fiscal politics that Moynihan could cast himself politically as the protector of Social Security, even though he was proposing to reduce its funding with a payroll tax cut of $55 billion a year.

Another bright idea about trust funds came from Judy Park, legislative director of the National Association of Retired Federal Employees. Her concern is protecting the trust fund for civil-service retirement benefits, and she has no problem with investing all the trust fund in government bonds. "Our feeling has always been that if you work for the government, you should invest in the government." But she adds: "Using the trust fund balances to balance the budget is something people need to think about. There should be a separate accounting for the trust funds to show them for what they are. Show the deficit without the trust fund money. I don't think that necessitates investing differently or pulling down the assets."

Like the Social Security trust fund, most federal trust fund surpluses are clearly temporary. Only those federal workers hired after 1984 have fully funded benefits. Most are only partly covered by the $214 billion in Treasury bonds now in the kitty. The discounted present value of payments to be made over the next seventy-five years exceeds those assets by $486 billion. Since 1985 the military retirement trust fund has received contributions for benefits currently earned, but holds a $498 billion actuarial deficit for benefits earned before 1985. The Medicare trust fund's actuarial deficiency is said to be $252 billion, although that number depends greatly on the cost of medical treatment, not just on demographic assumptions. The Social Security system's actuarial deficit is the biggest, at $6.1 trillion.

As with the Social Security system, federal financial managers intend to make up the difference by paying as they go, using

payments from tomorrow's workers to pay tomorrow's retirees.
It's high time this policy was put on the record so that citizens
could understand it. The federal government should freeze the
trust fund system dead in its tracks. It would incur no new
liabilities and would create what the private sector calls an im-
munized pension program—issuing sheaves of zero coupon
bonds today that will represent the monthly checks due Social
Security recipients and federal pensioners who are current participants in the system.

These bonds would resemble preprinted checkbooks—rip out
a check and deposit it in your bank on your due date. For those
who want to opt out of the system—for example, people who
fear inflation would be loath to hold these bonds—they would be
tradeable like any other federal bonds. A participant could cash
out at any time at a market price and roll the proceeds over into
investments more to his liking in a tax-sheltered IRA.

The point of this scheme is to get the government's liabilities
out in the open where citizens can debate the problem honestly.
It might ruin government finances, but we must acknowledge
that government finances are today a hidden ruin. After facing
that, we could make progress.

A SOUND ECONOMY

A long-term solution to the pension mess also must strengthen
the U.S. economy. We need to make every worker so much more
productive that the economy can support the retired citizens.

If a person in 1893 had made the accurate prediction that in
1993 there would only be two farmers in the United States supporting ninety-eight consumers, his audience would have been
shocked. The prognosticator and his audience lived in a world in
which two-thirds of the population lived in rural areas. They
would have been convinced, like Malthus, that the ninety-eight
consumers were doomed to misery and starvation. Instead, the
enormous increase in agricultural productivity of the past century has made it possible for two farmers to feed ninety-eight
consumers and at lower prices than thirty-four consumers paid
to be fed by sixty-six farmers.

Even if you could have made them believe that agriculture

could be so productive, the people of a century ago also would have been sure that there was no room in the industrial economy or the service sector for the displaced farmers and hired hands of the nation. In truth, the United States absorbed the mass migration off the farms and millions of immigrants besides, in a process of industrialization and urbanization that made the country the wealthiest in the world.

IS REFORM ENOUGH?

The record for pension reform is bleak. The pinnacle of achievement for the Reagan and Bush administrations was enactment of some meager reform of the Pension Benefit Guaranty Corp., increasing the premiums and giving the agency more power and privilege as a creditor in bankruptcy actions. Their more sweeping reforms were shoved aside in a Congress more concerned with tax revenue than with pension security.

The major Reagan reform package came out from the Labor Department in 1987, and proposed to allow companies to withdraw surpluses from their pension plans without having to terminate them. This was a nod in the direction of reality, for it recognized that companies could simply cease to fund a plan with a surplus, saving money for the right pocket by not putting it in the left pocket.

Better still, it would have provided a real incentive for companies to clean up the common situation of having several pension plans for different groups of employees, some with surpluses and some with deficits. The Reagan administration plan suggested that each and every plan would have to have assets covering 125 percent of liabilities before any surplus could be withdrawn from even the most overfunded plan. This was actually a pretty fair balance between competing interests, but neither advocates of mandatory pensions nor defenders of the employer's property right to pension assets were willing to compromise.

The Bush administration had its own ideas, with the central aim of barring PBGC insurance for pension increases by underfunded plans. But the centerpiece of the pension measures that eventually passed Congress was an increase in PBGC premiums.

In the fall of 1993, the Clinton administration also produced a proposal for some useful reforms. Although it rejected the pending Bush ideas, it also focused on the threat underfunded plans pose to the PBGC.

The new executive director of the PBGC, Martin Slate, took office to discover that underfunding among defined benefit plans had risen to an estimated $51 billion, most of which was insured by the PBGC. In what seemed to signal a new understanding of the problem, he spoke publicly about the fact that deeply underfunded plans—those least likely to reverse their fortunes—accounted for 80 percent of the total underfunding. Those firms were paying only 25 percent of PBGC premiums. The Clinton administration proposed raising premiums for underfunded plans to as much as $125 per participant per year from the $72 enacted in the Bush era. (Remember, however, that a rigorous, open-market premium to cover the real risk of underfunding would be more like $1,000 per participant per year.)

The Clinton administration also proposed reducing the grace period given to companies to cover shortfalls in their pension plans. But the proposal was to cut the period from thirty years to fifteen years and to apply it only to companies with funding ratios below 60 percent of liabilities. And it proposed that companies would have to start funding new promises as they were made, not as they took effect in future years. There would be a requirement that annual cash contributions always at least equal cash payouts from underfunded pension plans. The administration's outline also said it would change some actuarial methods, such as the way future interest rates are calculated and the life expectancies used, but details were not available.

In a more esoteric provision that showed a real appreciation of pension finance, the task force proposed eliminating a practice of counting investment earnings twice, once to reduce the regular annual minimum contribution and once to reduce the extra contribution required to make up underfunding.

Slate and Labor Secretary Robert Reich made brave statements about getting the new pension reform legislation passed in 1994. But President Clinton already had health care, welfare reform, military force reduction, and other major issues on his dance card. The amount of pension reform that would be enacted would be inversely proportional to its importance.

A Program for Reform

Is it possible to create a program for pension reform that would leave every American confident about the care taken to provide for his retirement? Probably not. The demographic bulge of the baby-boom generation is so overwhelming that it would strain the resources of a perfect system. But there are things we can do now to mitigate, postpone, and alleviate the effects of the coming collapse of the pension system. First, we have to ask the right questions, and then attempt to provide the right answers.

Should the pension system be voluntary? Yes. Employers should be free to start and stop pension plans, and so should employees be free to join them or withdraw.

What kind of pensions should be offered? All plans should be defined contribution, in the sense that every deposit would be made to a retirement trust and be the property of the beneficiary. If an employer wished to offer a defined benefit, he would agree to be billed by the trustee for the annual premium necessary to maintain the desired value of annuities for each beneficiary.

What about the tax angle? Retirement savings, whether deposited by employers or employees, should be tax-deductible without limit. Reinvested earnings on retirement savings accounts should be tax-deferred. All withdrawals should be subject to income tax, plus a tax penalty if the withdrawals occur before age sixty.

Who would insure benefits? Anybody or nobody. Pension trusts could offer a range of protections, including a pledge of their capital and guarantees from other financial institutions. In general, however, the stability of pension trust deposits would be their own best source of protection. They would be like mutual funds with the added security that would come from the tax system's disincentive to withdraw savings. Government regulation and government insurance have provided a false sense of security to the banking industry, while the discipline of the markets has created a mutual fund industry that enjoys the trust of American investors without much government protection. The PBGC should push healthy plans to buy private insurance, while any plan that could not or would not get private insurance would not be allowed to make new pension promises.

Where does Social Security fit in? The benefits that we now

pay to everyone for old age income under Social Security and old age medical services under Medicare should be paid from general revenue to people below the poverty line. Bluntly, they should be converted to welfare programs.

How do we get from here to there? Freeze Social Security liabilities and issue government annuity certificates—bonds by another name—to all individuals for the present value of the benefits they have been promised. The bonds would only be cashable at the time the benefits would come due.

It is not likely that America will recognize the coming crisis until it's too late to take effective steps. It's more likely that many pension promises will be dishonored, that the rescue of the system will place a heavy burden on the financial system and on each individual.

Part Four

ESCAPING
THE
PENSION
SYSTEM

15

SAVING YOURSELF FROM THE PENSION MESS

Have you been planning for your retirement? Are you going to count on Social Security plus a pension plan at work? By now you should realize you must do more. You must try to do everything you can to become financially secure, to protect yourself from the financial crisis of the twenty-first century and the possible collapse of our pension system.

How much do you need for comfortable retirement? An ideal goal is to have the same disposable income in retirement that you had in your last year of work and to have the wealth that generates that income protected from the ravages of inflation. That means building wealth equal to at least ten times your income.

The conventional wisdom of retirement planners says 70 percent of your final salary is enough, but you should aim higher. By this theory, the costs of working are 30 percent of your salary. That's ridiculous. Sure, you won't need business suits and you won't put miles on your car commuting to work. But in early retirement, you're going to want to do all the things you haven't had time for—and that won't be cheap unless the only thing you want to do is putter in your garden. Depending on your means, you might want to fly to Europe or vacation in the mountains or help with your grandkids' tuition.

Today's reality is that the average combined retirement income (Social Security, pension, and personal savings) of American retirees is about two-thirds of final working salary, and many find themselves too limited. Current workers, though, aren't even saving as much as their parents did. Americans on average are not preparing themselves to do even as well as two-thirds of final pay, yet they face the demographic and financial crises of the twenty-first century.

How many people save and invest enough? Better ask how many people save and invest at all. In a poll by the benefits consulting firm of Towers Perin, 77 percent of the 1,000 workers sampled said they are doing little or no saving to make up for shortfalls in employer and government retirement benefits. Sadly, they think they are on the right track. The poll shows people have higher expectations about retirement income than they should.

Inflation, ignored in the projection that assures a comfortable retirement on 70 percent of final pay, is also important for future retirees because life expectancies are growing. Even a little inflation can deeply erode purchasing power over a long period. After twenty-five years, even 3 percent inflation slashes the purchasing power of a fixed pension by more than half. Just ask today's retirees on pensions they earned in the 1940s, 1950s, 1960s, and 1970s.

You can measure the cost of inflation insurance this way: If a retiree receives a pension annuity indexed for inflation, the first year's retirement check will be only about half of an unindexed pension, though the amount will rise in later years according to the inflation rate. The extension of life does not guarantee the extension of health, happiness, or prosperity. More people are going to live past age eighty-five, when the chance of being frail, even disabled, rises dramatically. Thus expenses rise at the same time the purchasing power of old pensions declines.

INFLATION'S THREAT

Don't be fooled by the size of your pretax, preinflation lump of retirement savings. Your cash balances will rise in nominal terms while inflation pushes up the cost of living and depreciates the value of your savings.

Observe the life cycle of a nest egg. Its pretax, preinflation balance rises from, say, a little less than $3 million in 1992 to over $8 million in 2016. But the true value of the same nest egg in deflated after-tax dollars rises to a peak of less than $3.5 million in 2004 and declines steadily thereafter. That's reality. In nominal terms, everything looks great until a steep drop-off after 2024. The difference is that the person tracking his wealth in nominal terms is surprised to find its purchasing power evaporating at the same time that he is no longer capable of replenishing his capital.[1]

Everybody has heard about the hyperinflation in Germany in the 1920s, Israel in the 1980s, Russia in the 1990s, and Argentina and Brazil in every decade. But most Americans experienced inflation only in the seven lean years from 1974 to 1981, during which there were three years of double-digit price increases. That inflation, though it was traumatic for business and difficult for many individuals, was the kind of ill wind that blew good for many people. Many readers of this book, if they owned homes, will remember it as the time when their wealth grew as never before or since. Having made a $5,000 down payment on a $50,000 home, they saw the price of the house double to $100,000. All the appreciation was theirs to keep, and their salaries grew while their mortgage payments were frozen. The fact that this period planted the seeds of ruin for many savings and loan associations and banks that lent on those homes was not a problem for homeowners.

It's hard for Americans to imagine real hyperinflation. We've all heard that it took a wheelbarrowful of money to buy a loaf of bread in Germany; we've seen the postage stamps overprinted to cross out the old value with some absurd figure like 50 million marks. What we fail to appreciate is that the same wheelbarrowful of money was a day's salary the previous day, a week's salary the previous week, and a year's salary the previous month. We can understand that money became worthless; we don't easily understand that it used to be worth something and that real people lost real wealth just by leaving it in the bank.

Inflation is never an accident. It is always a government's conscious repudiation of its obligations. In the American inflation of the 1970s, the U.S. government chose to cheapen the dollar in order to make imported oil cheaper; it seems no stretch of the imagination to expect that the government someday will shrug off the accumulated weight of the national debt by inflating away its value. Woe then to those who store their wealth in currency or in fixed-rate securities.

Assuming Responsibility

Are you now scared? Do you want to know what you can do to increase your chances of a secure and happy retirement? Here is some basic advice.

1. Take a realistic look at your employer. Will this company be around until you reach retirement? Failing companies can't be trusted to preserve pension funds. All companies are going to be under stress in the twenty-first century, and some will meet the same sorry fate that inadequate steel companies and airlines met in the 1980s. You may be better off changing jobs now. If you are working in a shaky company or an industry with a questionable future, don't wait until you're helpless at the end of your career. Change jobs now. No skills? Too old? Many government jobs only require ten years of service to get generous pensions, and many are open to part-time political workers with no appreciable qualifications. If you have time to plan ahead, two or three years of part-time classes can earn you a public school teaching certificate. Of course you should try to pick a state with prospects for growth and a public employee retirement system that's soundly funded.

2. Exert as much control as you can over the retirement funds other people manage for you and stay informed about the investment philosophy of those who manage your money.

Demand that your company fund its defined benefit pension plans fully and honestly. If you have a union or a professional association, push them to become aware of this problem that they usually ignore. Don't assume that actuaries and accountants hired by your employer have your best interests at heart. Question these authorities and demand full disclosure and independent analysis of pension plan actions.

3. If you are a government worker, take an active voice in the affairs of your union; it's the only chance you've got. Don't let politicians raid your pension to buy other people's votes. Are you going to gamble your future on the proposition that the taxpayers can be made to pay on the promises made by the officials they elected? As a taxpayer, don't tolerate funny accounting and empty pension promises. Move now and avoid the rush. For an example of what happens to people who don't move, visit Detroit.

4. Don't trust the Social Security promise. The system will be in a state of crisis during your lifetime, so don't make Social Security a sacred cow. The system can't be reformed without reducing expected benefits. Find out how much the system will theoretically pay you and reduce your expectations by one-third—either by reduced benefits or a later retirement age. Support politicians who will tell you this truth. Oppose politicians and special-interest groups who will tell you lies to get your support.

5. Postpone your retirement—it's the simplest path to financial stability and the only one under your complete control. Almost all mandatory retirement rules were abolished by federal law in 1987, and that may turn out to be the single most important federal benefit for the baby-boom generation. It means that you accumulate more salary income when it's the greatest and maybe even when you need it the least. You also get a bonus from Social Security in the form of a bigger benefit. It also means that your investment portfolio can continue to grow, undiminished by withdrawals, when it's the largest. Even three years' delay in retirement can be the equivalent of twenty years of saving 5 percent of your income.

6. Run your own retirement savings plan in addition to the pension system supplied in your workplace. Use a payroll savings plan, a 401(k) plan, or a defined contribution plan. Plans where the worker is entitled to a pile of cash set aside for him are far more honest than a benefit promise of unknown reliability. If you don't have a defined contribution pension plan, try to get one started. If nothing else, start an IRA. Even if you're not eligible for the tax deduction, there's no tax on investment profits until you make withdrawals after retirement. However you do it, save and invest for yourself. Join an investment club, read financial publications, watch TV shows about business and investment.

When the time approaches to retire, know yourself and your means. The two most common mistakes about retirement are leaving too early with insufficient savings and leaving too late with insufficient preparation for a retirement lifestyle.

Find out how much Social Security thinks it's going to pay you. Your benefit is based on how many years you worked and how much you paid into the system, and that depends on whether Social Security's notoriously antiquated computers tallied your work history correctly. Well before you retire, and preferably every ten years, you should file Social Security's Request for Earnings and Benefit Estimate Statement form, just to be sure that you and the computers are on the same planet.

You could start collecting Social Security retirement benefits as early as age sixty-two, and many people who are sick of work or just sick do that. But your total monthly benefits are reduced 20 percent—a percentage that will increase as the normal retirement age is stretched out to age sixty-seven in the early years of the twenty-first century. So how's your health? By present law, you would have to live to age seventy-four just to make up the lost Social Security money and you would, of course, lose extra years of salary just when you might be able to really save a good chunk of your income. What's more, current law gives retirees an extra 3.5 percent a year in benefits for delaying retirement past age sixty-five, and this bonus will be increased to 8 percent a year by 2005.

WHAT DO YOU WANT?

Are you tired of your work? Or are you afraid to quit work?

Those questions may be too tough to answer at first, or the answers may be too tough to face, so ask yourself some related questions:

Are you elated or relieved when you finish a project?

Is the arrival of a paycheck the most meaningful event of your workweek, or is it the Wednesday afternoon slide out of the office to play golf?

Are there goals at work for you? Are you striving to achieve them?

If you made a list of all the things you would tell St. Peter to induce him to let you into Heaven, how many of them would have something to do with work? Is your list frighteningly short?

If you were young and could start all over, would you choose a different field?

BANKING ON RETIREMENT

When you do retire you will need sound advice about retirement finance.

Ideally, you are financially ready to retire when you can replace all your net income from work with earnings from investments, pensions, Social Security, and similar sources, and protect yourself from inflation. Although net income means you need not provide for work-related expenses, it's easy to exaggerate their share of your finances when you plan for retirement. Your office expenses may go down, and you may not wear suits every day, but you will still eat lunch, and it won't be tax-deductible.

Many of us will never reach this ideal, so we must make tradeoffs and decide how long to work, how hard to work, how much to save, how to cut expenses. When we make these tradeoffs for retirement, chances are we will only be continuing a lifelong pattern. Cutting expenses now is the surest way to a comfortable retirement income in the future.

Everyone planning for his future should make two balance

sheets and two income statements—one each for the present and the future. Get out a pencil and paper, or make a spreadsheet on a personal computer.

BALANCE SHEET

ADD ASSETS:
  Bank accounts
  Home real estate
    (Market value less mortgage debt)
  Personal items

SUBTRACT PERSONAL DEBTS:

ADD INVESTMENT ASSETS:
  Business
  Real estate other than home
  Stocks
  Bonds
  Insurance
  Vested pension benefits
  Collectibles
  Other investments

SUBTRACT INVESTMENT DEBTS:

NET WORTH:

INCOME STATEMENT

SALARY INCOME:
BUSINESS INCOME:
  Less business expense:

INVESTMENT INCOME:
  Business
  Real estate other than home
  Stocks
  Bonds

Insurance
Vested pension benefits
Collectibles
Other investments
    Less investment expense:

ADJUSTED GROSS INCOME:

SUBTRACT TAXES:

NET INCOME:

SUBTRACT EXPENSES:
Housing
    Mortgage or rent
    Taxes
    Insurance
    Utilities
    Maintenance
Food
    Groceries
    Restaurant
Clothing
Medical
    Health Insurance
    Other
Transportation
    Car lease or loan
    Gas
    Maintenance
    Transit
Entertainment
    Amusements
    Hobbies
    Travel
    Vacations

Insurance
  Life
  Disability
Charity
  Church
  Causes
  Other
Other expenses

TOTAL EXPENSES:

REMAINDER AVAILABLE FOR INVESTMENT:
Less other nonretirement investments:
College tuition fund:

OTHER INVESTMENTS MADE ON YOUR BEHALF:
Employer pension contributions
401(k) match

After you have worked up a balance sheet and an income statement for your current situation, push your assets forward to the year of your retirement. For the moment, ignore inflation and assume that your current investments will grow by 3 percent a year. Use a personal computer spreadsheet or a calculator to estimate the purchasing power your assets will command. Then do the same with the amounts that your contemporary income statement says you will invest each year. Add your employer's pension contributions or push forward the asset value of today's pension, but don't do both.

For easy figuring on the future income statement, assume that your investment assets can generate 5 percent a year, ignoring inflation. This may be somewhat optimistic unless you are willing to accept the risk of some fluctuation in income or principal.

When you do this the first time, you may tremble. And then you will start to think about the probabilities of higher taxes, lower investment returns, stock market crashes, real estate price swings, and you may not sleep well. But don't despair. Go back to your worksheets and find out what happens if you trim back on, for example, vacations.

Every thousand dollars you save and invest today will grow while waiting for you to retire. Benjamin Franklin was too conservative: a penny saved may be a penny earned, but a penny invested may be ten cents earned or more by the time you spend it in retirement.

MAKING AND MEETING RETIREMENT GOALS

As we have seen earlier, the federal government's pension policies are driven more by the thirst for tax revenue than by the idea of giving taxpayers a break for saving for retirement. It would be better to have a tax system that exempts money saved and taxes money consumed, but that doesn't look like it's coming anytime soon. Instead, almost every year brings another tax law change that reduces the tax deductions for corporate pension contributions or individual savings or both.

To replace an $85,000 salary requires more than $1 million in pension and private savings on top of Social Security, Medicare, and employer-paid supplemental health coverage. That's the cash it takes at age sixty-five to buy a life annuity that will bring your monthly income back to what you had when you were working. Of course, that assumes you are willing to spend your entire savings on retirement income, and that you are willing to live on a fixed income despite the constant threat of inflation. If you seek the more difficult, less risky goal of living on investment income alone, you will require more than twice as much capital. ($2.5 million invested at 5 percent pays dividends and interest of $125,000, less 40 percent or so for federal and local taxes leaves $75,000. Depending on retirement age, Social Security may add another $10,000.)

On an $85,000 salary, saving and investing enough money to have a million or two at retirement is no easy trick, nor is saving and investing to have half a million on a $42,500 salary, or saving and investing to have a quarter of a million on $21,000 a year. Saving alone will never get you there—you must put your capital to work for you and it must work hard.

For each income bracket these goals are magical sums of money. If you reach your goal on retirement day, you will hold a sum you have never seen before and probably never will see again. Only a disciplined savings program and an aggressive investment program can prepare you to meet the future with confidence.

But these goals are also minimal goals. What you need to save also increases with projected life span, or if you change jobs often, or if you work at a place with below-average benefits, or if you still have to meet other responsibilities, such as putting children through college or supporting an elderly relative.

Other reasons to save:

- Protection: Companies restructure and merge every day—any job, including yours, can disappear without warning. Living off savings may become an immediate necessity, even though it can damage your retirement income plans.
- Medical expenses continue to rise faster than inflation and health care reform is not likely to change that. Government reform of health care is aimed at helping those who can't afford medical insurance, not at helping the rich. After retirement, anybody with investment income is "rich." You will pay more for health care than you think, whether in direct charges or insurance premiums or in taxes.
- Inflation causes your wealth to shrink in value. If inflation averages even 5 percent, you'll need $26,500 in twenty years to match $10,000 in today's purchasing power. Saving is futile if your investment strategy is too timid. If all your savings are in a taxable money market account that pays 2.5 percent and you're in the 31 percent tax bracket, you have about a 1.7 percent return after tax. Inflation has not been that low since 1965. Even though returns on money market funds quickly rise to track inflation, the tax bite virtually guarantees that your account will never keep up with inflation.

Now that you have assessed your present and future resources, you have the answers to two of the important questions of personal finance:

1. What am I worth?
2. What will I be worth when I retire?

Now you must go on, and ask:

3. What are my financial objectives between now and the end of my life?

Write down the big-ticket items, such as paying college tuition, buying the dream house, the yachts and cars, enjoying a perfectly secure retirement, paying for a nursing home without impoverishing the rest of the family. Put specific dollar amounts on these objectives.
Now the bad news:

4. How far short of no. 3 is no. 2?

So you ask yourself:

5. Can I cut back my objectives or boost my income?

Put unrealistic goals out of your mind forever, or start developing a specific plan for getting from no. 1 to no. 3. Do you really want that yacht, and if you do, what field offers you the best prospect for a second income? You may even want to consider a career change to that occupation related to your field that you once disdained as "selling out." Now that you're older, you may have a better idea of what your price is. On a less cosmic scale, your plan should also include sharper budgeting, refinancing debt, and aggressive investing.
Then consider the strength of your plan:

6. What do I do if it all blows up?

Review your insurance coverage, both life and disability. If your employee benefit plan isn't enough to carry you through all your responsibilities, call several insurance agents. You should also consider long-term-care insurance, though you are likely to be better off doing your own investing to build enough wealth to meet any eventuality.
One of the most likely catastrophes is losing your job before you're ready to go. Are you sure you have twenty or thirty

more years to save for retirement? Most people reach the peak of their careers by around age fifty, plus or minus five years. The pyramid in a hierarchy gets very narrow at the top, and there just aren't enough top jobs to go around. Tough competition in virtually every American industry adds to the threat: can you honestly say that your company would not sell itself to outsiders, that it cannot be taken over, and that its prospects are so good that it will never feel the need to cast out superfluous workers? One American company where people from top to bottom sincerely believed that was IBM. More than 100,000 lost jobs later, they now know that lifetime employment is a myth.

Even more likely than losing your job is divorce, which may bring with it financial catastrophe for at least one partner. At the very least, a divorce pounds home the fact that one can't live as cheaply as two, and the lawyer's bill will give new meaning to the word "dependent."

DRAINING SAVINGS

Parkinson's Law was that work expands to fill the time allotted to a task. The demands on savings will probably consume any amount you save. As J. P. Morgan reputedly said, if you have to ask how much a yacht costs, you can't afford it. If you wonder if you are saving enough, you aren't. A rule of thumb would be to invest 10 percent of your pretax income before having children and 20 percent while they're growing up. After they leave the nest, keep going at the 20 percent rate.

If you have a pension plan at work, you may think you are not too far from this goal, but you should be convinced by now that many pension plans will fall short of the expectations of their sponsors and participants. So the total amount of money you ought to save may seem so overwhelming that you give up without trying.

Don't give up. Start tomorrow by putting away 2 percent of after-tax income and do it in the most invisible, painless way available to you. If you can, arrange a payroll deduction at work for a credit union, or a stock-purchase plan, or a voluntary contribution to a retirement plan. If no such thing is available, set up an automatic deduction from your checking account for a deposit into a savings account or a mutual fund. Then, every three months, increase the deduction by another percent of after-tax income. Keep going, at least until you hit 10 percent of pretax income.

16

INVESTMENT CHOICES

Now that you're saving money, how will you invest it? Investment earnings must eventually be the main source of retirement capital.

The American stock market is one of the great wonders of the world. Because of America's unequaled political stability and its enormous economic vitality, ownership of economic assets has always been more rewarding over any long period of time than mere lending. In other words, stocks outperform bonds. Although the price of stocks is far more variable, the variations cancel out over time and produce solid growth. The Standard & Poor's index of the five hundred largest stocks has outperformed all other broad-based financial investments for the past sixty years. A dollar invested in the S&P 500 in 1926 would have grown to $534 by the end of 1989 if all dividends had been reinvested. Adjusted for inflation, that dollar would still have grown immensely, to $76. The same dollar invested the same year in U.S. Treasury bills and rolled over at prevailing rates each year would have grown to only $1.38 after inflation.

If people who read this book take nothing away from it but the idea that they should put some of their bank savings or money-market fund balances into a mutual fund that invests in the S&P

500 and leave it there, they will earn themselves the price of the book many times over.

Stocks also can be an appropriate investment for the retiree who wants income. Unlike bonds, where the interest payment is fixed for the life of the bond, stockholders often find that successful companies increase their dividends, providing a cost-of-living increase in retirement earnings without any effort. (It works both ways, of course: companies in trouble often cut or eliminate their dividends.)

Many people don't like stocks because they go up and down so much. They read about people losing big sums in the market. They may remember the stories about the Crash of '29. They certainly remember the panic-tinged days of the market meltdown in 1987, when otherwise sane people talked seriously about the chance of another Great Depression.

But even if an investor picked the worst time in the twentieth century to invest in stocks—the peak of the market in 1929—stocks still outperformed Treasury bonds over the next forty years. And a real person saving for retirement doesn't just dump a pile of cash into the market on one day of his life; he adds a reasonable percentage of income each month, each quarter or each year. A young person with a long view might have put 10 percent of his income into the market in 1929, but if he was truly wise, he would also have invested in 1930, 1931, 1932, 1933, and thereafter.

Mark well: good returns in stocks are based on a strategy of buying and holding a diversified portfolio of stocks like the S&P 500. You cripple yourself if you let a crash or a panic stampede you out of the market. That's when you should be scraping up more money to invest. Interestingly, the contrary is not so true: in the market as a whole, selling at the top is not as important as investing at the bottom. (Individual stocks are a different story, because companies run in longer cycles and sometimes the down cycle ends in bankruptcy.)

Don't confuse volatility and risk: the long-term investor runs no more long-run risk of permanently losing principal than the trader does. He simply accepts the fact that his account balance will go up and down from month to month while it climbs steadily from decade to decade.

For the personal investor, action must be the priority. Don't let your money rot in a money-market fund unless it's your considered judgment that all other investments are less attractive than cash, and have a short-term expected return less than the inflation rate.

HIGH OR LOW

Although economic theory teaches that the stock market quickly incorporates all available information that affects the prices of stocks, it is a rare day on Wall Street when most market participants believe that stocks are correctly priced.

Wall Street's stock market strategists are always divided between those who think the market is too high in view of current and prospective economic conditions and those who think the near future will bring developments to justify those and even higher prices. This division holds true whether the market is high or low, rising or falling.

The best available advice is to ignore advice: ignore stock market strategists and market timers. Whether you are investing in mutual funds or a carefully selected portfolio of individual stocks, there is only one timing strategy that makes sense for the long-term investor: invest regular amounts of money regularly in the stock market. Whether it's 10 percent of salary once a year or 1 percent of salary every month, make that investment a regular feature on your calendar.

Regularity ensures that you will be in the market in good times—especially those rare and always unexpected occasions like the end of the summer of 1982, when the stock market took off on an upswing that ushered in a bull market that has lasted eleven years. Regularity also ensures that you will buy fewer shares of your selected investment when prices are high and more shares when prices are low.

Some advisers suggest mixing stocks and bonds to reduce the volatility of equity investments. For example, they suggest putting a percentage of your portfolio equal to your age in fixed-income investments. This makes no sense for the long-term investor in the accumulation phase of a retirement program, because he is trying to earn the increased average rate of return that financial markets pay to investors who are willing to accept extra volatility. A fifty-year-old with 50 percent of his portfolio in bonds is too timid. He has ten or fifteen or twenty years for his investments to grow—plenty of time for a portfolio of stocks to outpace bonds.

An important thing to emphasize about creating a retirement portfolio that's heavy in stocks is that it not be created all at once. Taking a large lump of cash and dumping it into stocks at what appears to be the top of a bull market is not what you want to do. A retirement plan heavy in stocks must be built slowly. Monthly or yearly investments in equities made over decades will purchase small quantities of overpriced stocks when prices are high and large amounts of cheap stocks when prices are low.

If you do receive a large sum ten years or more before you actually retire, what should you do? Start carefully: craft a balanced portfolio of one-third stocks, one-third intermediate to long bonds, and one-third money market to one-year bills. Each year, put 10 percent of each fixed-income account into the equity account.

The time for asset allocation is when retirement nears. Then it may make sense to put some money in an investment, such as one-year Treasury bills, that preserves capital even if it can't beat inflation.

MUTUAL FUNDS

Mutual funds give the individual investor a chance to diversify, placing small amounts of money in many investments. That reduces the risk of heavy loss because one key investment turns sour. The investor must pay a price for this service and so mutual funds charge fees.

The traditional price, a 6 percent sales charge up front, turns off many investors, and properly so. There are plenty of studies showing no difference in average long-term performance between funds with a sales charge, or "load," and "no-load" funds. An investor who holds a successful fund for many years will not find the front-end load onerous, although the investor who selects his own funds without aid should object to lining the pocket of a broker for his "advice."

No-load fund managers are not in the business for the joy of making somebody else rich; they earn their compensation with an annual fee, often more than 1 percent of the investor's balance per year. The long-term investor may well pay more to the manager of a no-load fund than to a load fund. There are also funds with exit fees, funds that charge nothing to get in and nothing much to stay in, but which take a share of the winnings—or remainder—on the way out. And there are combination fees: pay some on purchase of a fund; pay some more while the fund is held; pay some more on selling the fund.

The latest trend in fees is to let the customer decide when to pay. Some fund sponsors establish two classes of shares, one in which the investor pays the load up front in the traditional way, the other in which the investor pays a higher fee over the life of the investment, and an exit fee if he sells out. What this amounts to is an invitation to investors who like to switch from fund to fund to come and play with traditional front-end-loaded funds as well as in no-load funds. This may not be a blessing for the long-term investors who hold successful load funds for many years because it will make those funds more volatile without adding long-term value to the fund.

The key question is not the fee but what the fee is used for. The traditional sales load mostly goes to a broker as a reward for getting the investor to buy the fund. Some brokers are more interested in getting 6 percent of your money for themselves and their house than in what happens later to your 94 percent. No-load funds are usually marketed directly through newspaper ads, so the annual fee mostly goes to the fund managers and the media that sell the ad space. Since the managers make more when the fund grows, their interests are usually on the same side as the investors. The managers, however, may be more interested in fattening this year's compensation by bringing in new investors to enlarge the fund rather than improving their take over time by making the best long-term investments.

A mutual fund also charges investors its regular expenses, such as brokers' commissions. Though the National Association of Securities Dealers has new regulations that are supposed to limit sales charges to 8.5 percent of the initial investment regardless of the fee system, a mutual fund can be designed to separate investors from their money so painlessly that they thank the manager for letting them invest. The only defense is a close examination of each fund's prospectus, focusing clearly on long-term returns and on expense ratios. Quarterly fund reports in business and investment magazines are only a starting point because they exclude expenses and sales charges.

Mutual funds have become the most popular American investment vehicle. For thirty years, American households have been net sellers of stocks individually owned, and huge net buyers of mutual funds. This trend accelerated in the early 1990s when interest rates fell so much that alternative investments became less attractive. The Investment Company Institute reported net flow into mutual funds of $120 billion in the first half of 1993. That compared with $171 billion for all of 1992, a year that had smashed all previous records. Total assets of mutual funds totaled $1.25 trillion at the end of June 1993.

Most of this money was in open-end mutual funds, in which a sponsor manages a pool of money the way a bank trust department would—taking in deposits, investing them, and handing back cash on demand. A question that's rarely asked is whether mutual fund sponsors can really imitate banks: what happens if there are runs on funds?

Shareholders in most open-end mutual funds are told they can cash in their holdings with a single phone call, usually without a transaction fee. It's a great deal for the consumer as long as a limited number of fund shareholders take advantage of it. But if many shareholders run for the exit at once, the fund will exhaust its cash reserves (hardly ever as much as 10 percent of total assets and often as little as 3 percent) and be forced to sell securities from its portfolio. And it must sell to redeem its promise, regardless of whether the market is rising or, more likely, falling.

A run on funds will quickly become a run on the underlying market anyway, because mutual funds hold such a large proportion of the total American markets in stocks and bonds.

Remember the Jimmy Stewart movie *It's a Wonderful Life*? He's the manager of a little building and loan society, and he has to tell worried townspeople that he can't give them all cash at once. Their deposits are loans on houses in town, and he can't get cash unless he forces them to sell their houses.

What is not recognized by many fund investors is that the securities the funds hold may be just like Jimmy Stewart's home loans, far less liquid than the funds' shares. Though mutual fund investors expect that they can cash in their shares on any given day, some of the securities the funds hold would be hard to sell in a time of crisis, and asking the funds for cash would accelerate the market crisis.

Even holding on in the face of a panic, normally the wisest thing to do, may not pay off for investors in a real run. If buyers can't be found for illiquid securities like junk bonds and small company stocks, funds may be forced to sell what they can, their best investments, and hang on to the losers. Many funds have fine print in their prospectuses to allow for bank borrowing to meet redemptions, and funds also can distribute securities instead of cash. But employing these tactics to meet redemptions would also acknowledge the crisis, and possibly make it worse.

No safety net–like deposit insurance exists for mutual fund investors, nor should it. But people who invest in mutual funds ought to be aware of all the risks.

Some open-end funds acknowledge that they cannot liquidate their assets to pay off shareholders on demand. Exit fees serve the useful purpose of reminding investors about the costs of redemption. Other funds that invest in particularly illiquid markets only allow redemption once a quarter.

Another alternative is the closed-end mutual fund, which issues a set number of shares at the creation of the fund and invests the proceeds. After that, the mutual fund share price rises and falls on a stock exchange in accordance with the value of the investments, and with investors' projection of the future performance of the portfolio. (In the bull market of 1993, most closed-end funds sold at a premium to net asset value.)

Closed-end fund managers don't have to liquidate investments, but investors can still be burned in a panic. The price of closed-end funds will fall if the underlying securities fall, and can fall further. If enough fund holders sell, the fund shares may sell at a discount to the total value of the underlying securities. (That's probably a buying opportunity, if you like the long-term prospects of the fund.)

FROM THE BOTTOM UP

As long as investors are aware of the particular risks of mutual funds, some mutual funds should be the foundation of any retirement portfolio—specifically, index funds. An index fund purchases stocks or bonds in the same proportion used to compute a widely followed market average. There are funds that mimic the Standard & Poor's index of five hundred stocks on the New York Stock Exchange, funds that mimic the Russell 2000 index of over-the-counter stocks, funds that mimic an index of foreign stocks. Because a manager does not have to have much brains to read a list of stocks and buy them, many index funds are truly no-load and have low expense charges and fees besides.

Several of the major mutual fund companies, such as Fidelity, T. Rowe Price, and Vanguard, offer no-load S&P 500 index funds and funds pegged to other indexes. The Vanguard 500 Index Trust charges a bedrock 0.22 percent a year.

With index funds making up more than half of an individual's long-term retirement portfolio, there will be enough diversification, enough stability, and enough solid long-term growth built in to protect and enhance a retirement account. Investing only in the S&P index, however, leaves the investor with too conservative a position. After all, the S&P 500 is composed of the five hundred biggest nonfinancial stocks in the United States, weighted by market capitalization. (Market capitalization means the number of shares multiplied by the share price—essentially the stock market's judgment of the worth of the entire company.) As much as these stocks are the pillars of the American economy, they are the big success stories of yesteryear. Two old sayings are especially apt: "They have nowhere to go but down" and "The bigger they are, the harder they fall."

The investor should employ not one index fund but several: large stock and small stock funds, ones that invest in foreign stocks. The index funds should be sponsored by several different mutual fund management chains. With that solid foundation assured, the individual investor can be more adventurous with the rest of his money.

A substitute for index funds as the foundation of retirement investment is a portfolio of managed funds. One hopes that the fund managers you select can do what the majority of managers cannot do—beat the S&P index. The investor trying to cover the market should probably find a fund that invests in value stocks (those valued low in the market relative to their earnings), growth stocks (those with good prospects for business expansion), and small stocks (those value or growth stocks hidden from common view like truffles in a forest).

In addition, a managed mutual fund is probably the best way to invest in international stocks because some foreign stock indexes are skewed by local oddities. And foreign stocks should be an important part of any retirement portfolio, since these investments allow the investor to diversify away from the risk of crisis or depression in the United States.

In mutual funds, one can also take a stand on specific industries, such as biotechnology or energy or health care or banking, through industry-specific funds. And one might wish to put a small share of a portfolio into a gold fund to hedge against an American financial crisis. But anyone who has such firm views on industries or the economy probably should do the extra work of picking individual stocks.

A problem with mutual funds that's rarely recognized is that they are vulnerable to their own success. When a fund is popular or successful, money may come flooding in—more money than the manager can invest well. This either drags down earnings, if the manager just parks the money in cash, or drags down the quality of the portfolio, if the manager buys against his better judgment.

For example, one reason that the junk bond market became so junky in the late 1980s was that the high returns of junk bond funds earlier in the decade sucked in large sums of enthusiastic money. Fund managers felt they had to invest in something, thus creating a sellers' market in junk. Bond covenants, which are supposed to protect investors by limiting issuers' financial shenanigans, became weaker. Issuers and their investment bankers knew they could sell almost anything into a market of funds dripping cash. The natural result was a rising default rate, higher than the historical norms that most serious students of junk bonds anticipated. Similar enthusiasms have affected funds in small stocks, in convertible securities, in preferred stock, and especially in funds that invest in the stocks of single foreign countries.

The honest thing for a fund manager to do is to close the fund to new investment when there are more investors than good investments in a fund's specialty. Many of the funds that have closed, however, are not funds restricted to a popular sector but funds managed by a particularly successful investment adviser. These also have large swings in popularity, based on performance and the managers' appearances on television and the covers of investment magazines.

Sometimes the proprietors of a fund that closes itself have second thoughts and decide to clone the fund, appointing a different manager to pick securities according to the same basic philosophy. Logically, this is silly: the more the clone fund is like the old fund, the more it will suffer from the old fund's problems; or the less the clone fund is like the old fund, the less right it has to trade on the old fund's name. Nevertheless, clone funds often outperform the original fund, at least in the short term of two years or less.

UPS AND DOWNS

Just as investors don't like stocks that go up and down without warning, unexpected swings in the market and investment cycles can provoke even long-term stock investors to dump a fund at the worst time—just when a manager's investment style is out of fashion, the portfolio undervalued, or a run of bad luck is about to reverse itself.

An investor can prepare himself for swings in a fund's value by looking at its past volatility. Managers can choose the level of volatility their funds assume, and their choices are pretty consistent—more consistent than their earnings.

Beta, a term derived from regression analysis, is the statistician's most common measure of volatility. It measures the tendency of a fund (or a stock) to rise and fall faster or slower than the broad market index the statistician chooses for comparison. The Standard & Poor's 500 stock index is the most common measure, and a beta of 1 means a fund tracks the S&P quite closely. A beta of 1.5 means the fund is 50 percent more volatile than the S&P 500—when the index is up or down 10 percent, the fund rises or falls 15% on average. A beta of 0.6 means the fund is 40 percent more stable than the index.

Investors would like to find those funds and those stocks that have high beta on the upside and low beta on the downside. They can be found, but they tend to be funds and stocks that are changing character, for which beta is not as good a predictor of future performance as we would wish.

Since most investors are not disturbed by violent swings to the upside, another way of measuring risk is to look carefully at the fund's sharpest decline over the last ten years. Can you stand to see it happen again tomorrow? Another way to ask that question is this: if you put half your planned investment into this fund and it dropped 25 percent tomorrow because of a big drop in the market, would you put the other half of your investment in on the day after tomorrow? That's what you should do. Most people would sell. A sharp reversal of (unrealistic) expectations drives them out of investments, when the real problem is their failure to appreciate the difference between risk and volatility.

William F. Sharpe, a Stanford University economist whose Nobel Prize was awarded for his studies of risk-adjusted performance, stresses that investors who have the time, the patience, and the courage to ignore volatility will gain extra return on their investments. "You need to differentiate between risks where you will be compensated in the long run and risks where you won't," he says. Another investment style that provides adequate and occasionally generous compensation for accepting risk is a bias in favor of small stocks and overseas stocks. (Foreign investments include currency risk, and that risk runs against the dollar long-term, as it must run against any paper currency used as reserve currency.)

Funds that invest in a single industry or sector of the economy, he says, have higher risk and merely average returns. In 1993 Professor Sharpe reported that there seems to be a systematic underrewarding of investments in growth stocks and a small but significant extra compensation that goes to undervalued stocks. Growth investors follow rapidly rising earnings, which are widely recognized, and value investors look for unrecognized stocks that sell for low multiples of earnings or underlying assets. So for the moment, the extra rewards flow to the less easily practiced discipline. But one of the most important things to understand about markets is that they adjust to new information; if Sharpe's findings are widely accepted they are likely to be reversed.

For a final thought on mutual funds, consider the companies that manage them. Peter Lynch, who used to manage the Magellan Fund, the nation's largest, notes that he didn't follow his own advice about looking for investments in your own life. Thus he missed a terrific chance in the publicly traded mutual fund companies. "If you had divided your money equally among the eight mutual fund stocks and held them from the beginning of 1988 until the end of 1989, you would have outperformed 99 percent of the mutual funds these companies promote," he says in his book *Beating the Street*. Now ask yourself: at whose expense are mutual fund companies profiting? If the fund companies are making above-average profits, are they doing it by making above-average returns for their clients? Can any producer long make profits greater than the value he adds to his product?

EQUITY INVESTMENTS

In 1968 about a third of the average American's financial assets consisted of individual stock shares. Now the proportion is less than a sixth. Individuals now own less than half of corporate equities. There is probably an opportunity in something so many people abhor.

Investing in individual stocks on your own, especially those that grow but don't pay dividends, is a better strategy than a mutual fund for accounts that are not tax-sheltered. A mutual fund throws off regular income dividends and also capital gains dividends. Paying taxes on capital gains each year can kill you in comparison to letting all your profits run.

Small stocks of growing companies, in industries with long-term promise, are perfect for investors who are trying to accumulate a store of capital over decades. And the stocks of well-established companies, including giant concerns, are usually a secure way to participate in the success stories of the American economy.

With most of your retirement savings invested in a widely diversified portfolio of mutual funds, through a tax-sheltered savings or retirement plan, your personal unsheltered portfolio is the place to undertake some specific, even risky, investments. Dividends don't count here; you just pay tax on them. What you are after is capital gains.

Buy low, sell high? The key to capital gains is to buy low. Sell high is the other half of the well-worn phrase, but the real key is buying low. Sell high if you like, but a genuine solid success story of a company that grows and does well may have a generation or more of prosperity before it meets disaster.

Of course you should keep watching the finances of all your stocks. The problems of a faltering company often show up first on the balance sheet. Inventories that balloon out of proportion to sales may signal trouble, as may a sudden urge to borrow that's unmatched by any investments. Stock prices of course reflect all investors' judgments about a company—a company that suffers an unexplained drop of 10 percent, relative to the market, may soon produce an unpleasant explanation.

A reason you have your core holdings in a widely diversified portfolio is that nobody can predict the market as a whole, or the rise and fall of interest rates or the operation of the business cycle. The diversified portfolio is like a fishing net, spread wide to catch anything good that might be swimming along. Your individual portfolio of stocks is like a fishing line baited with a lure to attract mackerel—you have a specific object in mind and your energy is focused on that task.

Find the industries abhorred by the conventional wisdom and pick the companies with the best prospects in those industries. How do you do that? Keep your eyes and ears open. Read, read, read. Translate every trend in supermarkets and department stores and daily life into an angle on some company. Peter Lynch has written two sensible books on investing this way, *One Up on Wall Street* and *Beating the Street*. Jane Bryant Quinn, the columnist, has a book on financial issues that combines technical excellence and down-to-earth simplicity called *Making the Most of Your Money*. The American Association of Individual Investors, based in Chicago, issues a wealth of information on securities, including a monthly journal, a guide to mutual funds, and a financial planning guide. Financial magazines and newspapers like *Barron's* and *The Wall Street Journal* provide a continuing course in investments. In one of the few federal subsidies for savings and investment, all your reading material may be tax-deductible as an investment expense. (Miscellaneous business expenses are deductible to the extent they exceed two percent of income.)

If you are suited to have a long-term portfolio of stocks you manage yourself, you have a chance to do very well for yourself. The idea is to be in the leading companies in growing industries. For an example, look at computer technology, in which the leading companies are those that produce new equipment and new software, not those that produce knockoffs. A beaten-down sector with continued long-term growth prospects (pharmaceuticals fit that description in 1993) is a double advantage. Be careful investing in something really new, such as biotechnology. While anyone can tell that gene splicing is a basic science invention that will be as important to the twenty-first century as the transistor was to the second half of the twentieth century, it is impossible to guess which of the hundreds of biotechnology companies will become the IBM, the Digital Equipment, the Hewlett-Packard, or the Intel of its field.

Beware of buying any stock where the assets go home at night. Talented people are unpredictably mobile. The classic example is advertising, where businesses have virtually nothing but what's in the heads of the best people. Computer software is not much less quirky.

A Second Job

Buying stocks should be nearly as hard work as a part-time job, though probably more rewarding. To research industries and companies and keep track of your holdings requires at least a few hours of direct concentrated effort every week, such as sitting down on Saturday morning and reading *Barron's* intensively. You should also have enough intellectual interest in business and economics to keep you reading on the subject for fun. If *The Wall Street Journal* and *Business Week* don't hold your interest separately from any direct news you can use, direct investing in stocks may not be for you. Stock investing is brain work, and brain work that's drudgery is often not successful.

Start with what you know from business or personal experience. A customer or supplier or competitor, a chain of stores that seems to have a key to success, local companies that haven't come to notice in New York. You can pool your knowledge and your money with others through investment clubs. Many are members of the National Association of Investment Clubs and some have long and impressive track records.

Investment clubs serve as support groups, bolstering members' courage and reminding them of their long-term investment strategies. A stockbroker used to do that, and a few good, old-fashioned ones still do. But these days, big brokerage firms, intent on fat commissions and on bolstering their image as financial consultants, push their brokers to promote "products" such as annuities, mutual funds, and limited partnerships to their customers.

Most employees of public companies can get some stock almost without trying. Stock purchase plans, company matching in savings plans, and stock options are all paid in the same coin—the employer's stock. The employer likes to do this because it ties the fortunes of the employee very firmly to the company, but perhaps too firmly. For every worker who took home a bundle of stock and got rich, there may be a worker whose wealth turned to waste paper when the company ran into trouble. People Express, the innovative airline of the 1980s, paid every employee a 25 percent bonus in stock. While the airline grew and the stock rose, flight attendants and ground personnel worked with passionate enthusiasm because they could see themselves getting richer every day. But when People Express overexpanded, lost money, and the stock fell, bitter workers helped kick the company down to oblivion.

People Express went from rags to riches to rags in less than seven years, but the experience of IBM demonstrates the same problem on a longer time scale. Tens of thousands of IBMers lost their jobs in the early 1990s and saw their accumulated IBM stock decline in value by 75 percent. They were forcibly retired just as their investments were less able to support them; and their investments were less able to support them because of the ill fortune that forced them into retirement.

If there's one stock you should not load up on, it's the one of the company on which you already depend for a salary and a pension.

FEARFULLY VULNERABLE

Many investors believe they have steeled themselves to the volatility in stocks, but in fact they are still afraid. The only thing a diversified investor ought to fear is fear itself and the people who play on fear. Ask yourself if you find this offering attractive:

You can buy a certificate of deposit that offers "stock market returns" while also offering FDIC insurance like a bank. That means, as the ads in *The Wall Street Journal* trumpeted, "zero risk to principal."

If you're attracted by the combination of zero risk and stock market returns, you are ready to be suckered. Marketed heavily by Citibank in 1992, these CDs are a classic example of investment mislabeling.

Here's how the Citibank CDs work: invest at least $10,000 for five years, just like a regular CD. But instead of paying a steady, if paltry, interest rate, the CD just sits there in the bank. At the end of the five years, Citibank promises to average all the end-of-the-month prices of the Standard & Poors index of 500 stocks during the five years. Then that average is compared with the value of the S&P index when the CD was purchased. That difference is then doubled, and paid to the customer.

The minimum rate of return on this instrument is zero and zero is what might be paid even if the S&P index five years out is much higher than the starting point. If the S&P first sinks and stays low for several years, and then rises dramatically at the end of the five-year term, a stock investor could be up substantially, while the CD holder is stuck at the starting gate because all the prices for five years were averaged. Worse, the Citibank CD is much less liquid than an index fund. A discouraged investor or one who needs to liquidate his investment to meet an emergency must pay a 30 percent penalty for withdrawal in the first year—25 percent in the second year, 20 percent in the third year, 15 percent in the fourth year, and 10 percent in the fifth year.

Even winners don't win big. The so-called stock market returns don't include dividends, even though many S&P 500 stocks pay generous dividends. Even in 1993, when yields were at historic lows, the S&P 500 stocks paid nearly 3 percent a year in dividends—not a trivial addition to the long-term 10 percent or 11 percent average annual price increase that the S&P index tends to tally over most five-year periods. Those ignored dividends, by the way, go a long way toward matching Citibank's guaranteed principal: the last losing five-year stretch for the S&P 500 index ran from 1973 to 1978, when the index of stock prices declined nearly 20 percent. But even in that sad span, the holder who reinvested dividends would have posted a loss of merely 1.1 percent. What Citibank offers to do with federal deposit insurance the stocks themselves do with dividends. A no-load mutual fund investing in the S&P 500, such as those offered by Vanguard and Fidelity, charges much less than 1 percent a year in expenses.

Residential Equity

Like generals preparing to fight the last war, a majority of Americans are concentrating their long-term equity investments in the one asset class that offered the best return in their formative years—their houses.

Houses appreciated in value dramatically from 1970 to 1990, the very years when most members of the baby-boom generation were settling down, raising families, and buying houses. Many saw the price of their first house double or triple, and on a house financed with a down payment of 10 percent or less, that means they saw their equity investment increase tenfold or more. Few people ever get so lucky in the stock market, and almost nobody ever consistently does that well in any investment.

Now Americans continue to put as much money as they can into houses, but they may not be doing it the right way. During the record low interest rates of 1993, many homeowners who refinanced did so in order to shorten the term of their mortgage, thus increasing their equity in their house and reducing interest charges over the life of the loan.[1]

Reducing interest charges is a tax-free form of investment, even though the returns must be discounted because they happen so far in the future. But mortgage interest rates in 1993 sank below 7 percent, with deep discounts for shorter terms and adjustable rates. With the tax deduction for home mortgage interest, a householder would pay less on his loan than the average inflation rate of the previous five, ten, or twenty years. Real interest rates, after inflation and after tax, were negative, which is another way of saying that banks were paying you to borrow. The last time mortgage interest rates were negative was in the late 1970s, and that period was followed by a large inflation that rewarded borrowers, such as the people who bought homes with low down payments, and penalized lenders, such as the bankers who made those loans. When you take the side of a lender, you run a lender's risks.

Equity in a home is an investment that pays no dividends except the interest avoided at the end of the loan term. If it pays capital gains, in the form of price appreciation, it pays the same gain to the homeowner with a great deal of equity as it does to the homeowner with very little equity. On the downside, if the price of homes should collapse, the loss comes out of equity. A homeowner with substantial equity will lose money if he sells while the highly leveraged homeowner may just walk away without a loss of cash (morally reprehensible, but financially shrewd). And in the static case of a house market where prices stay roughly the same, the homeowner who refinances and takes money out can put his money in another investment; the homeowner who refinances and increases his equity will register a subpar return on his investment.

17

FIXED-INCOME
INVESTMENTS

THE BULK OF a personal retirement fund should be held in stocks, directly or through mutual funds. But most investors want some part of their future to be a little more secure, even if it means sacrificing growth. Younger investors, those under fifty, should certainly have three-quarters to 90 percent of their investment portfolio in stocks, but when the stock market starts reaching historic highs it's understandable that even aggressive growth-oriented investors would want to pull back a little. "Sell high" makes sense, and you can't "buy low" if you buy high.

So here are some words on fixed-income investments, from bank deposits to bonds. Generally, selecting a fixed-income investment means guessing about interest rates during the term of the investment: if you think interest rates are high or going lower, then you should look for a long-term investment to "lock in" a yield that will look better and better as time goes on—if you're right. If you think rates are low or going higher, you should consider a short-term investment that will give you a chance to reinvest later when rates are higher.

Think of a fixed-income investment as the flip side of a decision about financing a home. In mortgage finance you try to lock in the lowest, most favorable rates, and you try to have floating rates or balloon payments when rates are high and might drop to more favorable levels.

Inflation and taxes must be factored in when deciding whether rates are high or low. You want to guess whether or not inflation and taxes will reduce the value of your investment faster than interest payments increase it. This is called the real after-tax rate of return, adjusted for inflation. The nominal rate of return, without adjustments, may be very high, but if inflation is even higher, a fixed-income investment becomes a way of destroying wealth. Taxes, of course, mean that every dollar earned as interest is worth no more than eighty-five cents and as little as fifty cents.

The most basic fixed-income investment, the one everybody used to start with, is a savings account in a bank. Perhaps you remember the days of 5 percent passbook savings accounts—5.25 percent if your account was with a savings and loan. Before inflation drove the deregulation of financial services, that was about all that a small-time saver could choose.

Today, anyone with $1,000 or more probably stashes it in a money-market mutual fund or an interest-bearing checking account. Money-market funds are mutual funds that hold very short-term obligations of corporations, banks, and government agencies. They usually credit interest daily, keep the price of a share at exactly one dollar, and allow depositors to withdraw money using special checks. They are not insured by the federal government. Interest-bearing checking accounts at insured banks operate just like regular checking accounts, and are covered by federal deposit insurance.

For terms of three months or more, banks offer a wall chart full of certificates of deposit, at various yields and terms to maturity. Certificates at federally insured banks carry the guarantee of the Federal Deposit Insurance Corp., up to $100,000 per account holder per bank. A person with more than $100,000 to deposit should open accounts at several banks to be sure that he never exceeds the $100,000 insurance limit at any one bank.

CHANGING INCOME

Many "fixed-income" investors received shocks in the early 1990s when their longer-term certificates of deposit started coming due in a period of sharply lower interest rates. Somebody who had a five-year CD at 11 percent could easily be shocked when offered the chance to reinvest at only 6 percent for a five-year certificate and even less for a shorter term. And a shocked investor is often a foolish investor: reaching for a higher yield requires an investor to assume more risk. Not everybody who listened to a broker or a TV ad and bought Ginnie Mae certificates, junk bond mutual funds, zero-coupon Treasury bonds, or other vehicles with attractive yields really understood the important point that high yields are paid to compensate for higher risk to principal.

A sensible tactic for a person trying to figure out how to reinvest a maturing CD may be to split the original sum into several parts. Take your $10,000 CD and invest $5,000 for one year, and $5,000 for five years. Or, if you really think rates are low, maybe $2,500 for six months, $2,500 for one year, and $5,000 for two years would be the strategy that feels right.

But more importantly, retirement assets don't really belong in a bank certificate of deposit. Fixed rates of return are a trap when interest rates rise, and all securities, both equity and debt, tend to go up when interest rates fall. Bank deposits are for people too lazy or too fearful to work on their investments themselves. Federal deposit insurance helps the banks play on this fear. Your money is safe because it's backed by Uncle Sam, they say, never mentioning that the flip side of safety is a submarket rate of return.

In 1993, moreover, the federal government quietly reduced the safety margin for risk-averse depositors. Effective December 19, 1993, FDIC insurance was reduced on self-directed retirement accounts, such as Individual Retirement Accounts, Keogh plans for self-employed people, 401(k) workplace savings plans, and 457 plans for employees of nonprofit corporations and state and local governments. Instead of being able to have $100,000 of FDIC insurance for each of the four types of plans, the rule cut insurance to $100,000 total. So a depositor with, say, $75,000 in a Keogh and $85,000 in an IRA at the same bank has $60,000 uninsured. This person would not have so much money in a bank if he were not so frightened of losing principal that he depends on federal deposit insurance to help him sleep at night. To get full insurance, he would have to take some of his money to another bank.

Actually, he ought to walk over to the stockbroker's desk now found in many banks and open an account. The same federal government that insures his bank account will sell him Treasury bonds, or the broker will help him select a T-bond mutual fund with an average maturity that suits him.

There's usually a little better yield in a Treasury security at any maturity term than in a bank certificate of deposit, and there may be a little extra security investing directly in the federal government, as compared to the federal guarantee of deposit insurance. Even better, the interest payments on all Treasury securities are free of state and local income tax, though not federal tax.

Treasury securities are also more liquid than fixed-term CDs. There is always an active trading market in "seasoned" Treasury securities, and a broker or bank can convert them to cash readily. This attractive feature can, however, be a two-edged sword. Just as with stocks, it's easy enough to look up the quote on your investment in the newspaper and be frightened by a drop in the market into selling low or bullied by a high price into selling to lock in a profit. An active investor must be disciplined, buying or selling for a good reason, not for a twinge of fear or greed.

All fixed-income securities trade in an aftermarket, and there are a few simple keys to understanding that market. Regardless of maturity, a fixed-income security is just that: it pays a particular amount of interest over its life. When the money market moves to raise or lower the general rate of interest, the interest payment associated with a fixed-income security does not change. So the price of the security moves instead. The prices of fixed-income securities move inversely with interest rates—up when rates fall, down when rates rise.

If the market rate and the interest rate of the fixed payment happen to coincide, the security sells at par, or one hundred cents on the dollar. If the market rate is higher than the fixed payment rate, the security sells at a discount, less than one hundred cents on the dollar. And if the market rate is lower, the security sells at a premium, more than 100 cents on the dollar.

One further factor affects the market for non-Treasury debt securities. At least in theory, market prices assume that the U.S. Treasury will not default on its obligations. Corporations and municipalities, however, may find it impossible to pay back what they owe. So the price of every security incorporates the market rate of return plus a risk premium to compensate investors for assuming the risk of default. The risk premium expands and contracts according to the mood of the marketplace and the market's assessment of each borrower.

Most short-term fixed-income securities with maturities of less than a year, whether Treasury bills or corporate debt instruments, don't make periodic interest payments. Instead, they pay all interest at maturity, and they do so by redeeming at par a security that was sold at a discount. Thus a one-year bill intended to pay 5 percent per year sells at 95.24 cents on the dollar and is redeemed at one hundred cents on the dollar. (Note that the interest is earned on the 95.24 cents invested, not on the dollar that represents return of principal and payment of interest.) During the year, interest rates will fluctuate, and the price of the bill will rise and fall with the market rate for the remaining term of the bill.

Debt securities with longer terms pay interest at intervals, usually every six months. They sell at a discount or premium representing the present value of the stream of interest payments plus the present value of the future repayment of principal. The longer the term of the debt security, the more the market price must change to incorporate the appropriate adjustment for a change in interest rates. So long bonds—thirty years is usually the longest term—are the most volatile debt securities in the marketplace.

The most volatile long bonds, moreover, are zero-coupon bonds, which are bonds that promise to pay principal and all accumulated interest in one lump sum at the end of their term. They are sold at deep discounts and redeemed at par. In the meantime, their price fluctuates to reflect the present value at present interest rates of all the unpaid interest that's accumulating. Zero-coupon bonds are sold by corporations and government agencies. Some financiers also convert Treasury bonds into zero-coupon bonds by stripping the right to receive interest payments from the right to receive repayment of principal.

One feature of zero-coupon bonds makes them tricky for the individual investor. The IRS wants investors to pay tax on zero-coupon bonds as the interest is earned, even though it won't be paid in cash for years to come. This makes them unattractive to tax-paying accounts, and more suitable for tax-sheltered accounts such as Individual Retirement Accounts.

Some corporate and municipal bonds are short-term instruments masquerading as long-term investments. They have call provisions, which allow the issuer to pay them off at par or some price near par long before their stated maturity. Issuers do this when interest rates are so far below the issuing rate that they can replace high-cost debt with new debt that will cost less to service. An investor who buys a bond without noting a call provision can lose a lot of anticipated interest, and be forced to reinvest at a lower rate.

BUYING BILLS AND BONDS

An investor buys Treasury securities through a bank or a broker, to be held in his account. They can be original issue or they can be purchased in the trading market, which is highly efficient and gives a price that accurately reflects the money market. Either way, a bank or a broker will charge a service fee or commission—not large but not insignificant. To avoid any charge, you can buy original issue securities direct from the Treasury, though this requires a little more work on your part.

Tender forms for Treasury securities are available by phone, by mail, or in person from any of thirty-seven servicing offices throughout the country. You fill out the form, checking the box marked "noncompetitive," which means that you will accept the average rate at the next Treasury auction, and specifying the amount and type of security you wish to buy. The minimum for T-bills is $10,000 face amount, increasing by multiples of $5,000. You may pay with certified personal checks, teller's checks, matured Treasury securities, Treasury redemption checks, or even cash. Checks must be payable to your regional

Federal Reserve Bank or to the Bureau of the Public Debt if you buy direct from the Treasury in Washington. Part of the process requires opening a Treasury Direct Account so that the government can pay principal and interest directly into your checking account. When purchasing bills, you may request that your money be reinvested, for up to eight reinvestments of a thirteen-week bill, up to four reinvestments of a twenty-six-week bill, and up to two reinvestments for a fifty-two-week bill.

You submit your tender to the Federal Reserve Bank or branch serving your area, or to the Bureau of Public Debt if you live in the Washington, D.C., area. You may go in person on the morning of the auction, but it's more convenient to use the mail. A bid must be received by the date of the auction and postmarked no later than midnight the day before the auction.

Many individual investors buy another kind of federal debt security that is not a fixed-income security at all. Some investors, sadly, are not aware of the strange variable features of mortgage pass-through securities issued mostly by "Ginnie Mae," the Government National Mortgage Corp.; "Freddie Mac," the Federal Home Loan Mortgage Corp.; and "Fannie Mae," the Federal National Mortgage Assn. They are pools of home mortgages, and the security entitles the holder to receive a share of the principal and interest payments on those mortgages. Timely payment is not the issue, since the lure for most such securities is that payments are guaranteed by a government agency. The issue is that homeowners pay off their mortgages early when they move or when they refinance. The amount the investor receives each month fluctuates according to the repayments that happen to take place in the particular pool of mortgages.

In a further complication, financiers have seized on the pre-payment problem and created derivative securities known as Collateralized Mortgage Obligations and Real Estate Mortgage Investment Conduits, which arrange different shares and different orders of payments of principal and interest or just one or the other. By picking different slices of the total pool, an investor bets on future interest rates and on the pattern of future prepayments. These securities are too weird for the average individual, but brokers are willing, even eager, to sell them to investors hungry for yield. They come in amounts down to $1,000. Usually there's no commission; instead the individual pays a price subject to a markup or markdown. Many individuals are involved in CMOs and REMICs without knowing it, because managers of fixed-income mutual funds use them to boost their yields.

There is one simple, old-fashioned savings vehicle that is still attractive in the modern market. U.S. Series EE Savings Bonds offer a competitive fixed rate (of 4–7 percent in mid-1994), or 85 percent of the average yield on five-year Treasury notes issued during the preceding six months—whichever is higher. For small investors, this is a fixed-income investment if rates fall and a variable-rate investment if rates rise. Heads you win, tails Uncle Sam loses. In addition, the interest is not subject to federal income tax until the savings bonds are cashed in, and it may not be taxable at all if they are used to pay college tuition. A savings bond must be held for six months, and then it can be cashed in at any bank. The minimum investment is fifty dollars, and they are for sale at banks, free of commission or sales charge.

UNDERSTANDING ANNUITIES

Bank deposits, debt securities, and savings bonds all keep principal and interest payments separate. Another fixed-income investment, the annuity, combines them. The word "annuity" is related to the word "annual," and it means a yearly payment. In finance, an annuity is a stream of periodic payments for a term of years, at an interest rate. Given statements of the size and frequency of the payments, the term, and the interest rate, it is a fairly simple compound-interest calculation to determine the present, lump-sum value of a future stream of payments—in other words, to state the price of an annuity. The calculation is simply the reverse of the calculation to determine how much money will be in a savings account after a term of years if one makes regular deposits of a certain size at a fixed interest rate compounded periodically.

Financiers (usually insurance companies) can then add complexity: delayed annuities that don't begin to pay for years after the price is first paid; variable annuities that don't pay at a fixed interest rate but instead pay according to the earnings of some investment; annuities that pay for a lifetime rather than for a fixed term. A defined benefit pension that is funded 100 percent is an annuity of deposits followed by a lifetime annuity of withdrawals to the employee. However, it must be recalculated every time the deposit amount changes because of pay raises, every time the payment amount changes because of benefit increases, every time interest rates of available investments change, and every time life expectancies change. Making this calculation for every individual employee and then adding the results to determine whether a pension plan is adequately funded is a job for an actuary.

Fixed annuities, which attracted $23.3 billion in 1992, are like certificates of deposit. You hand over a lump sum—usually $5,000 or more—and the insurer guarantees payments of principal and interest based on a fixed rate of interest for one to five years. The annuity is reset with a market rate when the term expires. Variable annuities are similar to tax-deferred mutual funds; they let you put your money in the insurer's stock and bond portfolios and the yield varies with those investments. They attracted $14.6 billion of investment in 1992.

Annuities of both types carry expense charges that average 2.25 percent a year, and insurance companies levy surrender charges of up to 7 percent the first year, dropping by one percentage point each subsequent year. As with other tax-deferred retirement investments, the government charges a 10 percent tax penalty on earnings withdrawn before the age of fifty-nine and one-half.

The key point in an annuity is that it pays out both principal and interest for the term, and when that term, whether an indefinite term such as a lifetime, or a definite term of years, is finished, the annuity expires and there is no remaining balance. Most defined benefit pensions are paid as annuities—when the pensioner dies, the benefit ends. For individual investors planning retirement, the annuity increases income and reduces one's estate. This matters a great deal to people who have worked all their lives in part to provide an estate for their children and grandchildren. Such people would prefer to live on the income and not invade principal, and should avoid annuities in their personal investments.

CHAPTER

18

TAX SHELTERS

EVEN BEFORE THE hefty personal income tax increases of 1993, there was no long-term investment that could not benefit from a healthy tax shelter. There's nothing like having Uncle Sam for a silent partner, both in the good old days of a 28 percent maximum federal tax rate, and in the contemporary case of a 39 percent federal tax rate plus 11 percent more in state and local income tax.

Tax-free municipal and state bonds have long been the favorite tax shelter for the wealthy. The federal government gives a subsidy to the borrowing of lower levels of government, so that municipal and state bond interest is not taxed as income by federal, state, or local governments. That means people in the highest tax brackets, in high-tax states like Massachusetts, California, and New York, can earn as much as twice the stated yield on these bonds. Mutual funds comprising portfolios of bonds from single states are readily available.

Municipal bond investors may, however, be subject to the alternative minimum tax, by which the government takes back with the left hand some of what it gave with the right. The alternative minimum tax is levied according to the taxpayer's use of many tax preferences, including municipal bonds. It may bite you when you least expect it.

There are huge quantities of municipal bonds outstanding and many more billions issued every year. States and counties and towns vary widely in their credit quality, and bond rating agencies can't keep up with every shift of the political and economic winds in every corner of our nation. So although defaults are uncommon, sudden rating changes and price changes can surprise the municipal bond investor.

Another problem often arises in the municipal bond market, most recently in the summer of 1993. When Congress legislates a tax increase, investors sometimes crowd together in search of a tax-sheltered investment. They cash out of other investments and bid up the price of municipal bonds, up to and beyond the point of erasing the new tax advantage. It's another, predictable variation on "buy low, sell high." Municipal bonds also become popular at the end of the year and in March and April, when people are thinking seriously about taxes.

Fortunately, the retirement investor has other tax-exempt options, ones that can even cover securities and other investments that are not normally tax-free.

Meeting IRA

An Individual Retirement Account is the basic low-budget tax shelter. You may contribute up to $2,000 a year, and it may be tax-deductible, depending on your income and whether you're covered by a pension plan at work. Workers with no employer-sponsored retirement plan, and workers earning less than $25,000 who do have retirement plans, may deduct the full $2,000. Partial deductions are allowed for higher incomes. An eligible married worker whose spouse does not work may deduct $2,250. Anyone may make a nondeductible contribution of up to $2,000 to an IRA, and all earnings are tax-deferred until withdrawal.

A person in the 28 percent tax bracket who makes monthly deposits of $167 to a savings account paying 8 percent will have $75,728 after 20 years; a person who calls the account an IRA, so that there is no tax due on the interest earned, will have $82,354. Since the tax you're avoiding is levied on interest and dividends but not on capital gains, an IRA is the right vehicle for the high-yield part of your personal portfolio—such investments as bonds, certificates of deposit, and stocks that pay substantial dividends.

IRAs are portable investments. Once a year, you can move them to or from banks, mutual funds, or brokerages, and you may switch investments at the same custodian as often as you like. Virtually any kind of security is an acceptable IRA investment. To make a switch, you can personally withdraw your money from the old IRA and transfer the money into the new IRA, but if you hold the money more than sixty days, you'll pay taxes and penalties, and the feds will withhold 20 percent of the withdrawal. The direct transfer is a better route: set up a new account and have the new custodian transfer the money directly from the old account. Many new account forms include the forms for a transfer from another custodian.

Although it's not a good idea, some people are forced to withdraw their money from an IRA before retirement. A normal withdrawal before age fifty-nine and one-half carries the usual tax plus 10 percent penalty, but you can get some of your money at any age with tax but no penalty by taking "substantially equal periodic payments." Divide the total in the fund by your life expectancy to find the allowable annual payment. Once you start taking equal periodic payments, you must continue for at least five years or until you reach fifty-nine, whichever is longer.

So don't let the fear of locking your money up deter you from making annual deposits to an IRA. Besides, if you have such a financial emergency that you are tapping your IRA, one of your problems is likely to be loss of income. You will pay less tax if you do withdraw. The benefits of tax-free appreciation before the crisis will outweigh the penalty for early withdrawal.

IRAs have been around long enough for the government to make a serious muddle out of them. At times, such as the early to mid-1980s, anybody could make a tax-deductible $2,000 contribution, regardless of income. At other times, many people's contributions could not be deducted. Beware of having an IRA that contains both deducted and nondeducted contributions.

When the time comes to withdraw, you will (if tax law stays the same) have to calculate what part of your withdrawal is tax-free as a return of your nondeducted contribution, and pay taxes on the deducted contributions and the earnings. Don't get involved: establish separate IRAs for deducted and nondeducted contributions.

WORKING KEOGH

A Keogh plan (named for the otherwise obscure congressman who wrote the enabling provision of the tax law) is a retirement plan for self-employed persons and unincorporated businesses. Keoghs can be used for persons who have some self-employment income in addition to a regular salary, though the contribution percentages are figured only on the self-employment income. Most Keoghs are defined contribution plans—that is, you define how much you put in every year, without regard to ultimate payout. There are two basic types of defined contribution Keoghs: money-purchase plans and profit-sharing plans. A third variation, called a paired plan, is a combination of the two.

In a money-purchase plan, participants are allowed to contribute up to what the IRS calls 25 percent of earnings, but that's earnings less the contribution, so it works out to just over 20 percent. There is also a limit of $30,000 on the annual contribution. Once established, the percentage must be contributed every year. Any change in the percentage of earnings contributed requires a legal amendment.

Profit-sharing plans don't commit the business to any fixed percentage of earnings, and a contribution doesn't have to be made at all. The maximum contribution is 15 percent of earnings less the contribution, or about 13 percent of earnings.

To open a Keogh, you do not have to be self-employed full-time. So nothing stops you from having other kinds of retirement savings plans, such as an IRA, at the same time.

Keogh plans have a reputation for complexity, and they are too complicated for businesses that have employees. But they are simple for people with self-employment income.

KEEP IT SIMPLE

Simplified Employee Pensions work like a combination of the IRA and the Keogh and are best suited to small businesses with some employees. If your business isn't incorporated, you can contribute a tax-deductible 20 percent of net income, up to $30,000, to a Simplified Employee Pension.

The SEP offers more flexibility with less paperwork. As with a regular IRA or a Keogh profit-sharing plan, you do not have to put in any specific amount per year. The maximum contribution is 15 percent, IRS style, which works out to about 13 percent of business income. And the maximum is $30,000 a year for each participant.

In effect, the employer sets up Individual Retirement Accounts for each worker and contributes to each account up to 15 percent of pay or $30,000, whichever is less. These IRAs are administered by a financial institution, such as a bank, brokerage, mutual fund company, or insurance company, under contract with the employer. The contributions are tax-deductible to the employer and not taxed as employee income. Just as in an IRA, the employee owns the money in the account, and can even withdraw it, subject to the usual IRA penalties. There are no federal filing or reporting requirements, although the employer must comply with certain rules. These include a requirement to include every worker over age twenty-one employed at least three of the past five years, including part-timers who make as little as $363 a year, and a restriction on "top-heavy" plans in which more than 60 percent of the contributions go to owners, officers, or high-paid employees.

Any business, no matter how small or large, can set up a Simplified Employee Pension. For businesses with no more than twenty-five employees, there is a Salary Reduction Simplified Employee Pension, created under a 1986 law. In this one, which can be set up if at least half the employees agree, workers can contribute to their own accounts up to 15 percent of their pretax wages or $8,728, whichever is less. At the same time employers can contribute to their workers' regular Simplified Employee Pension accounts, as long as the total contributions don't exceed the annual limit of 15 percent or $30,000.

The Simplified Employee Pension is a good straightforward and honest tax shelter for both employer and employee. Everyone in a small business ought to have one. But the Small Business Administration reports that less than 5 percent of the 41 million employees of small businesses have access to a Simplified Employee Pension plan, and the Bureau of Labor Statistics, working from a different survey that excluded part-time workers, says 1 percent of small-business employees participate in a Simplified Employee Pension.[1] So what's the matter?

Employers, remember, do not sponsor pension plans out of the goodness of their hearts, or to solve social problems of the United States in the twenty-first century. They want to compete successfully in the market for labor. They want to attract productive workers and encourage work effort. They may want to reduce turnover, but that may not be very important in low-skill, low-wage jobs.

Small-business associations and the government officials assigned to help small businesses report that any kind of pension arrangement is just too costly for most small businesses. They are already paying all they can to attract the workers they have, who are generally younger, lower-paid, less likely to be in a union, and more likely to leave for reasons unrelated to the job than other workers. Also, the Simplified Employee Pension is just too simple. It covers virtually all workers, whether they want to be covered or not. It sets the pension contribution as a percentage of pay rather than a share of profit, which seems too dangerous to the proprietor of a new or shaky business.

Also, many employers are sophisticated enough to realize that a Congress that passes major changes in pension law every year is not going to leave the Simplified Employee Pension alone. Every change in rules costs money to administer.

Another important reason for the failure of the Simplified Employee Pension is that it may be a little bit too fair. Employers who care at all about pensions probably want to use them to hold workers' loyalty. They would rather delay vesting of retirement benefits, and so they choose some other form of deferred compensation (stock options are popular in high-tech, high-skill start-ups) or they forget the whole thing. A bigger fairness item, however, is the restriction on top-heavy plans. A small business with one owner and one clerical employee is inevitably top-heavy. All too often those rules create a paperwork mess, and less security, and no pension at all, fair or not.

Use the 401(k)

An employer may offer a company-sponsored savings plan under section 401(k) of the tax law. There are also 403(b) and 457 plans for nonprofit and government employers. If your employer creates a 401(k) plan, you can set aside a percentage of your pretax income for a contribution, up to a maximum of $9,240 in 1994. Successive years' limits will be increased with inflation. The 403(b) allows up to $9,500 and the 457 allows up to $7,500, but they are not indexed. The employer may choose to match your contributions, and about three-fourths of them do.

Benefits to you are an immediate tax deduction, tax-deferred compounding of your investment, extra pay from the employer, and a relatively painless automatic deduction system for your savings. There's no better deal around, and most people recognize it. After only a decade, 401(k) plans hold more than $400 billion, some 14 percent of private pension assets. Most analysts expect 401(k) plans to become the dominant retirement vehicle of the twenty-first century.

A typical 401(k) program calls for the company to deposit stock in your plan at the rate of fifty cents' worth for every dollar you contribute, up to 6 percent of your pay. This is not much of a pension contribution but it's a great return on your savings. Every dollar you put into this bank at work is as good as putting $1.76 in a regular bank on Main Street if you are in the lowest tax bracket. It's as good as depositing $2.54 if you are in the highest bracket. All persons, of any age and any income, should contribute the maximum to a 401(k). They are simply throwing money away if they don't deposit at least enough to attract the maximum match from their employers.

Some workers treat their 401(k) plans as part of current pay: the employee puts in money to attract the employer's match and leaves it in just long enough to avoid penalties. Then it's withdrawn. The worker may think he's fooling somebody. In fact, he's only fooling himself.

Even if current income is what workers want, it makes more

sense for them to take their money in the form of a loan. Then they will pay money back to their own account with interest, perhaps more interest than the money would have earned in the 401(k) account. Also, the money they receive as a loan is not taxable, as cash taken from their paychecks would be, so Uncle Sam doesn't take a share.

Investments for most 401(k) and similar plans are directed by each participant. Unfortunately, many 401(k) plans offer too few investment choices, too little flexibility, and hardly any information about performance and expenses. Workers, who directly pay the administrative costs of 401(k) plans at many companies, have little or no say about the choice of managers or investments.

As of 1994, the government is requiring employers to offer at least three different investment types, and to explain the risks of each vehicle. Companies and sponsors, however, are reluctant to give advice because that would increase their responsibility to participants.

A company could comply with the new rule by offering its own stock, a fund of Guaranteed Investment Contracts, and a stock fund. That's far too little choice, though it would be an improvement at some companies that haven't yet even bothered to offer the stock fund.

The Securities and Exchange Commission is considering a requirement that all retirement savings plans file annual reports and prospectuses as mutual funds do. The report would also reveal fees and expenses. Currently, employees have the right to receive annual reports of their 401(k) plans. They do list assets and investments and provide some performance measures.

As with many defined contribution plans, there are problems in the 401(k) system with employees' investing too conservatively and withdrawing the money instead of leaving it to grow. The Wyatt Company, a pension consulting firm, has compared the rates of return on retirement plans directed by individuals with professionally directed retirement plans. Wyatt found individuals sacrificed two to three percentage points of return by their too-conservative investment choices.

The biggest mistake 401(k) participants make is putting too much money in fixed-income investments, such as bonds, Guaranteed Investment Contracts, and money-market funds. They should be putting more of their money in stocks. Unfortunately, a 1991 survey of large 401(k) plans by Hewitt Associates showed that employees put 47 percent of their money in fixed-income investments, primarily Guaranteed Investment Contracts, 7 percent into investments balanced between growth and income, 15 percent in pure equity investment vehicles, and 25 percent in company stock. The rest was categorized as miscellaneous.

Although 401(k) investors should be more heavily in the stock market, buying company stock is the second biggest investment mistake participants make. A worker already depends on his company for his salary, his benefits, and his pension. He should take every opportunity to diversify into other equities that would prosper if his company falters. Some companies, though, push their employees to load up on company stock: Anheuser-Busch will not match employees' 401(k) contributions unless half the contribution goes to company shares. All of the company's match, of course, comes in the form of stock.

If you change jobs, you can choose to stay in the 401(k) plan until you retire or you can roll over your account into an IRA, being sure to establish the IRA first and order a direct transfer to avoid the 20 percent withholding. Leaving your savings in the 401(k) may be an advantage if you want the money in a lump sum on retirement, because you can reduce your tax somewhat with a five-year forward averaging method. If you want gradual payouts or to wait until age seventy and one-half to begin payouts, roll it over to an IRA.

Generally speaking, 401(k) and 403(b) savings plans are as safe as the underlying investments. Employers do not directly affect safety because the investments are fully funded and held in trust at banks or other independent institutions. That does not apply to Section 457 savings plans, an investment vehicle for more than 700,000 state and local government employees.

These plans offer tax-sheltered deposits of up to one-third of income or $7,500, whichever is less, but unlike a 401(k) or a 403(b), the money in a 457 plan belongs to the state or local government that offers the program, not to the employee. The municipality or state could confiscate or "borrow" 457 assets to pay damages in a lawsuit or satisfy creditors in a bankruptcy, even if the employees were not involved in the lawsuit and did not contribute to the bankruptcy.

It's never happened yet, but it could. Creditors have never attached 457 assets, and no municipality that has gone bankrupt since the creation of 457 plans has used employee assets to pay creditors. No state has gone bankrupt since the early nineteenth century. Most 457 accounts are kept and managed separately from other government accounts, which may reduce risk. Better, though, are the governments and agencies that use 403(b) plans, which cannot be attached by creditors. But if the only choice is between a risky tax-deferred savings plan and a safer taxable plan, go with the tax deferral but keep your eyes open. Be aware of the added risk, but don't be frightened away unnecessarily.

The rise of 401(k) plans, justly popular among workers and employers, has given rise to critics. Some people say that savings plans are unfair to people who can't afford to save. Karen Ferguson, a consumer advocate from the Pension Rights Center in Washington, would actually end 401(k) plans entirely, or at least sharply cut the tax preferences for them. She argues that no amount of education will induce lower-paid workers to save, while higher-paid workers would save even without the tax benefits. And she says 401(k)s are too cheap an alternative for the employer: "If companies no longer had the easy escape route of 401(k)s, most would reinstate or improve their traditional pension and profit-sharing plans."[2]

Ferguson's preference is to force workers to save by fooling them—either with a mandate that employers create private pension systems or by creating another public retirement system on top of Social Security. Both ideas will raise the cost of hiring a worker and reduce the number of jobs available in the economy. The benefits received in retirement by those who do work will probably not match the increased cost of unemployment benefits and welfare for those driven out of work.

Surveys of 401(k) participants that show lower-paid workers with less participation in savings plans also show that these workers are younger, less experienced, and more likely to be women. They save more as they age and rise in the company, and enough of the women are covered by a husband's savings to equalize the percentage of savers by gender.

LIVE WITH INSURANCE

The most traditional form of tax-deferred investment is life insurance. There are two basic types of life insurance—term and cash-value. Term is pure insurance—pay until you die, then they pay. You pay an annual premium for a year's coverage, although some policies allow the premium to rise every year and others hold it steady over a longer period by overcharging at the beginning of the period and undercharging at the end.

The other forms of life insurance, such as whole life, universal life, and variable life, combine term insurance and a tax-sheltered investment account. After commissions and expenses, the premium is invested with the insurance company. Depending on the form, the company guarantees a rate of return, offers a variable return that will track a stock or bond portfolio, or fudges the issue.

This permanent, cash-value life insurance is a tax shelter—the earnings on invested premiums (known as inside buildup) aren't taxed as long as the insurance company holds the money. But it takes ten to fifteen years for the tax-deferred buildup inside a life insurance policy to overcome the initial weight of commissions and expenses.

If you have funded your IRA and your 401(k) to the limits and still have money to invest long-term, then you might consider some form of permanent insurance. Under current law, there's no limit on the amount of money that can be put to work tax-deferred in an insurance policy. There have been many attempts in Congress to reduce the tax shelter of life insurance, but the insurance lobby has beaten them all.

For many years, life insurance was a poor investment. After subtracting the true cost of the financial protection against sudden death, the remaining investment value of whole life insurance was often negligible, which meant in turn that the tax advantage was often irrelevant. More recently, insurance companies have been teaming up with brokers to offer a combination mutual fund and life insurance option called variable life. The advantage over mutual funds is the tax deferral on inside buildup; the advantage over life insurance is the mutual fund investment, which may provide a better return on money invested.

In addition to basic variable life insurance, companies also offer a retirement vehicle called a variable annuity. This policy also is invested in mutual funds and gives returns based on the specific funds the purchaser chooses.

Variable annuities became popular in the 1980s because they combine the tax shelter available to life insurance products with the attractive returns that mutual funds have tallied. The investor buys shares in a mutual fund and a life insurance benefit at the same time. The life insurance policy states that even if the mutual funds lose value, the insurance company will pay at least the amount of contributions if the investor dies before receiving all contributions back from the annuity. This little gimmick is sufficient to defer all taxes on income and capital gains from the mutual fund, just as the inside buildup of policy values is deferred on life insurance.

A small additional advantage of a variable annuity is that the sheltered account need not begin paying taxable benefits as soon as other instruments, such as the 401(k), the Keogh, and the IRA. Most insurance companies offering variable annuities allow the investor to wait until age eighty-five to start drawing on them.

There can be a catch, or more than one. As with any insurance policy, beware of the insurance companies that drastically overcharge for the guaranteed death benefit, so that an investor gives his tax saving and more to the insurance company. As with any mutual fund investment, beware of the mutual funds that impose heavy up-front sales charges that reduce the amount being put to work on behalf of the investor. Also, exit fees and tax penalties require the investor to lock himself into a mutual fund investment for many years—almost certainly long enough for the investment manager to change and quite probably long enough for the fund to post a few bad years. At best, the investor will be offered the chance to switch into other funds of the same sponsor. The long horizon of the investment also may be long enough for the tax laws to change enough to make the whole thing less attractive.

One major advantage for variable policies in years past was they could serve as powerful contemporaneous tax shelters. The Internal Revenue Service had deemed that no tax was due on loans from the policy to the policyholder. Sponsoring insurance companies rigged up payout plans to take advantage of this feature so that the life insurance tax shelter extended beyond investment earnings to the actual payout of benefits. Congress firmly closed this loophole in 1990. Now any payment, including a loan, from a variable policy to a policyholder is subject to income tax, and if the policyholder is younger than age fifty-nine and one-half he must pay a 10 percent penalty tax as well.

Variable life plans also are limited to particular mutual funds, sometimes not many of them, in which one's payments may be invested. If those particular funds don't perform well, the investor can do little except hope for improvement: withdrawals for any reason will bear the tax and penalty if the owner is under age fifty-nine and one-half. The insurance company and mutual fund manager often add surrender penalties as well.

A variable annuity should not be your first tax-sheltered investment. An employer's defined contribution plan may accept employee contributions; you should certainly make the maximum tax-deductible contribution to a 401(k) and put $2,000 into an IRA.

Annual fees on variable annuities average 2.12 percent according to the VARDS Report, an annuity tracking service. That compares to 1.5 percent or less for the typical equity mutual fund. So if you consider a variable annuity, you should compare it to a similar low-fee mutual fund to be sure you aren't paying too much for the tax benefits.

Variable annuities are offered in every flavor and spin. Two good sources of independent information about them are the monthly publication *Annuity & Life Insurance Shopper* and the quarterly *Morningstar Variable Annuity/Life Performance Report*.

SPECIAL SHELTERS

With its higher marginal tax rates and lower rate on capital gains, the Clinton tax package of 1993 brought back much of the incentive and ability to create tax shelters. The idea is to convert personal income into capital gains, often by starting with a deductible expense. The human mind is infinitely variable, and nobody can foresee all the tax shelter dodges that will come before the public under the term tax-advantaged investment. Still, it is worth remembering that in all of these schemes, the expense that erases personal income is a certainty, while the capital gains are estimated and will be received some time in the future. In the heyday of tax shelters in the early 1980s, the capital gains all too often never came at all.

Any individual investor will find that his brokers and advisers can generate more tax-avoidance strategies than he ever imagined. Here's a sample:

- Congress wants to invest in low-income housing but doesn't want to invest tax money or directly increase the deficit. So tax law encourages creation of partnerships for tax advantage to invest in low-income housing. An investor who puts in $10,000 may stand to receive about $15,000 of tax credits, spread over twelve years. The more interesting question, though, is whether at the end of the period the investor gets his $10,000 back. Low-income housing wouldn't need a subsidy if it were a good investment on its own, and it's a rare housing project that's more valuable after years of wear and tear.
- The first $3,000 of losses on investments can be deducted against current income, and all investment losses can be deducted against present and future investment gains. A person who realizes a capital gain can sell some other investment at a loss to reduce income. And even if the investor really thought the stock would come back, he can sell at a loss and buy it back again thirty-one days later without having to erase the tax benefit. The lower new cost will mean that if the stock does rebound, there will be more taxable profit when it's sold, but the 1993 tax act has set the tax on capital gains at roughly 28 percent while raising the tax value of the loss deduction to as much as 48 percent. Commissions will eat into the benefit, though.
- Mutual fund investors sometimes avoid investing in funds with large unrealized capital gains because they will have to pay tax on those gains when they are realized and distributed as dividends. But an investor who sells stock at a loss can use those losses, even from prior years, to offset the

distribution gains. In effect, this increases his after-tax return.

- A person who makes charitable contributions can donate investments that have appreciated in value and take a tax deduction for the market price, rather than the cost. The alternative minimum tax limits the benefit of this strategy.

19

LIVING AFTER RETIREMENT

WHAT'S IT LIKE to be old?

Put on dark glasses, preferably scratched, to simulate the loss of acuity and the effect of cataracts on aging eyes. Stick cotton in your ears. Put a nose clip on and breathe through a straw, to simulate decreased lung capacity. Wear rubber gloves to simulate loss of feeling from arthritis. Now: Count the change in your pocket. Dump some pills from various bottles in your medicine chest and try to figure out what's what. Would such a person like to travel, play tennis, or do any of the things that once brought pleasure?[1]

Does this sound depressing? Sure, and the stereotypes include drinking too much or taking too much medication. Fortunately, however, there's some scientific knowledge about aging, also. The Baltimore Longitudinal Study on Aging has been giving psychological and physiological tests to a group of more than a thousand men since 1958. (Women were added to the study in 1978.) Here are some facts from the study:

- Mental performance rarely declines much before age seventy, even among those who complain that their memory seems to be failing them. Interestingly, women are better at recalling verbal information; men's memory works better on digits.

- Physical aging is related to a gradual decline in the effectiveness of the immune system. Old people get sicker more often and more seriously; they lose the ability to resist cancer. Men lose their hearing faster; women have slower reaction times.

The Health and Retirement Study being conducted by the University of Michigan's Institute for Social Research for the National Institute on Aging has also turned up many other important findings about the real world of aging:[2]

- Early retirement is often not a luxury but a painful necessity: poor health is the most important reason why people say they left their last job, and they cite chronic conditions like heart disease, back problems, diabetes, stroke, and lung disease.
- About 4.5 million Americans aged fifty-one to sixty-one had no health insurance in 1990.
- The median (half above and half below) household income of people in their fifties was $37,500 a year, and they had median assets of about $80,000.
- About 20 percent of people in this age bracket have virtually no assets.
- About 40 percent have no pension in sight at all.
- About half the people in this age bracket believe there is at least some chance they could be laid off within a year and believe, if that happens, that their chances of landing a new job are less than even.
- Nearly three-quarters wish there was some way they could retire gradually, phasing down from full-time to part-time work.

These slices of real life show that planning and foresight are required to complete a healthy life.

Vicki Robin, one of the authors of *Your Money or Your Life*, suggests a thought experiment for evaluating your interest in retirement. Think of something you really want, big or little, and compute how many hours you would have to work to earn the money for it. That new sports car of your dreams might take six months. Now: which would you rather have, a new sports car or six months of leisure? All right, scratch the car. A new carpet for the living room might represent three days' work. Which would you rather have, a carpet or three days of freedom? How about a day off or a week's groceries for the family? The beauty of this exercise is that you establish your own values for the constant trades anyone must make among labor, leisure, possessions, subsistence, and liberty. Not surprisingly, Ms. Robin wrote her book while living on $6,000 a year.

It's easy to say your job-related clothing costs and dry-cleaning bills will shrink, but how big a part of your budget are they anyway? You'll cut costs of commuting, but you won't stay home. Do you really think that both partners in a forty-year marriage will share so many activities happily enough that you can get by with one car? You can if you have to, but the point of planning for retirement is to be able to do it without sacrificing your favorite luxuries.

WHERE THE GRASS IS GREENER

Many people are ready to make one change: they move after retirement, seeking greater comfort, a less troublesome house, and lower expense. One type of place to look for a retirement home is in the kind of community tailor-made for impecunious transients, with many business opportunities in retailing and services and real estate: a university town. Palo Alto and Princeton have been bid out of reach, but towns like Ithaca, New York; Ann Arbor, Michigan; Eugene, Oregon; Austin, Texas; and Knoxville, Tennessee, combine a cost of living suitable for a student's budget with the cultural, artistic, and business opportunities of a big city.

In a 1992 Roper survey, only 18 percent of 1,296 people polled said that they felt their careers were personally and financially rewarding. All the rest, presumably, are good candidates for early retirement. But for your sake and the sake of everyone around you, don't retire too soon. You have too much ability to throw it all away. What's so terrible about that job, anyway? You're used to it. And if you enjoy your job, why quit? Keep on earning and saving and investing. When you finally retire, your retirement will be that much more comfortable. Consider how much of your social life is job-related. Do you really want to abandon all your friends at work?

If you do quit, don't stop working altogether. The saddest retiree is the driven manager who stops working and dies six months later because there was nothing driving him. Slow down, but don't stop.

Plan to work a few months a year or some hours a week. Maybe your old employer will need a consultant in your field, or maybe there's a new business in your new home that needs a part-time worker who comes without a need for benefits. Doctors and health care professionals probably have the biggest advantage here—among the cheapest places to live are the rural places often in great need of a doctor. Writers can write anywhere, if they can write at all; investment managers are on Wall Street if they have a personal computer and a couple of phone lines. Starting your own business is a risky but potentially rewarding way to enter a new community.

Financially, you ought to try to keep working at your regular job until age seventy-one. Under current law, you must be seventy-one to receive a decent-sized paycheck and Social Security benefits at the same time—though it may be different by the time you reach that age. Later retirement is also a contribution to the nation. Neither the defined benefit pension system nor Social Security can survive if Americans both retire earlier and keep on living longer.

Employers, however, may have other ideas. Even though federal age discrimination laws have virtually wiped out mandatory retirement, many corporations try to get the older folks to leave. Managers tend to believe that younger workers are more productive, that older workers stand in the way of promotions and cause younger workers to leave, and that if they must get rid of workers for some economic reason, the right ones to force out are the old ones with the fewest dependents.

Some 70 percent of nine hundred companies responding to a Wyatt Company survey said they subsidize early retirement.[3] Companies sometimes open a window for bigger subsidies, offering early-retirement bonuses and other inducements for a limited time. During the 1980s, 80 percent of the *Fortune* 500 opened a retirement incentive window. But wait: what goes around comes around, and 60 percent of the 500 companies opened a window more than once.[4] How do you decide if it's time to take the boss up on his offer?

Sometimes it's painfully obvious that you need to get out while the getting is good. If your company is having financial trouble, or consistently losing market share, you ought to be looking for a way out anyway. You're better off taking a buy-out, especially a lump-sum buy-out, from a troubled company than waiting around for layoffs to begin. IBM has, or had, a lot of smart people on the payroll. In 1992 at least 32,000 employees— almost 10 percent of its worldwide workforce and 60 percent more than expected—retired early under a lucrative buy-out plan. The company followed up with involuntary layoffs and far less generous deals.

In any case, you want to take as much as possible with you when you leave. Incentives may include lump-sum severance pay, enhanced pension benefits, Social Security supplements, more life insurance, or some improvement in retiree health benefits. Eligibility is often computed on some scale of years of service and age, just as regular pension benefits are. It's possible that the terms of retirement are so generous and your prospects for new employment are so good that you could come out ahead.

But you may not want to buy what the smart money is selling. What will you give up on retirement? A chance for promotion when somebody else goes through the retirement window? Stock options that might be worth more if the company gets lean and earnings surge? Be careful and examine all offers. Always look a gift horse in the mouth.

A Retirement That Works

One piece of good news is that more and more employers are offering part-time work, especially for older employees. According to a 1992 survey of six hundred major corporations by Towers Perrin, about one-third regularly hired retirees part-time. Du Pont, for example, even offers full-time benefits to half-time workers. Hewlett-Packard pays half on benefits for a half-time worker.

Elective office is just about the best retirement job any community has to offer. Run for Congress, or state legislature, or city council. These jobs pay pretty well, they have their own, often ridiculously generous, retirement plans, and they're perfectly suited to people with a lifetime of experience, time on their hands, and diminished physical resources. Term limits may make elective office less attractive as a career; instead it could become the perfect end of a career.

If you're really well-off, in your own terms, and you don't need to value yourself in dollars, give something back to the community. Find a full-time volunteer job at a museum or hospital or school or library; otherwise, stay in the economy. If you have professional skills, use them. Financial experts can join or create an accounting or investment firm. Managers can find a new business or product in their old field and sell it on commission. Builders and tradesmen can manage real estate properties, or go in with a group to own and manage an apartment building. Open a restaurant, or hire on as the breakfast cook. Become a real estate broker, or a yacht broker (often no training or license is required), or take any other commission job, such as telemarketing, where you can select your own hours. Become the polite, caring receptionist you always wished your doctor had hired.

Do such opportunities really exist?

A study of 2,000 large companies for the International Foundation of Employee Benefit Plans in 1991 found only 12.8 percent that claimed to hire workers who had retired from other companies. And only 8.9 percent reported facing an acute shortage of younger workers.[5] But companies are learning. More than 50 percent of the employees of Walt Disney World in Orlando are retirees from another corporation.

John Snodgrass, president of Days Inn, the motel chain, has instituted a program to hire retirees and says, "America's employers are walking past an unbelievable resource of talented, reliable, trained, and educated employees when they fail to hire older workers." Days Inn started to hire older people as telephone reservation agents in 1986, and found them more stable. They stayed with the company an average of three years, compared with one year for younger people. A seventy-seven-year-old employee was the highest-performing telemarketer in the company one year. The Travelers Corp., the insurance company in Hartford, Connecticut, found that older workers learned sophisticated computer software as quickly as did younger trainees.

Merrill Lynch and other brokers recently began recruiting new stockbrokers from the ranks of the retired. The theory is that successful brokers are personal financial consultants, and the best ones are people with experience. Of course, it also helps that a retired executive may know wealthy potential investors whose accounts are at other firms. Successful stockbrokering is mostly based on whom you know and how well you sell to them.

Airline work is attractive to some older people for the same reasons it draws young workers: free travel supplements the low pay, and employers are looking for people who don't mind the irregular schedules that are such a bother to people with families.

Markets respond to numbers. Chances are the baby boom will see increased opportunities for older workers, just as there were increased opportunities for its women, who were the first large generation of college-educated women. But for the reader as individual, opportunities will exist where you make them exist. If you are a manager, this is the time to create the part-time jobs that will be there for you to take when you want to slack off. If you have any power over pensions at work, this is the time to start changing the rules, such as a pension computation based on the final working years' salary that might deny you retirement income if you choose to work fewer hours at a lower salary in the last few years of your career.

If you don't have power, you could still have a say. Send this book, or a copy of this page, to your union benefits committee or your management pension consultant. Point out that you can keep working for as long as you like at full salary and then draw a full pension—the company might benefit if you postponed your pension and drew less than full salary.

INVESTMENT ADJUSTMENTS AFTER RETIREMENT

So you made it. You saved $1 million or more and you are about to retire. "What do we do now?"

Be careful. You are not really a member of the leisure class; you are a retired worker skating on the edge of financial crisis. This year, the first year of your retirement, could be the first year of a long downhill spiral. You have to invest as wisely as you did to get to this point. You need a portfolio that will increase your income to offset inflation ahead.

Whatever your target for retirement income was, inflation will rob you unless you keep a large portion of your portfolio growing and accept less current income than your wealth is capable of generating. You want assets such as growth and value stocks that take a long time to ripen. Age will not wither your need to expand your wealth, and the longer you can wait until you are forced to milk your wealth for income, the greater that income will be.

Speaking of income, are you sure you know what your pension will be worth? Really sure?

Your pension and other benefits, such as profit-sharing and a 401(k), may breach the ceiling on tax-deferrals for retirement. If that happens, your employer may be forced to reduce your pension to stay within tax limits or pay you the difference without a tax subsidy. A Hewitt Associates survey in 1992 found that 30 percent of industrial companies and 18 percent of financial companies don't take the honorable, unsubsidized path: they just chop the pension. Every company is different in the details; make sure you know how yours operates.

Assuming you know the value of your company pension, you have choices to make when you retire. How will you take your pension benefit? The law requires that you be given at least two options, the single-life option that pays a monthly sum for your life, and the two-life or joint and survivor option that pays a reduced sum for the lifetime of yourself and your spouse, whoever lives longer.

A quick look at life expectancy tables will convince anyone that men, on average, should take the two-life option and that women should take the one-life option, because women aged sixty-two to sixty-five will live, on average, four to five years longer than men of the same age. Add in the fact that men usually marry women younger than themselves.

It's a more difficult calculation to figure out for yourself whether the likely extension of pension payments by several years offsets the reduction in the size of the monthly check. You must discount to present value the sum of payments that would come to a couple of your life expectancies and a single person of your life expectancy. Take the bigger discounted total benefit. If you can't do this yourself and get the same answer three times in a row, find someone who can, such as an accountant or a financial planner.

Make sure that the person you go to for advice doesn't have a sales pitch up his sleeve. Many accountants and financial planners, and nearly all stockbrokers, including those who style themselves as personal financial consultants, receive a commission for putting you into a particular type of investment. It's too much of a strain on human nature to imagine they will steer you clear of an investment if they will profit from selling it to you.

There's a gimmick every year and every year there's a new gimmick. Insurance gimmicks are often the most confusing and are often sold with heavy pressure. For example, how about this idea, for the person trying to decide whether to take his pension as a single-life or a two-life payout?

Take the higher single-life payment, and use the extra money to buy a life insurance policy on yourself with your spouse as beneficiary. The policy takes care of replacing the pension if you die first, and if your spouse dies first the insurance benefit will pass to your heirs. It's called "pension max," and your insurance agent will have a computer program that will show you how much you save.

Ask yourself how it can be such a good deal for you if the insurance company has to take the same money that you were going to get from your pension and give you that good deal, plus cover its expenses and make a profit for itself, plus pay the sales agent a commission. The catch usually lies in the kind of insurance policy offered in a pension max plan. While the sales agent's computer program works from today's interest rate, the life insurance varies as tomorrow's interest rates vary. You may have to pay higher premiums to keep the policy in force, or your spouse will receive a lower death benefit and not be able to replace your pension. Other risks are that the value of the death benefit may not keep pace with inflation or with future increases in the pension under a cost-of-living clause or an ad hoc increase from a generous employer. The worst trap of all could close on you if your company's retiree health benefits are only available for people actually receiving a company pension.

GETTING PAID

A important choice to make on retirement may be whether to take a lump-sum payment or an annuity. All companies with defined contribution plans and about a third of companies with defined benefit plans offer a lump-sum payment when an employee leaves the company. All 401(k) and similar plans are paid as lump sums. Considering the experience of Republic Steel, it is astonishing that any responsible defined benefit plan still offers a lump sum, but there it is—grab it if you can and roll it over into a tax-deferred Individual Retirement Account. It's most likely to be available from a defined benefit plan as part of an early-retirement or layoff settlement.

As interest rates have fallen, the amount needed to finance a given pension promise has risen, and thus the lump sums are going up, too.

The two possible reasons not to take a lump sum are if you think you or your spouse will far outlive the life expectancy that governs the calculation of the lump sum, or if you think you haven't got what it will take to invest the lump sum carefully. Only then should you be interested in the monthly pension fund check, and in the federal pension insurance that backs the monthly payment but would not insure your future investments if you take the lump sum. It is also possible that your employer might grant cost-of-living increases that you didn't earn, but it's more likely that you can earn them yourself from the investments you make.

There are two good reasons not to take an annuity. First, when you take a lump sum, you can spread it around among several investments and custodians, but an annuity rests on the soundness of a single financial institution, either the pension fund that pays you or the insurance company that sells you the annuity. The pension fund is backed by the Pension Benefit Guaranty Corp., and you're out of luck if the pension fund fails and your benefits exceed the maximum PBGC coverage of about $2,500 a month. The insurance company is backed by a state insurance guaranty fund, and the firmness of that backing in a crisis will depend on prevailing politics and economics. Second, you can redeploy your personal investments if interest rates change, but annuity payments will be fixed.

If you do take a lump sum, how do you take it? The easy way hurts the most. You pay taxes on the whole wad, although you use a five-year averaging method that softens the blow somewhat. If your retirement occurs before age fifty-nine and one-half, whether voluntary or involuntary, the government adds a 10 percent tax and doesn't allow income averaging. A better idea at any age is to roll over your lump sum into an Individual Retirement Account. You only pay tax on the money you take out of the IRA and you don't have to start taking money out until age seventy and one-half. The minimum withdrawal is based on your life expectancy. The only pitfall is the possibility that the government will increase tax rates so much in the future that you'd rather pay currently.

In a rollover IRA you make your own investments, selecting mutual funds, bank CDs, or individual stocks through a brokerage account, just like any other IRA. You would give up the tax-deferred compounding of your big stake if you have some other investment opportunity that is such a sure thing that it will pay your taxes and beat the market besides. But if you have such a sure thing, you don't need investment advice at all. Most people are far better off with tax-deferred earnings on good stocks. If you have some other investment opportunity, such as your own business, you should draw down some other savings vehicle that doesn't enjoy a tax advantage.

One further word on the rollover of a lump sum: don't take a check from your employer because it's subject to a 20 percent withholding tax. You'd get a refund eventually, but there's no reason to let your money work for the government instead of for you.

CONFRONTING RETIREMENT

Investment strategies must change as you approach retirement. Now preservation of capital becomes an important goal, and wringing income from your portfolio is the chief determinant of your retirement investment plan.

If your nest egg is on a thin branch, you will want to be very cautious. But don't be too cautious. If you retired at sixty-five or seventy, you may have fifteen to twenty-five years to live. Changing all your investments around to a fixed income is an invitation to let inflation blow you away. Your last ten years could be very disappointing.

So don't sell all those stocks on the day after you retire. Keep working the long-term growth strategy. Only capital appreciation can ward off inflation.

Inflation is the biggest enemy of a retired person. Once you can't earn more wealth, you must live on what you have earned. You should not count on cost-of-living increases, even those that are written into law, like Social Security, because COLAs inevitably bankrupt every pension plan that employs them.

You must keep your assets growing, even at the expense of current income. That expense can be stiff: an annuity from an insurance company that's indexed to the inflation rate will deliver less than half the current income in the first payment year that an unprotected annuity will deliver. That's the hardheaded judgment of people who stand to lose their money if they guess wrong—you should be as hardheaded.

HOME SWEET HOME

For many people, the largest chunk of appreciated capital in their portfolio is their home. It may well be paid off, or nearly so, and it may have doubled or quintupled in value since purchase. For the past decade or so, the government has given a tax break to retirees who sold their houses, allowing them to escape capital gains tax on $125,000 of house profit. This is allowed once, after age fifty-five, for any individual or couple. Under current law, a prospective bride and groom who think about getting married in their golden years should sell their homes separately before marriage so they can each escape capital gains tax. (Current law also establishes a substantial marriage penalty, so they should not marry anyway.) Inflation is eating away the value of this capital gains tax shelter and we should not expect a revenue-hungry government to make it more generous.

There are two good alternatives to selling the homestead: one is renting it out as an income-producing property; the other is a reverse-annuity mortgage, in which a bank agrees to pay you monthly checks in exchange for a share in your equity. In effect, this is a monthly regularization of a home-equity line of credit, so you draw on the capital tied up in your home. Every dollar you draw is, of course, a dollar borrowed, using a dollar of equity in the home as security. Interest must be paid on this loan like any other. On the sale of the house or your death, the bank gets its share of the home equity, with interest.

A number of different reverse-annuity mortgages are available. In most states, they include insurance by the Federal Housing Administration. Some are simply staged borrowing, others are very much like regular insurance company annuities, in which you promise to pay a lump sum in exchange for a lifetime monthly income, so that in effect you are betting you will live long enough to beat the mortality tables. In no case should a borrower pledge more than 75 percent of the equity in his or her home, and the borrower should be very careful to understand what the transaction really promises: lifetime extra income paid for by a reduction in one's wealth.

Another income-producing strategy is to sell the house but provide financing yourself. Taking back paper speeds the sale of the house, increases the nominal price, and provides you with a steady monthly income. But there is a financial catch that you should understand. Some of the money you will receive is not interest; it's the borrower returning your principal. And in any amortization schedule, the principal share of each monthly payment increases and the interest share of the payment decreases. To keep your wealth intact, you must reinvest each principal payment received. Not to do this will leave you with less wealth than you imagine.

This is why a sum of money left in an interest-bearing account to compound will produce a greater final balance at the end of a term of years than money lent out. The money in the deposit account is automatically reinvested, while the interest payments from a bond or the combined interest and principal payments from a mortgage or other amortized loan must be reinvested. A deposit of $10,000 left for ten years at 10 percent will grow to $25,937. But a bond will pay $1,000 per year and the $10,000 principal at the end of ten years, and so the bondholder will have $20,000 unless he reinvests the interest payments. The owner of a 10 percent mortgage for $10,000 amortized over ten years will receive $16,275 in principal and interest, because interest is earned on a declining principal balance.

In real life, markets even out these competing investments. There are no 10 percent savings accounts available when mortgages offer 10 percent. Markets also price investments according to risk. A danger arises when people ignore the messages of the markets. If you are trying to sell your house, you may not immediately grasp all the subtleties of mortgage lending, and you may ask too much or too little without realizing it. Not every real estate agent is well versed in finance, either. If you want to take back a loan when you sell your house, you would do well to find a knowledgeable agent who also invests in real estate for himself.

RETIREMENT IN SHELTER

Unless you are very close to retirement, the tax laws are likely to be different then than they are now. In general, though, remember that preservation of capital includes preserving it from the tax man and from the hidden tax of inflation. Remember that assets have to earn their keep.

The final tactic for preserving capital is very final indeed. Though estate planning is beyond the scope of this book, you may wish to arrange your affairs to avoid estate tax, the 37 percent to 50 percent federal levy on wealth in excess of $600,000 that you leave to anyone other than your spouse. (State taxes vary widely.) There are dozens of sophisticated strategies for protecting your estate from the tax man; most involve trusts and would take an entire book to explain. See a lawyer and a bank trust department. And be careful about pitchmen who sell life insurance in the guise of tax avoidance. Unless your wealth is tied up in nonliquid assets, such as a farm or other business that you are leaving to your beneficiaries, you will be just as well off paying the damn tax as paying commissions on life insurance to pay the tax. Even if your estate will need ready cash to pay taxes, the first thing you should do is work to reduce your taxable estate, through gifts. A husband and wife can give away

$20,000 a year (in cash or in minority interests in that nonliquid business) to any number of people, even the beneficiaries of their wills, without incurring gift tax or estate tax.

THE GREATEST FEAR

Practically every elderly person fears entering a nursing home. They fear that they will never leave. They fear that they will not receive good care. They fear that the cost will bankrupt them or their spouse.

The first two fears are justifiable and far beyond the scope of this book, except to say that some people who manage their affairs successfully and whose illnesses also can be managed may be able to choose to have home health care at a cost not too far above that of a good nursing home.

The chances of elderly persons' entering a nursing home at some time in their lives are quite substantial, and of course rise with age. About 15 percent of men and about 30 percent of women spend a year or more in a nursing home at some time in their lives. Less than 5 percent of people between ages sixty-five and seventy have a nursing home stay, but it's 30 percent for people between ages eighty and eighty-five. And 60 percent of all Americans over age ninety spend time in a nursing home.

In 1993 nursing home costs were between $25,000 and $50,000 a year. Medicare covered only 2 percent of all dollars spent on nursing homes, under a benefit restriction that requires a person to be coming straight from a hospital stay. (Medicare saw nursing homes as a cheap substitute for hospital care, not as an expensive substitute for family care or no care.) The government enters the nursing home scene only after people have impoverished themselves. Most state Medicaid programs pay for nursing care for people who have virtually no cash and few other assets.

Like retirement costs in general, covering the risk of needing to pay for long-term care is a proposition in long-term savings. The difference is that everyone who retires will need to generate income without working, but not everyone will need nursing care. The answer, naturally, is insurance. But what kind?

If you were going to design long-term-care insurance, it would probably look very much like an idealized defined benefit pension plan. A lot of people pay in during their working lives and those that need the benefits receive them. The amount to be paid in is determined by actuaries estimating life expectancies, investment returns, the cost of future bills, and other factors. Unfortunately, if you do this, you get an expensive product that most insurance companies consider to be unmarketable. Younger people, with the same certainty of the young that leads some not to bother with health insurance, say that they would rather have their money now, or just put it into general savings, than prepare for a contingency they'd rather avoid anyway.

So long-term care looks more like life insurance. Policies vary, but Health Insurance Association of America reports that coverage worth eighty dollars a day for up to four years, with protection against inflation of 5 percent a year, will run $1,781 per year for a person aged sixty-five. Policies are almost always sold on a "guaranteed renewable" basis. In life-insurance-speak, this reassuring term actually means that premiums can be raised every year. Permanently fixed premiums are guaranteed only by another, less frequently seen term, "noncancellable."

For insurance, an initial low price can represent a high price over the life of the policy, just like any other bait-and-switch sales tactic. A low price attracts customers, and then a rate increase drives them away before they can collect any benefits. Unscrupulous companies do this on purpose; even the best-intentioned insurance company must be as optimistic as possible to sell policies, and will push the edge of optimism as long as it knows it can do well with a rate increase.

It may come to pass that long-term-care insurance will become part of standard health insurance, but given the current burden of health care costs, it's hard to imagine who will pay for it.

Another way that people handle the risk of long-term care is to buy it as part of a real estate deal. Life-care facilities offer several levels of resident services in one building, from apartments for a totally independent lifestyle, through dining rooms and services like those of a residence hotel, through "assisted living" and on to full-blown nursing care. A typical life-care facility requires a large payment up front and substantial rents, but promises that the resident will be able to have any level of care that's needed.

Recently, the Internal Revenue Service has given its blessing to a form of insurance that may belong in a complete plan for living in retirement, because it allows for the payment of catastrophic medical expenses. Insurers can offer "qualified accelerated death benefits," which isn't quite as bad as it sounds. Insurers prefer to call it a "living needs" benefit, and it means the policyholder can tap the death benefit to pay for medical care or other expenses when the policyholder has a terminal illness and isn't expected to live more than a year. New IRS rules, which took effect July 1, 1993, lift the threat that these benefits would subject the policyholder and his heirs to a huge sudden tax liability. There are limits on the amount of living needs benefits, and if they go beyond what the IRS deems excessive, some of the life insurance will lose its tax break, but not all.

The cost of medical care when death is near often exceeds the cost of all other medical care during a person's life, and a catastrophic illness is the most frequent reason for the collapse of a retirement plan. The IRS-sanctioned "qualified accelerated death benefits" is a much better deal for the terminally ill person than the only previous option—a taxable sale of life insurance benefits to a "vulture firm" that buys your death benefits.

CONCLUSION: CYCLE OF LIFE

A pension system is the social form of deferred gratification—it's a financial structure that helps you take money away from yourself in your youth that you would have been able to use to make yourself happier, in hopes that the money will make you happier in your oldest age.

A baby cannot defer gratification. It's very hard for some children to trade an ice cream cone now for two ice cream cones next week. The proverbial anxiety of teenagers may have its roots in the dawning realization that present actions have future consequences. With luck and guidance, they begin to provide for their own future. Perhaps they wear seat belts. Perhaps they don't smoke.

We don't fully understand the unstoppable passage of time until we watch children grow up, or until we watch parents grow old. These soul-disturbing experiences gradually prove our own mortality, and the inadequacy of our attempts to deny our inevitable fate.

This book was meant to be, as I said in the Introduction, "an alarm bell to the entire postwar generation, warning that they are depending on an economic system that is not strong enough to bear their weight. It is a call to action to reinforce the American pension system and a survival kit that can reduce our reliance on that system."

I hope it has been all that, and more. I hope it will provide some readers with the strength of heart and the determination to face their lives honestly, and to realize that they must provide for themselves.

WHAT QUESTIONS SHOULD I ASK?

"I'M WORRIED ABOUT the security of my pension, and I don't even know what to ask. What should I do?"

There are lots of questions you might want to ask, and we'll review that shortly. But first the bad news: there is very little that employers must tell plan participants about their pensions.

A pension participant gets almost no information automatically. The summary annual statement just tells the value of plan assets—but not liabilities—and certifies that the plan is in compliance with minimum ERISA funding requirements—which, as we've seen, can be far less than adequate funding. It also tells the participant that other information is available on written request.

On written request, an employer who sponsors a defined benefit pension plan must give a worker a statement describing benefits the worker has already earned—which is not much use until the worker approaches the age of retirement. There's no requirement that the worker be told what his projected pension benefit would be if he works until retirement age.

And that information, the Form 5500 annual report filed by pension funds with the Labor Department, isn't much better. For example, employers are allowed to treat plan assets held in a master trust as though they were a class of investment assets.

Thus employers often do not disclose how much of a fund is held in stocks or bonds or cash or other investment classes. Even worse, the so-called annual report isn't due until two years after the end of the plan year. A worker concerned about how his plan weathered the 1987 market meltdown would not have received any official information, no matter how inadequate, until early in 1990.

There are a number of questions you should ask your defined benefit pension plan sponsor.

The most basic question is, "What kind of a plan am I in?" There is more to this than the difference between a defined benefit plan and a defined contribution plan. Some of your pension benefits may be promised through a "nonqualified" pension plan. It's nonqualified because it's not tax-exempt, and it's not tax-exempt because some part of your benefit was too rich to satisfy the IRS. So your employer promised those benefits but didn't take the normal tax deduction. ERISA basically doesn't cover nonqualified plans, so your employer can fund these benefits any way he wishes, or not at all. In the extreme case, these benefits can be increased, decreased, or canceled at will, and the employee has no claim or recourse. Sometimes employers fund nonqualified benefits and put them in a trust but even then they are not secure if the firm goes bankrupt.

Some people only find out that their benefits were promised in a nonqualified plan at the worst possible time—after years of service when the company has a financial crisis.

How can you tell if your pension includes a nonqualified benefit? You can't. You have to ask. If a defined benefit paid in 1993 exceeded $115,641, it's almost certain that the excess amount came from a nonqualified plan. If an employer contributed more than $30,000 or more than 25 percent of pay to a defined contribution plan, it's almost certain the excess was nonqualified and may not have been real cash on the barrelhead. Unfortunately, these are maximums, and it's possible for lesser benefits also to have come from nonqualified plans. Early-retirement benefits reduce these maximums. If you have both a defined benefit plan and a defined contribution plan, the maximum qualified benefit is reduced to 125 percent of the two maximums. Tax-exempt health benefits and dependent-care benefits may also reduce the maximums.

Is this plan fully funded? If it's overfunded, has the sponsor cut back on its contributions? Are there any provisions that would give overfunding amounts to the participants if the plan were terminated? Does the employer intend to do that? Has the employer ever used overfunded balances to finance a cost-of-living increase for pensioners? Would the employer ever do that?

If the plan is underfunded, can the employer explain how it got that way? What is the funding history over the past ten years? Is it trending toward greater overfunding? Why? Is the employer complying with the minimum funding standards of ERISA, or doing more to bring the plan back to full funding? Are there contingent liabilities that the plan might have to finance, such as early retirements or shutdown benefits?

How are plan assets invested? How much of this fund is currently in cash? In stocks? Bonds? Real estate? Venture capital? Derivatives? Who are the investment advisers? What are their styles or specialties? How are they selected? What are they paid? What is the performance history of the fund, and of each adviser? How does the fund's performance compare to the average fund performance? How do its earnings in stocks compare with stock indexes? In bonds with bond indexes? In real estate?

Asking the questions may be easier than getting the answers. At some companies you may be able to sit down with a knowledgeable benefits counselor and receive all the information you want, accurate, dependable, and timely. But don't be surprised if you can't find anyone to ask, and if the people you do ask don't know the answers. In that case, you will have to dig some of the answers out yourself.

Start with the company's annual report, if it's a publicly traded company. There will be some pension information, and of course there will be some information about the basic financial health of the firm as well. The funding status of pension plans will be found in footnotes to the financial statements, although it's likely that all pension funds will be aggregated. A company could hide the existence of a poorly funded plan by surrounding it with overfunded plans.

For specific information on your pension plan, you must ask for a copy of the Form 5500, and you will probably have to pay copying costs at fifteen cents a page for a document that can run to one hundred pages. If you don't want to make waves at work by asking questions, you can ask the government for the Form 5500 by sending your employer's identification number (on your tax form W-2) and the plan number (on the summary plan description) to the U.S. Department of Labor, PWBA Public Document Facility, 200 Constitution Ave., N.W., N5507, Washington, D.C. 20210. (The government will definitely charge you fifteen cents per page for copying.)

As with most financial documents, start at the back. Read the actuary's report and make sure that there are no reservations about the financial health of the pension plan. Then read the footnotes. If there are any bodies, that's where they are buried.

Then go back to the front and read it all through. The Form 5500 will tell you the fair market value of the investment assets in the plan, though it may not tell you how they're invested. It will tell you the accumulated benefit obligation, but that's the amount that would be due if the plan terminated, and does not include contingent liabilities such as shutdown benefits and early-retirement benefits.

The Form 5500 will also tell you the discount rate that was used to calculate the estimate of benefit liability. With this, you can get an idea of the true funding status of your plan. Look up the yield on thirty-year Treasury bonds listed in the financial section of the newspaper. If the discount rate is the same as the bond rate, then you can make a straight comparison of the accumulated benefit obligation and the market value of plan assets. Assets should be bigger than the benefit obligation. If your company used a discount rate that's higher than the current thirty-year Treasury bond rate, you should increase the figure for the benefit obligation. You can make a rough adjustment by adding 10 percent to the benefit obligation for every percentage point that your company's discount rate exceeds the bond rate. (If the discount rate is lower than the bond rate, you can decrease the obligation figure by the same proportion.) Now compare the market value of assets to the adjusted estimate of benefit obligations, and hope that assets are still greater than obligations.

Find the section on income and outgo. It's unsettling if the plan is paying more in benefits than the sponsor is contributing. And it's unhealthy if the company has asked for a waiver of its required annual contribution.

Read the Form 5500 closely. The sponsor must disclose if it is considering terminating the plan, though the information may be more than two years old by the time you get the form. If the employer chooses, the form may show how the plan assets are invested. It's best if investments are not all one class.

It Could Be Better

This very cumbersome process of learning about the health of a defined benefit plan contrasts with the simplicity of an annual report for a defined contribution plan. The worker receives an annual report that reminds the worker how he has allocated his investments, shows the earnings on those investments, and specifies the employer's and the worker's contributions. There's a bottom line that shows how much the account is worth. The company should tell the worker how much monthly pension that sum would buy him at age sixty-five, but if the company doesn't do it the worker can price annuities for himself by calling insurance agents.

The difference is that the assets of a defined contribution plan are the worker's property. Many employers believe that they have no obligation to the workers to disclose anything more than their earned benefit and the way the defined benefit would be computed when the worker decides to retire.

In December 1993, the Department of Labor asked for employers' comments on whether they should be required to make a better disclosure of the financial health of defined benefit pension plans. Specifically, the department asked if employers should notify workers when pension funds are underfunded or when employers apply for funding waivers, rather than making workers ferret out that information for themselves. Also the department asked if annual reports to workers should disclose a projected benefit and state how much of that benefit would be insured by the Pension Benefit Guaranty Corp.

Employer trade associations immediately denounced the proposals, saying that workers would be confused and worried needlessly if they were given such information.

A better stance was taken by the American Institute of Certified Public Accountants, which has urged that companies be required to give workers simple, readily understandable pension fund report cards that disclose funding position, benefits, and the actuarial assumptions used to calculate them. The AICPA also endorses a report on the investment portfolio and returns on its assets.

Glossary

Actuary: A professional trained to estimate probable future earnings and expenses of pension plans and other long-range financial institutions.

Annuity: A stream of regular payments from principal and accumulated interest for a term of years or a life span. A typical defined benefit pension plan (q.v.) is an annuity.

Beneficiary: A person who receives or may become eligible to receive a distribution from a pension plan.

Current liability: What a pension plan would owe to beneficiaries if it terminated.

Defined benefit pension plan: A retirement plan maintained by an employer that pays out a predetermined annual amount to eligible employees after retirement. A lump-sum payment may sometimes be substituted, but the size of the cash payment will be based on the present value of the defined benefit pension.

Defined contribution pension plan: A retirement plan that accumulates contributions that will be used to pay a lump-sum benefit after retirement. The size of the benefit is based on the total of contributions, plus their investment earnings. The lump sum may be used to purchase an annuity but the size of this annuity will depend on market conditions and interest rates at the time of retirement.

Derivative: A financial contract to pay or receive money in the future based on the performance of some underlying asset such as a currency or a portfolio of stocks or bonds.

Discount: The process of using interest rates to compute the present value of future payments. Discounting answers questions like "What would my pension be worth in a lump sum payable to me right now?" A high discount rate implies that a sum of money invested today could earn more than if interest rates were lower. Thus low discount rates force high lump-sum values. Conversely, low discount rates force employers to make larger present contributions to fund pension plans

ERISA: The Employee Retirement Income Security Act of 1974, which sets the federal rules regulating pension management. It also established the Pension Benefit Guaranty Corp.

Fiduciary: A person who has control over the management of assets for the benefit of another person, or who gives advice regarding the management of such assets. Managers and advisers of pension plans have fiduciary responsibilities to the beneficiaries.

Form 5500: The annual financial report filed with the Internal Revenue Service by pension plans with more than one hundred participants. Smaller plans file Form 5500-C every third year and the shorter Form 5500-R in the other years. Participants do not receive Form 5500 unless they ask for it. Instead, they are given a summary annual report with almost no useful information.

401(k) plan: A tax-deferred employee savings plan named for the section of the tax code that authorizes it. Employees can contribute pretax earnings and select investments in stocks, bonds, mutual funds, or bank accounts from the investment vehicles chosen by the employer. An employer typically will match a percentage of an employee's contributions. The contributions and earnings are not available to the employee until the employee retires or leaves the company, and are not taxed until the employee receives the money.

Fund: An account in which money may be held, invested, administered, and supervised.

Guaranteed Interest Contract (GIC): A contract from an insurance company that promises to pay a fixed interest rate guaranteed for a certain period of time. The only guarantee is the insurance company's promise. GICs are frequently options in defined contribution plans, and they have been popular with managers of defined benefit plans also.

Highly compensated employee: An employee who earns more than $75,000, or is a member of the highest-paid group of employees, or who owns more than 5 percent of the corporation, or any officer of a corporation who receives more than $45,000.

Individual Retirement Account: A tax-deferred savings plan in which persons with income under $25,000 or who do not have a pension plan at work may deposit up to $2,000 a year, tax-deductible. Other persons may also make the deposit, but may not claim a tax deduction. Persons receiving lump-sum distributions from other retirement plans may roll their receipts into an IRA without paying tax on the distribution. Balances and earnings in IRAs are not taxed until they are withdrawn, and withdrawal may begin after age fifty-nine and one-half and must begin by age seventy and one-half.

Keogh plan: A defined contribution retirement plan, for self-employed individuals and small businesses, that features simplified tax and reporting requirements. Keogh plans may be money purchase plans requiring a fixed percentage contribution of income or they may be profit-sharing plans.

Lump-sum distribution: Payment of the total amount a person is entitled to receive from a retirement plan. The relationship of a lump sum to a pension depends on the interest rate used to discount the present value of future pension payments.

Mutual fund: An investment vehicle that takes in money by selling shares and invests the proceeds in stocks, bonds, money-market instruments, or a combination. Mutual funds usually pay all their realized profits as dividends each year, and the value of unrealized profits or losses is reflected in their share prices. There are general mutual funds specializing in nearly every kind of security investment. They come in two main types:

Open-end mutual funds sell new shares to new investors and redeem shares for cash on demand, usually at the net asset value of the underlying investments of stocks, bonds- or short-term money-market instruments.

Closed-end mutual funds sell a fixed number of shares at formation, and these shares then trade on the open market, usually on a stock exchange, and usually at a discount or premium to net asset value, depending on investors' opinion of the prospects of the underlying portfolio of stocks or bonds and on the supply of and demand for the shares.

Pension: A sum of money paid periodically to replace wages.

Pension Benefit Guaranty Corp.: The federal agency established by ERISA to insure benefits of terminated defined benefit pension plans. The PBGC insures benefits up to $2,556.82 per month in 1994, an amount that increases in rough concord with inflation. (The insured benefit was $750 in 1974.) Insured benefits are reduced for people who retired before age sixty-five or if the benefit was not a single-life annuity. Employers pay insurance premiums to the agency.

Pension coverage: Anyone eligible for pension membership is said to be covered by a pension plan.

Pension participant: Anyone in a pension plan, whether employed or not, for whom contributions are being made, or who is retired receiving benefits.

Pension plan: The legal arrangements establishing a pension promise for a group of workers and setting up savings arrangements to fund it.

Plan administrator: The person who oversees a pension plan and the contact for participants who request information.

Profit-sharing plan: A defined contribution plan in which the size of employer contributions depends upon the employer's profitability.

Reversion: Capture of surplus assets in a pension fund by a plan sponsor.

Rollover: A transfer of assets from one retirement plan type to another, such as the deposit into an IRA of a lump-sum benefit paid from a defined contribution plan.

Self-employed: Anyone who has income as a sole proprietor or as a partner, on a full- or part-time basis, and who reports such income on Schedule C or Schedule K of his or her tax return.

Trust fund: A fund that is administered for the benefit of specified beneficiaries by an independent trustee, appointed by the giver of money into the fund and subject to supervision by a court.

Vesting: Anyone who has worked long enough to have earned an entitlement to receive a benefit is said to be vested. Current federal law governing defined benefit plans allows "cliff" vesting after five years, meaning that an employee has no right to a pension until he has worked five years, but obtains 100 percent of his pension rights after five years. Companies also may give partial pension credit for each year of service, but if they do they must give full vesting by the end of the seventh year of service.

Appendix

Companies with the Greatest Underfunded Pension Liabilities (1992)*

Company	Total liability (In millions)	Underfunded (percent)
Ravenswood Aluminum	$ 106	$ 95 (89%)
LTV	$ 3,375	$ 2,102 (62%)
New Valley	$ 698	$ 429 (61%)
Tenneco	$ 444	$ 249 (56%)
Keystone Consolidated Indus.	$ 215	$ 120 (56%)
Loews	$ 328	$ 170 (52%)
Uniroyal Goodrich Tire	$ 1,018	$ 501 (49%)
Laclede Steel	$ 216	$ 101 (47%)
Rockwell International	$ 842	$ 380 (45%)
Trans World Airlines	$ 1,071	$ 479 (45%)
Bridgestone-Firestone	$ 547	$ 245 (45%)
Anchor Glass	$ 296	$ 126 (43%)
ACF Industries	$ 214	$ 90 (42%)
Bethlehem Steel	$ 5,857	$ 2,431 (42%)
PacifiCorp	$ 736	$ 262 (36%)
White Consolidated Indus.	$ 388	$ 136 (35%)
Clark Equipment	$ 276	$ 95 (35%)
Maxxam	$ 888	$ 302 (34%)
General Motors	$59,754	$20,182 (34%)
American National Can	$ 1,637	$ 546 (33%)
Budd	$ 535	$ 173 (32%)
Mack Trucks	$ 583	$ 183 (31%)
Allegheny Ludlum	$ 466	$ 143 (31%)
Rohr	$ 493	$ 146 (30%)
Crown Cork & Seal	$ 1,179	$ 339 (29%)
B.F. Goodrich	$ 537	$ 151 (28%)
James River Corp. of Va.	$ 370	$ 104 (28%)
Bull HN Information Systems	$ 483	$ 133 (28%)
National Intergroup	$ 719	$ 187 (26%)
CSX	$ 1,080	$ 268 (25%)

Appendix

Companies with the Greatest Underfunded Pension Liabilities (1992)*
(continued)

Company	Total liability (in millions)	Underfunded (percent)
Westinghouse Electric	$ 5,189	$ 1,271 (24%)
Reynolds Metals	$ 1,248	$ 304 (24%)
PPG Industries	$ 1,203	$ 279 (23%)
Goodyear Tire & Rubber	$ 1,622	$ 346 (21%)
Navistar International	$ 2,614	$ 544 (21%)
Northwest Airlines	$ 1,523	$ 311 (20%)
Woolworth	$ 664	$ 118 (18%)
Allied-Signal	$ 740	$ 133 (18%)
Ceridan	$ 685	$ 120 (18%)
National Steel	$ 1,157	$ 194 (17%)
Deere & Co.	$ 1,617	$ 250 (15%)
Warner-Lambert	$ 1,209	$ 183 (15%)
Honeywell	$ 2,530	$ 368 (15%)
Armco	$ 2,088	$ 298 (14%)
Chrysler	$ 9,692	$ 1,360 (14%)
Greyhound Lines	$ 1,070	$ 142 (13%)
United Technologies	$ 1,616	$ 171 (11%)
Unisys	$ 3,055	$ 307 (10%)
Inland Steel	$ 1,844	$ 157 (9%)

*Compiled by the Pension Benefit Guaranty Corp. and announced in a press release, November 22, 1993.

Notes

Introduction   *Legal Looting*

1. The legal looting of the Republic Steel plan was investigated for LTV Corp. by Washington lawyer Frank Cummings after LTV took over Republic. LTV and Cummings supplied his report to the Office of Enforcement of the Pension and Welfare Benefit Administration at the Department of Labor, which made it available pursuant to a Freedom of Information request.

Chapter 1   *Construction*

1. Samuel H. Williamson, "U.S. and Canadian Pensions Before 1930: A Historical Perspective," in *Trends in Pensions 1992*, U.S. Department of Labor Pension and Welfare Benefits Administration. U.S. Government Printing Office, Washington, D.C., 1992.
2. Phillip Longman, "The Great Train Robbery," *Washington Monthly*, December 1987, p. 12.
3. Julie Kosterlitz, "Pension Losers Attract a Few Key Allies," *National Journal*, January. 5, 1991, p. 28.

Chapter 2   *Over- and Underfunding*

1. *In re C.D. Moyer Co. Trust Fund*, 441 F.Supp. 1128 (E.D. Pa. 1977).
2. *Washington-Baltimore Newspaper Guild Local 35 v. The Washington Star Co.*, 555 F.Supp. 257 (1983).
3. Julie Kosterlitz, "That's My Money!" *National Journal*, February 25, 1989, p. 454.
4. American Academy of Actuaries, press release and news briefing, June 24, 1992.
5. Interview.
6. Jonathan Peterson and Robert A. Rosenblatt, "Business Is Shaking Pension Fund Piggy Bank," *Los Angeles Times*, May 12, 1985, Part 5, p. 1.
7. Ibid.

Chapter 3 *The Looting Continues*

1. American Academy of Actuaries report, June 1992.
2. Susan Pulliam, "Retirees at Risk," *Wall Street Journal,* September 2, 1993, p. A1.
3. Liz Pinto, "UAW Pact Looks Out for No. 2," *Automotive News,* September 20, 1993, p. 4.
4. "G.M.'s Pension Plan Adds Stock to Cash," letter to *New York Times,* January 9, 1994, section 4, p. 20.
5. *USA Today,* November 23, 1993, p. A1.
6. "Ohio Companies on Underfunded List," *Cleveland Plain Dealer,* November 23, 1993, p. 8F.

Chapter 4 *The Government Example*

1. U.S. Department of Labor, *Employee Benefits of Medium and Large Firms, 1989,* Bureau of Labor Statistics, Bulletin 2336, August 1989.
2. "Golden Parachutes; New Attention on Retirement Bonanzas," *Newsday,* December 20, 1992, p. 6.
3. Tom Dunkel, "Do You Know Where Your Nest Egg Is?" *Washington Times,* April 19, 1993, p. 16.
4. *Florida Trends,* September 1992, p. 31.
5. *BNA Government Employee Relations Report,* February 15, 1993, p. 219.
6. Ibid.
7. Jeffrey S. Eisenberg, "A Rendell Report Card," *Focus Magazine,* January 1993, p. 24.

Chapter 5 *Defined Contribution Plans*

1. Daniel J. Beller and Helen H. Lawrence, "Trends in Private Pension Plan Coverage," in *Trends in Pensions 1992,* U.S. Department of Labor.
2. Ibid.
3. Ibid.
4. "Taking the Controls," *Dallas Morning News,* July 6, 1993, p. D5.
5. *On Employee Benefits,* a newsletter of Hewitt Associates. March–April 1993, p. 3.
6. Estimate by David Langer, a New York consulting actuary.
7. *Washington Post,* May 30, 1993, p. H3.

Chapter 6 *The Pension Industry*

1. Patricia B. Limbacher, "Pension Assets Up 9.6%," *Pensions & Investments*, April 4, 1994, p. 1.
2. *Pensions & Investments*, May 17, 1993, p. 20.
3. Kenneth R. Harney, "Tax Bill Winners?" *Barron's*, August 16, 1993, p. 48.
4. Steven Hemmerick, "Some Hear the 'Death Rattle' of Indexing," *Pensions & Investments*, July 26, 1993, p. 1.
5. Claire Makin, "Passive Resistance: Is Indexing's Heyday Over?" *Institutional Investor*, July 1993, p. 175.
6. *Business Week*, July 13, 1992, p. 22.
7. *Wall Street Journal*, July 20, 1993, p. C1.
8. Donald Woutat, "State Pension Fund Returns Not What They Used to Be," *Los Angeles Times*, April 4, 1993, p. 3.
9. Ibid.

Chapter 7 *The Insurance Game*

1. Patricia B. Limbacher, "Exec Life Action Proposed," *Pensions & Investments*, January 10, 1994, p. 15.
2. During the 1980s the PBGC repeatedly refused my requests for information on companies providing annuities. It later turned out that the computer database did not work.
3. General Accounting Office study of annuity conversions, April 1991.

Chapter 8 *Dangerous Investing*

1. James Srodes, "Trojan Horses," *Financial World*, October 27, 1992, p. 32.
2. Campbell press release July 15, 1993, and "Campbell Soup Fund to Take Activist Role," *Wall Street Journal*, July 15, 1993, p. C1.
3. James Sterngold, "Japanese Companies Rebuff Mighty U.S. Pension Funds," *New York Times*, June 30, 1993, p. D1.
4. Victor F. Zonana, "Pension Funds Flex Muscles," *Los Angeles Times*, June 21, 1991, p. A1.
5. Patrick M. Fitzgibbons, "Economically Targeted Investments Are Key to Funds' Portfolios," *The Bond Buyer*, August 3, 1993, p. 2.
6. "Economically Targeted Investments," a report by the Institute for Fiduciary Education, Sacramento, Calif., June 1993.
7. David A. Vise, "A Billion-Dollar Battle Over Pension Plans' Purpose," *Washington Post*, December 6, 1992, p. H1.

8. Leslie Wayne, "Seeking Investment with Principle," *New York Times*, August 10, 1993, p. D1.
9. "Berg Advises Pension Fund Managers to Invest in Firms That Develop Skills," *BNA Pension & Benefits Reporter*, September 13, 1993, p. 1915.

Chapter 9 *Pension Regulators*

1. Social Security Administration, Office of Research and Statistics, cited in Virginia P. Reno, "The Role of Pensions in Retirement Income," in *Pensions in a Changing Economy*, Employee Benefit Research Institute Education and Research Fund.
2. Julie Kosterlitz, "Promises to Keep," *National Journal*, August 29, 1987, p. 2138.
3. Munnell's paper to the Pension Research Council, also press releases by an opponent.
4. Letter to Rep. Tom Lantos, D-Calif., chairman of the Government Operations Subcommittee on Employment and Housing, September 1989.
5. Brenda Sapino, "No Plaudits for Audits," *Legal Times*, July 27, 1993, p. 9.
6. *Pension Reporter*, July 6, 1992, p. 1179.
7. Calculation by Sylvester Schieber of the Wyatt Company.
8. *Highlights, a Monthly Summary of Benefit News*, Foster Higgins Consultants, December 1993, p. 4.
9. *Mertens* v. *Hewitt Associates.*
10. "Reversing Mertens a DOL Priority," *BNA Pension and Labor Reporter*, September 13, 1993, p. 1919.

Chapter 10 *Pension Insurance*

1. Robert Litan, "Deposit Insurance, Gas on S&L Fire," *Wall Street Journal*, July 29, 1993, p. A11.
2. Interviews and letters in *Business Insurance*, January 25, 1993; February 15, 1993; and March 8, 1993. Langer's views were also reported in *BNA Pension Reporter*, January 18, 1993, p. 122.

Chapter 11 *From Benefits to Contributions*

1. Grant Thornton study, cited in Donald Jay Korn, "Skewed Retirement Plans Help Owners at Workers' Expense," *Financial Planning*, June 1993, p. 112.
2. "Pension Evolution in a Changing Economy," *EBRI Issue Brief 141*,

September 1993. Some data come from the Labor Department's *Trends in Pensions*, and other data come from tabulations of pension plans' annual reports to the IRS.
3. Celia Silverman and Jack VanDerhei, "Private Plan Sponsorship Trends in the 1980s," cited in *EBRI Issue Brief 141*.
4. Christine Philip, "Top 1,000 Funds Increase by 9 Percent," *Pensions & Investments*, January 25, 1993, p. 1.

Chapter 12 *The Aging of America*

1. Gregory Spencer, *Projections of the Population of the United States, by Age, Sex, and Race: 1988 to 2080*, U.S. Bureau of the Census, January 1989.
2. *Sixty-five Plus in America*, U.S. Bureau of the Census, Current Population Reports, Special Studies, U.S. Govt. Printing Office, Washington, D.C., 1992.

Chapter 13 *The Social Security Crisis*

1. Congressional Budget Office, *Baby Boomers in Retirement: An Early Perspective*, Washington, D.C., 1993.
2. 1994 Trustees' Report, footnote to Table III, B.2, p. 176.
3. 1994 Trustees' Report, Table II, D.1, p. 52.
4. 1994 Trustees' Report, Table III, D.1, p. 191.
5. EBRI, *Future Financial Resources of the Elderly*, 1993.
6. Laurance J. Kotlikoff, *Generational Accounting: Knowing Who Pays, and When, for What We Spend*. New York: Free Press, 1992. See also papers by Kotlikoff, Alan J. Auerbach, and Jagadeesh Gokhale.
7. U.S. Government Office of Management and Budget. *Budget Baselines, Historical Data and Alternatives for the Future*. Table F-5, p. 536. U.S. Govt. Printing Office, January 1993.
8. Federal Reserve Bank of Cleveland, *Economic Commentary*, July 1, 1992.

Chapter 14 *Fixing Pension Policy*

1. Phyllis Borzi, "A Congressional Response to Pension Reform," in *Pensions in a Changing Economy*, Employee Benefit Research Institute, 1993, p. 111.
2. Karen W. Ferguson, "A Consumer Advocate's Response to Pension Reform," in *Pensions in a Changing Economy*, EBRI, 1993, p. 110.

3. J. J. Pickle, "Pensions: Grand Plans Short on Funds," *New York Times*, July 11, 1993, section 3, p. 11.

Chapter 15 *Saving Yourself from the Pension Mess*

1. Arthur Andersen newsletter, Spring 1993, p. 6.

Chapter 16 *Investment Choices*

1. Jeanne B. Pinder, "Owners Refinancing Homes to Cut Debt, Not Payments," *New York Times*, August 9, 1993, p. A1.

Chapter 18 *Tax Shelters*

1. Cited in General Accounting Office HRD-92-119, "Changes Can Produce a Modest Increase in Use of Simplified Employee Pensions."
2. Karen W. Ferguson, "A Consumer Advocate's Response to Pension Reform," in *Pensions in a Changing Economy*, EBRI, 1993, p. 109.

Chapter 19 *Living After Retirement*

1. This role-playing comes from an Age Wave presentation reported in the *Los Angeles Times*, June 16, 1991, Orange County Edition, p. 1.
2. News conference materials, National Alliance for Aging Research, 1993.
3. Wyatt's 1990 COMPARE survey, as cited in Sylvester J. Schieber, "Retirement Policy Schizophrenia," *Contingencies*, March–April 1993, p. 22.
4. George E. Bell III and Dennis R. Coleman, "The Right Way to Open a Window," *Contingencies*, September–October 1991, p. 36.
5. Arthur G. Dobbelaere and Kathleen H. Goeppinger, "Older Workers: With All Their Experience, Why Aren't They Still Employed?" *Contingencies*, March–April 1993.

Acknowledgments

Many of the people I would like to thank for helping me to prepare this book have clients and other business relationships that might be damaged if they were associated with an iconoclastic book. It would be poor thanks to name them, but I am very grateful to them. Some read the manuscript at early stages, others provided valuable leads or documents, many took time to discuss difficult issues.

There are many public officials I would thank, especially the ones who tolerated aggressive, skeptical questioning and patiently explained their views and policies. I single out three executive directors of the Pension Benefit Guaranty Corp., Kathleen Utgoff, James Lockhart, and Martin Slate. Also at the PBGC, Judith Beckelman and Jane Hoden of the public affairs office patiently supplied information and documents.

The committees and subcommittees of Congress provide a permanent floating university lecture series to any reporter who wishes to study any subject, with the added benefit of publishing transcripts of all the past lectures. I would like to thank the Congressional Information Service for putting all the transcripts of all the tens of thousands of hearings on microfiche, and for producing a workable index to this mountain of material. I look forward to the day when it all goes on line, searchable by computer. My thanks also to one subscriber to CIS, the library of George Mason University Law School, for the welcome it gave to this unaffiliated researcher.

The General Accounting Office and the Congressional Research Service work hard to provide background that congressmen ought to have before they make decisions on important issues. They are not as unappreciated as congressional actions often indicate.

The professional organizations with a stake in pension issues were unfailingly cooperative, and I would thank particularly the Employee Benefits Research Institute, the Pension Research Council, the American Academy of Actuaries, the American Institute of Certified Public Accountants, the American Council of Life Insurance, and the staffs of their Washington offices.

Jim Smalhout, a pension economist and critic of the Pension Benefit Guaranty Corp., was particularly generous in sharing his insights, his research, and his encyclopedic familiarity with the academic literature on pensions. I hope his forthcoming book on the PBGC will improve the prospects for pension insurance reform.

In any major reporting project about business, a journalist builds on the work of other journalists, particularly the painstaking reporters of the trade press. *Pensions & Investments* magazine and the newsletters of the Bureau of National Affairs let no sparrows fall without notice in the world of pension finance.

At *Barron's*, I thank editor Jim Meagher, former editor Alan Abelson, and former editor and publisher Robert Bleiberg, for their encouragement and instruction through twelve years of challenging fun as a business reporter in Washington. They saw fit to push me up to the position of editor of the editorial page three years ago, and I thank them for making a great job even better.

Most important, I thank the people who made it possible to turn an idea into a book: agent Rafe Sagalyn, who helped create a proposal an editor could believe in; editor Fred Hills, who believed in the proposal and helped establish the shape of the book, copy supervisor Leslie Ellen and copy editor Ann Keene, who helped the book's details match each other and reality.

Always, thanks are insufficient to express my gratitude in everything to my wife, Carol Knopes Donlan, whose high standards continue to challenge me. She is my best editor and my best friend.

Index

DATE DUE

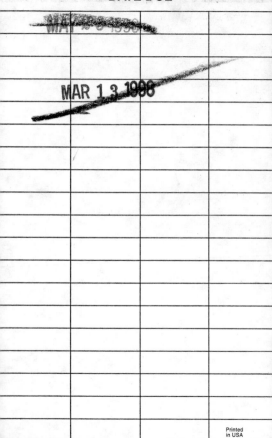

MAR 3 0 1996

MAR 1 3 1996